SUSTAINABLE DEVELOPMENT AND INTEGRATED APPRAISAL IN A DEVELOPING WORLD

Sustainable Development and Integrated Appraisal in a Developing World

Edited by

Norman Lee

Senior Research Fellow, Institute for Development Policy and Management, and Environmental Impact Assessment Centre, University of Manchester, UK

Colin Kirkpatrick

Professor of Development Economics and Director of the Institute for Development Policy and Management, University of Manchester, UK

Edward Elgar
Cheltenham, UK • Northampton, MA, USA

Published by
Edward Elgar Publishing Limited
Glensanda House
Montpellier Parade
Cheltenham
Glos GL50 1UA
UK

Edward Elgar Publishing, Inc.
136 West Street
Suite 202
Northampton
Massachusetts 01060
USA

A catalogue record for this book
is available from the British Library

Library of Congress Cataloguing in Publication Data

Sustainable development and integrated appraisal in a developing world
  /edited by Norman Lee, Colin Kirkpatrick.
    Papers presented at a conference on Impact assessment in the
  development process, held at the Univ. of Manchester, Oct. 1998.
    1. Sustainable development Congresses.   2. Environmental impact
  analysis Congresses.   3. Economic development—Environmental aspects
  Congresses.   I. Lee, Norman, 1936–   .   II. Kirkpatrick, C. H.
  (Colin H.), 1944–   .
  HD75.6.S8652   2000
  333.7'14—dc21   99–39625
                                                               CIP

ISBN 1 84064 162 2

Typeset by Manton Typesetters, Louth, Lincolnshire, UK.

Printed and bound in Great Britain by Bookcraft (Bath) Ltd.

Contents

Figures

Tables and boxes

Boxes

Contributors

W. Neil Adger is Lecturer in Environmental Economics, School of Environmental Sciences, University of East Anglia and Senior Research Fellow, Centre for Social and Economic Research on the Global Environment (CSERGE), University of East Anglia and University College London, UK.

Peter Bacon is Professor in the Department of Zoology, University of the West Indies, St Augustine, Trinidad.

Katrina Brown is Senior Lecturer in Natural Resource Development, School of Development Studies, University of East Anglia, and Senior Research Fellow, Centre for Social and Economic Research on the Global Environment (CSERGE), University of East Anglia and University College London, UK.

A. Lex Brown is Professor and Head of the School of Environmental Planning in the Faculty of Environmental Sciences, Griffith University, Brisbane, Australia.

Aleg Cherp is currently a researcher at the Department of Planning and Landscape, University of Manchester, UK.

Michael Common is Senior Lecturer in the Graduate School of Environmental Studies at the University of Strathclyde, Glasgow, UK.

Lourdes Cooper is an independent environmental planning consultant and researcher at the University of Brighton, UK.

Jennifer Elliott is a Senior Lecturer in Geography at the University of Brighton, UK.

Clive George is Research Associate at the Environmental Impact Assessment Centre at the University of Manchester, UK.

David Hulme is Professor of Development Studies, Institute for Development Policy and Management, University of Manchester, UK.

Murray G. Jones is Senior Environment and Social Adviser with Shell International Exploration and Production in The Hague, The Netherlands.

Colin Kirkpatrick is Professor of Development Economics and Director, Institute for Development Policy and Management, University of Manchester, UK.

Norman Lee is Senior Research Fellow, Institute for Development Policy and Management and Environmental Impact Assessment Centre, University of Manchester, UK.

Danette Leslie is a researcher at the Institute of Ecology and Resource Management at the University of Edinburgh, UK.

Reinoud Post is Technical Secretary of the Commission for Environmental Impact Assessment at Utrecht, The Netherlands.

Sanzidur Rahman is Visiting Fellow in Agricultural Economics at the Department of Agricultural and Food Economics, University of Reading, UK, and Senior Staff Economist, Research and Evaluation Division, Bangladesh Rural Advancement Committee (BRAC), Dhaka, Bangladesh.

Jayant Routray is Associate Professor of Regional–Rural Development Planning at the School of Environment, Resources and Development, Asian Institute of Technology, Bangkok, Thailand.

Jules Scholten is Secretary General of the Commission for Environmental Impact Assessment in Utrecht, The Netherlands.

David Shim is Marine Park Manager for the Department of Fisheries, Tobago.

Russell Taylor is Resource Ecologist with the World Wide Fund for Nature Southern Africa Regional Programme Office in Harare, Zimbabwe.

Dirgha Tiwari is an Environmental Economist and Consultant in Kathmandu, Nepal.

Emma Tompkins is Research Associate in the Overseas Development Group and School of Development Studies, University of East Anglia, UK.

Kathy Young is Research Associate in the Department of Zoology, University of the West Indies, St Augustine, Trinidad.

Preface

In recent years there has been a growing recognition that sustainable development can only be achieved on the basis of a balanced appraisal of the
environmental, economic and social impacts of a country's major development projects, as well as its development policies, plans and programmes.
This has highlighted the need for an integrated approach to impact assessment and decision making, which allows equal consideration to be given to
the goals of economic advancement, improved quality of the environment
and a more equitable distribution of benefits.

In October 1998, a conference on 'Impact Assessment in the Development
Process: Advances in Integrating Environmental Assessment with Economic
and Social Appraisal' was held at the University of Manchester to review
recent advances in the theory and practice of integrating assessment techniques and decision making. The conference followed a similar one in 1996
at the University of Bradford on the integration of environmental assessment
with economic and social appraisal. A selection of the 1996 conference
papers were published in *Sustainable Development in a Developing World:
Integrating Socio-Economic Appraisal and Environmental Assessment*, Edward
Elgar, 1997, edited by Colin Kirkpatrick and Norman Lee, and in a Special
Issue of *Project Appraisal*, **11** (4), 1996.

Both conferences were organized as part of the Collaborative Programme
in Environmental Assessment and Economic and Social Appraisal in the
Development Process, which brings together the resources of the Development and Project Planning Centre, University of Bradford and the
Environmental Impact Assessment (EIA) Centre and Institute for Development Policy and Management, University of Manchester.

More than 100 delegates attended the 1998 conference, from 30 countries,
and 41 papers were presented. Twelve of the conference papers have been
included, after revision, in this volume. A further eight papers were published
as a Special Issue of *Environmental Impact Assessment Review*, May 1999.

The 1998 conference received generous financial support from the Department for International Development (DFID). The conference, and the workshop
that preceded it, were organized by a committee consisting of David Howlett,
Clive George, Norman Lee, Colin Kirkpatrick and Debra Whitehead. We are
grateful to our colleagues for their support and assistance in planning both
events. We are especially grateful to Debra Whitehead who acted throughout
as conference administrator, and who also undertook the task of preparing the

manuscripts for the post-conference publications. Without her dedication, efficiency and enthusiasm the conference would not have taken place and this book would not have been written.

Colin Kirkpatrick
Norman Lee
Manchester, April 1999

1 Integrated appraisal, decision making and sustainable development: an overview

Norman Lee and Colin Kirkpatrick

1.1 Introduction

The need for closer integration between environmental assessment and economic and social appraisal in the development process is widely recognized. Interest in integrated appraisal continues to increase, at the level of both policy and research. Also, the agenda is broadening to include different approaches to integrated appraisal and its use for planning and decision-making purposes, particularly in the context of sustainable development.[1]

The purpose of this book is to contribute to the understanding of integrated appraisal and decision making for sustainable development in developing and transitional economies, first, by presenting alternative perspectives and methods and second, by providing case studies of the application of integrated appraisals.[2]

The aim of this opening chapter is to position the current trend towards integration, as represented in the other chapters, in the broader context of developments in studies and practice relating to appraisal, planning, decision making and sustainable development. Second, we identify a number of issues which require further consideration, either through more detailed investigation or through greater attention to the practicalities of implementation. Finally, we outline our own thinking on the desirable directions and forms of future work covering both research studies and improvements in appraisal practice.

Section 1.2 places the current trend towards integration (in some cases, 're-integration') in its historical setting and categorizes the different kinds of integration which are being proposed and the reasons for these. Section 1.3 outlines the contents of each of the chapters included in this volume, indicating how they reflect the differing facets of the integration theme covered in the book. Based on these chapters, and the wider literature, Section 1.4 examines a number of issues, which are important to the future understanding and practical application of integrated appraisal and decision making for sustainable development. In Section 1.5 we recommend a number of further studies and other ways of strengthening the practical application of integrated appraisals.

The collection of chapters included in this volume relates mainly to low- and middle-income countries in the developing world (LDCs) or in the transitional economies of Central and Eastern Europe and Central Asia (CITs). Our principal concern in this overview is with the same range of countries.

1.2   Integrated appraisal and decision making: an historical perspective

The *ex-ante* appraisal of projects has a long history (Prest and Turvey 1965; Squire 1989; Kirkpatrick and Weiss 1996; Francis and Jacobs 1999). The formalized appraisal of policies, plans and programmes has existed for a shorter time and is less well developed (Kanbur 1990; Devarajan et al. 1997; Harberger 1997; Bourguignon and Morrison 1989). In the former case, this first developed through technical and financial or economic appraisals. Because there were few different types of appraisal, their 'coordination' or 'integration' was not seen to be an important concern and it attracted little attention in the literature. In practice, however, it was quite frequently stated that engineers, accountants and economists did not work sufficiently closely together and, even when they did, the results of their appraisals received insufficient consideration when decisions were being made (Little and Mirrlees 1991; Devarajan et al. 1996).

The enactment of the National Environmental Policy Act (1969) in the United States was an important milestone in a trend *away from* integrated appraisal. It introduced a specialized form of appraisal, environmental impact assessment, which was separate from and largely considered additional to the existing forms of appraisal (Canter 1996, ch. 1; Clark and Canter 1997; Wood 1995, ch. 2). Also, it enjoyed the special status of being a regulatory requirement.

Since 1970, the growth of influence of this new form of appraisal on general appraisal practice has been dramatic.

● Regulatory provisions for project-level environmental appraisals now exist in well over 100 countries and many of these provisions require that the findings of these appraisals are 'taken into account' (that is, integrated) in decision making (Bellinger et al. 1999 forthcoming; Donnelly et al. 1998; George 1999 forthcoming; Sadler 1996).
● Regulatory provisions, as well as less formalized arrangements, for environmental appraisals are now being extended to cover earlier stages in the planning cycle (that is, policies, plans and programmes) in the form of strategic environmental assessments (Sadler et al. 1998; Sadler and Verheem 1996).
● International development banks and bilateral aid agencies are incorporating provisions for environmental appraisal into their own institutional procedures, even where there is no direct regulatory requirement for them to do so (OECD 1996; Rees 1999).

This is not the full extent of its influence. The growth in formalized environmental appraisal has stimulated the development of many other specialized forms of appraisal. This has taken place either under the regulatory umbrella of environmental impact assessment (EIA), or as a separate form of non-mandatory appraisal coexisting alongside other environmental, economic, financial and technical appraisals.

The list of these newer, more specialized, forms of appraisal is already long and it is getting longer. For example, Vanclay and Bronstein (1995) refer to social impact assessment, health impact assessment, risk assessment, climate impact assessment, development impact assessment and environmental sustainability assessment. More recent additions to the list include ecological impact assessment (Institute of Environmental Assessment 1995) and gender impact assessment (Kolhoff 1996).

The reasons for the increasing number of different types of appraisal merit further study. In some cases it has been due to concern that certain impacts were being overlooked or insufficiently examined within existing appraisals. In other cases, the concern was that inappropriate methods of appraisal were being used (for example, insufficient use of participatory methods of appraisal). Additionally, the motivation in some cases has been to give greater prominence to particular impacts so that they are given greater weight in the decision-making process. In some instances, the use of more specialized forms of appraisal has been promoted under the EIA umbrella, where they benefit from its regulatory/mandatory status. In other cases, where the regulatory scope of EIA is more narrowly defined, the new specialisms seek accommodation within the broader, overall appraisal and decision-making process.[3]

The proliferation of different forms of appraisal has brought a number of benefits which their supporters will be reluctant to lose, but it has also created a number of difficulties. At the *procedural* level, it has become more difficult to coordinate the timings of separate appraisals and to synchronize these with the timings of the decisions within the planning and project to which they are intended to contribute (see Scholten and Post, Chapter 2). At the *methodological* level, there is an increased likelihood of inconsistencies between the appraisal methods being used, of interdependencies between certain types of impacts being overlooked, and of increasing difficulties in constructing overall appraisals for use in decision making (Lee and Kirkpatrick 1997). In *organizational* terms, the extra workload of managing and coordinating separate appraisals, as part of the project planning and management process, has grown considerably. In under-resourced organizations (in LDCs, CITs and donor organizations), which are expected to comply with regulatory, fiscal and time constraints, this has become burdensome and causes a deterioration in appraisal and decision-making performance (see Scholten and Post, Chapter 2).

Growing awareness of these difficulties is encouraging a reassessment of the benefits and costs of a more integrated appraisal and decision-making approach to the development process. Two other policy changes are re-enforcing this.

- Increasing acceptance of sustainable development as an overarching policy goal for the development process.
- Increasing acceptance of the need for more strategic-level forms of appraisal for policies, plans and programmes to supplement those which have already been developed for use at the project level.

Since the sustainable development goal has interdependent economic, social and environmental components, it is argued that appraisal procedures and methodologies should use interconnected economic, social and environmental appraisal criteria which are consistent with achieving this goal. This has a bearing on a more general need to strengthen appraisal methods for use at more strategic levels of decision making relating to development policies, plans and programmes (PPPs). At present, existing specialized methods of appraisal at the project level (cost–benefit analysis, environmental impact assessment, localized public participation and social impact studies) do not have sufficiently developed counterparts at the PPP level. Hence, some ask, should strategic appraisal methodology and procedures be developed on a more integrated basis from the start?

For the above reasons, the calls for more integrated appraisals, and for their more effective use in development planning, decision making and implementation, have grown over recent years. However, views on the precise nature of the problem and the type of integration which is needed to address this, vary considerably. There is, it would seem, a need to establish the scope of the integration agenda, to identify and classify the main components which are contained within it and to clarify the relationships which exist between these components.

Based upon the contents of the chapters contained in this volume, and the wider literature which exists on the subject, we have identified the following types of integration measure which have been suggested as desirable, by different authors, to address different deficiencies in appraisal and decision-making practice.

- Synchronize the timings and standardize the requirements of separate procedures for the different appraisals to which a development proposal is to be subjected. This should enable the overall appraisal to be better coordinated or to be fully integrated into a single appraisal procedure (see Scholten and Post, Chapter 2).

- Synchronize the timings of appraisal procedures with those of the decision procedures to which they relate so that the outputs from the appraisal process are provided, when needed, as inputs to the decision-making process (Lee 1999 forthcoming; Mwalyosi and Hughes 1998).
- Ensure that appraisals are taken into account at all key stages of decision making in relation to a given action and not only at the stage where the formal approval of the action by the authorities (or funding agencies) is being given (Lee 1999 forthcoming).
- Ensure that appraisals and decisions at one phase in the planning cycle are 'tiered' (integrated) into appraisals and decision making at previous and subsequent phases in the cycle (Lee and Walsh 1992; Niekerk and Arts 1996).
- Ensure that neglected types of impact (for example, health, gender and other types of social impacts) are satisfactorily assessed and taken into account in overall appraisal and decision making (Birley 1995; Canter 1998; Kolhoff 1996; Vanclay 1999 forthcoming).
- Ensure that greater methodological consistency is achieved between the different methods of appraisal used in assessing and aggregating different types of impacts (economic, social and environmental) (Lee and Kirkpatrick 1997).
- Ensure that different assessment paradigms (scientific, humanities, participative) are used in a balanced, integrative manner (see Hulme and Taylor, Chapter 6).
- Ensure that the goals of sustainable development and the means of achieving these are sufficiently reflected in integrated appraisals of impacts and in their use for decision-making purposes (Dalal-Clayton and Sadler 1998).

Each measure, taken individually, is only a partial response to the range of appraisal and decision-making concerns that have been raised. Further study is needed to determine whether, collectively, they are sufficiently complete and logically consistent to provide a comprehensive solution. However, their full implementation would imply, in most countries, fairly extensive changes to the appraisal, planning, decision making and management of the development process. It would require significant institution strengthening and changes to the procedures, appraisal approaches and methodologies that are used. This would be very demanding, particularly in most LDCs and CITs. We return to this issue in Section 1.4, after presenting the main findings of the other chapters contained in this volume.

1.3   Review of chapters

The chapters included in this volume have been chosen for the contribution they make to the understanding of integrated appraisal and decision making for sustainable development in developing countries and transitional economies. They are arranged into two main themes: Part I: Alternative Perspectives and Methods (Chapters 2–7) and Part II: Case Studies (Chapters 8–13).

Part I contains seven chapters which examine the different approaches and methods used in integrated appraisal and decision making.

In Chapter 2, Scholten and Post highlight two deficiencies in development aid programmes. These are (i) insufficient attention to thematic policies (environment, culture, equity, gender and so on) in project design, appraisal and decision making and (ii) the complexity and greater time and resource requirements associated with increasing numbers of aspect-by-aspect appraisals which have to be processed by hard-pressed project officers. The authors argue for a more comprehensive *and* integrated approach to impact assessment to deal with these deficiencies. They distinguish different degrees of integration, which may be achieved on a step-by-step basis (for example, starting with 'procedural tuning', which may be used to harmonize the timing of separate appraisal procedures). They also suggest that the coordinating or lead authority for integrated appraisals may vary depending, for example, on the leading theme of the project being appraised.

In Chapter 3, Brown pursues a similar theme – the need to include other 'crosscutting' issues (such as gender, poverty and sustainable livelihoods) in a broadened assessment process for development assistance projects. He argues that these types of issues are of growing policy significance in the development agencies but, for a combination of logistical and practical reasons, satisfactory separate appraisals cannot be undertaken for each of them. He suggests that environmental assessment (EA) is the most appropriate home for most crosscutting issues and shows how rapid appraisal tools, in the form of an 'environmental overview' at the project level and 'strategic overview' at the policy, plan or programme level, may be adapted to serve this purpose.

In Chapter 4, Common presents an economist's perspective on the integration issue. He explores the potential use of an environmental cost–benefit analysis (ECBA), which is developed as an extension to an EIA study, as an appraisal tool for project-level sustainability. For this purpose, he draws upon standard welfare theory and ecological economics (which studies the interdependence between economic and ecological systems). He focuses upon an important bridging topic between economic, environmental and social assessment – the role of the public in valuing environmental impacts. A number of appraisal methods, including the contingent valuation method, are investigated. He shows that both public views and their valuations can be very sensitive to the nature and extent of the information at their disposal and the process by which views and values are formulated.

In Chapter 5, George considers how the goals of sustainable development might shape the appraisal criteria that are used in impact assessments, distinguishing between industrialized and developing countries. His analysis focuses upon the appraisal criteria that may be derived from the sustainability principles of inter-generational and intra-generational equity. He also explores the differing implications of adopting strong and weak versions of sustainability, depending on the degree of substitutability for natural capital which is assumed. These criteria are then used to assess the sustainability content of a number of environmental impact statements produced in the UK and in certain developing countries, and to appraise the likely sustainability of the particular projects to which the these statements relate. He detects a number of deficiencies of both kinds in each type of country, although the nature of the deficiencies appears to differ between them.

In Chapter 6, Hulme and Taylor distinguish three appraisal paradigms, which are used in the planning and implementation of development programmes. These are labelled 'scientific', 'humanities based' and 'participatory'. They argue that existing attempts to produce satisfactory integrated appraisals have often failed due to insufficient consideration of how to combine these three approaches, as well as to a failure to consider sufficiently who should be involved in the appraisals and in what ways. One of the difficulties, they suggest, is that the paradigms often compete rather than complement each other, with natural scientists and quantitative economists favouring the first paradigm and other interest groups and disciplines favouring more participative approaches. The authors use a case study of a wildlife programme in Zimbabwe to illustrate how the three appraisal paradigms might be integrated. A feature of this approach is its adaptive character in which distinctions between planning, appraisal and management are blurred as appraisal becomes more fully integrated in an ongoing, iterative planning and management process.

In Chapter 7, Cherp examines how environmental assessments are being integrated into overall appraisal and decision making in transitional countries. He distinguishes two EIA models which have been followed since the breakup of the USSR. One group of countries is following the model inherited from the USSR which is based on State Ecological Review (SER) and the Assessment of Environmental Impacts (OVOS) systems. The other group of countries is seeking future membership of the European Union and is adapting to the requirements of Directives 85/337/EEC and 97/11/EC. The author shows, using information relating to Belarus and Slovakia, that the relationship between environmental assessment, overall appraisal and decision making is quite complex in practice. This is partly because of differences between the formal requirements of the two systems and the ways in which they operate. The author concludes that the choice of model needs to take account of the set of conditions prevailing in the transitional society concerned. He suggests 'it is more appropriate for developed countries and for international aid agencies to support professionals, officials and representatives of the civic society from the region in finding the right approaches to their EA systems, than to offer them ready-made procedures borrowed from elsewhere'.

Part II contains six case studies relating to integrated appraisal and decision making in Peru, Guyana, Tobago, the Philippines, Nepal and Bangladesh.

In Chapter 8, Jones describes the adaptive appraisal and planning process that was used in the early stages of planning a large-scale gas project which was to be located in a sensitive forest area in Peru. It involved a substantial number of environmental, social, economic and technical studies, the preparation of seven EIAs and extensive consultations with a wide range of stakeholders at different stages of the planning process. These were used in combination to shape and modify the project's design and operations to meet the project's objectives, which included the provision of 'net capital' to the local communities in support of their long-term sustainability. The author highlights how stakeholder participation, supported by the various studies, was central to the adaptive process and led to a greater consensus and shared vision among many of the stakeholders.

In Chapter 9, Leslie describes the preparation and subsequent use of an integrated environmental and social impact assessment (ESIA) which was designed to improve the sustainability of the forest operations of a multinational timber company operating in the north-west district of Guyana. The ESIA examined the environmental and socio-economic context of the company's forestry operations, the potential negative and positive impacts that would result and recommended measures to be implemented by the company and the Government of Guyana in the light of these. The case study is essentially a post-audit of the ESIA and its implementation. It shows that although a number of the recommendations were implemented and had the desired effect, others were not or were implemented incompletely (including those relating to local community liaison). As a result, the author suggests, the long-term performance of the scheme has been less satisfactory than it might have been. Various recommendations are presented to make future impact studies of this kind more effective.

In Chapter 10, Adger and colleagues outline an appraisal method which is being developed to assist in decision making relating to the use and protection of marine and coastal resources. This is illustrated in a case study involving a choice between different development scenarios for a reef marine park in Tobago. The method involves (i) identification of alternatives and stakeholders, (ii) assessment of the economic, social and environmental impacts of alternative scenarios, (iii) use of multi-criteria analysis to assist in choosing between alternatives and (iv) use of stakeholder participation to inform each stage in the process. For illustrative purposes, a limited number of alternatives are investigated, using a combination of economic, social and environmental criteria. Initial preference ranking of the alternatives is undertaken which is then subject to stakeholder analysis and conflict resolution in seeking a consensus on the preferred alternative.

In Chapter 11, Cooper and Elliott analyse the growing attention to social acceptability factors in project EIA and decision making in the Philippines. Although the EIA system in this country dates from 1977, it was only in the late 1980s, after the introduction of more democratic forms of government, that public participation in the EIA process began to be politically feasible. In 1992, social acceptability criteria were written into the EIA procedural requirements and these were given greater operational force in 1996. The authors provide a number of examples of more recent cases where social acceptability criteria have been taken into consideration. They identify a number of favourable consequences, notably improvements in the quality of EIAs, and in the projects themselves, and reductions in the social conflicts which otherwise were growing. At the same time, they record a number of practical difficulties that have arisen in the application of these criteria. They conclude that the net balance is positive but consider that various improvements are needed before the system will work in a fully satisfactory way.

In Chapter 12, Tiwari focuses upon deficiencies in integrating the extent of damage to human health from polluted water into decision making within the development process. In response, he develops an analytical framework for decentralized decision making which combines the use of public valuation techniques with the analysis of public perceptions. He illustrates this approach through a case study located in rural Nepal. The components of his method include a simplified health risk analysis and the application of a user's perception and contingent valuation method (CVM) to assess willingness to pay. The study compares the costs of water provision with willingness to pay and examines the extent to which water requirements can be met on a financially self-sustainable basis, taking into account equity considerations in the charging schemes which are used. The author concludes that this methodology can be applied in the Nepalese situation and that it yields a number of useful policy findings.

In Chapter 13, Rahman and Routray describe the methods and main findings of an evaluation of the application of 'green revolution' technology in the agricultural sector in Bangladesh. Their evaluation considers the economic, social/distributional and environmental impacts arising from the use of high-yielding grain varieties of wheat and rice. A combination of multiple regression analyses, social surveys and bio-physio-chemical tests are used to derive the principal empirical findings. These findings, although provisional in a number of respects, identify a number of negative consequences. Crop production and productivity have increased but their long-term sustainability is questioned, particularly in the case of rice, and it may have exacerbated regional inequalities in income. The diffusion of modern technology has raised incomes for certain groups but poverty may have increased within the landless and tenant groups. Negative environmental effects are reported in relation to soil fertility, crop disease and water contamination. The authors conclude that the model of a 'middle' rather than 'high' technology village may be the best one to follow – balanced technology diffusion, crop and economic activity diversification, soil fertility management and greater emphasis on 'bottom-up' planning and the provision of agricultural extension services.

1.4 Some issues
A variety of issues, arising from the chapters summarized in the previous section and the wider literature on integrated appraisal and decision making, have been identified for further consideration. These are discussed below.

Procedural integration
A number of writers have recommended better synchronization in the timings of separate appraisal procedures and between appraisal procedures and decision making at different stages in the planning and project cycle (see Scholten and Post, Chapter 2). Where more than one competent authority and/or funding agency is involved, it has been proposed that one of these should be nominated as lead authority to coordinate their appraisal and decision-making requirements (assuming that organizational integration is judged an undesirable or unfeasible solution).

These suggestions should be pursued. However, the causes of existing difficulties need to be probed more deeply. Each stakeholder group has its own mission and procedures and its conduct during the planning and project cycle reflects these. 'Real' (as distinct from formal) decisions may be taken before appraisals are completed, and the completion of appraisals may be delayed until after important decisions have been taken. The form and method of the appraisal and the decision criteria which, *in practice*, are applied may be similarly affected. In this context, the choice of a lead authority is not only a question of administrative efficiency but also entails modifying the distribution of authority between the stakeholders. Changing the extent of stakeholder participation within the planning and project process (see 'Integrating paradigms' below) has similar consequences. Whether this results in more or less procedural integration cannot be deduced a priori. Deeper studies of conflict and cooperation in integrated appraisal and decision making, at an individual case level, are needed for further insights into this.

Vertical procedural integration (that is, integration between different tiers of appraisal and decision making) is subject to similar influences. Conflicts of interest between tier levels, as well as the dynamics and uncertainties of changing situations, help to explain why planning and project cycles are not as orderly as rational thinking may consider desirable. Only deeper analysis will indicate whether stronger procedural integration, or alternative measures to reduce tier conflicts, are likely to be more effective.

Integrating paradigms
Attention has been drawn to the existence of different 'paradigms' or 'approaches' for appraisal, planning and management in the development process (see Hulme and Taylor, Chapter 6). It has been suggested that economic appraisal operates within a primarily technical paradigm, social impact assessment within a stakeholder participation paradigm and that environmental impact assessment draws upon varying combinations of each. It has also been suggested that a cause of deficiencies in appraisal and decision-making practice is over-reliance on one paradigm and that a multiple paradigm approach could be more effective. This may be so, and it deserves further investigation. On the other hand, if different paradigms are underpinned by different stakeholder missions and corporate practices, the opposite effect could occur. Encouragingly, some papers indicate that economic appraisal is making more use of participatory methods in its valuation studies and that social impact assessment is giving more attention to the content of social analysis as well as to the process of stakeholder participation (see Common, Chapter 4; Francis and Jacobs 1999). Additional studies, involving the use of multiple paradigms in integrated appraisals, are needed to evaluate different hybrid approaches.

Integration of appraisal methods
Previous work has drawn attention to the need for greater consistency between the appraisal methods that are used to assess different types of impacts (Lee and Kirkpatrick 1997). For example, when comparing cost–benefit analysis (CBA) and environmental impact assessment, a number of possible inconsistencies have been identified, including the use of different assumptions, data and predictive methods, discounting procedures and significance criteria as well as different approaches to double-counting problems. Similar, if not greater, discrepancies are likely to be encountered when social impact assessment is drawn into the comparison. If, as seems probable, integrated appraisals are to be undertaken more frequently, it is important that the extent

and seriousness of these inconsistencies are examined in a number of case studies and that steps are taken to remove any significant problems of these kinds. Given the level of professional commitment to different appraisal paradigms and disciplines, eradicating such problems may take some time.

Integrated appraisal for sustainable development
The full implications for integrated appraisal of adopting sustainable development (SD) as the overarching development goal are still being elaborated. For some (see George, Chapter 5) the key concern is to work through the logical implications, for appraisal criteria, of inter-generational and intra-generational equity. For others, emphasis is placed on maximizing economic and social development subject to constraints on resource utilization (distinguishing between renewable and non-renewable capital, and critical and non-critical capital) and the pollution load that can be accommodated within the carrying capacity of the environment. Whichever concept of SD is used, and all involve significant value judgements, the task remains of translating this into operational appraisal criteria.

A broad distinction can be drawn between target-related indicators and process-related indicators (MacGillivray and Zadek 1995; Moldan and Billharz 1997). The former involves expressing SD goals in terms of a set of targets (economic, social and environmental) to be achieved at a specified future point in time. Corresponding to these, a set of indicators needs to be developed which measure progress over time towards the attainment of these targets. The choice of meaningful indicators, obtaining good quality data for their use and interpreting the rate of progress towards SD goals, can be problematic.

Attempts to construct SD targets and appraisal criteria for development proposals in small systems (for example, local development plans or individual development projects) are additionally problematic. This is because they relate to very open systems, with extensive exports and imports of resources and residuals to and from other areas. The SD consequences of these, for the larger systems of which they form part, are often difficult to evaluate. In practice, fairly simple averaging devices are often used to establish SD targets at these lower levels of aggregation (George 1997).

SD process indicators relate to the soundness of the institutional planning and management processes and the appropriateness of the policies in place to achieve SD goals. Appraisal procedures may have a dual significance in this respect. First, they may contribute to the soundness of the institutional, planning and management processes in place where they strengthen the capacity to shape new development along an SD path. Second, if the appraisal criteria are based on SD principles, the planning and management decisions themselves are more likely to be consistent with SD goals.

It has to be recognized that there is a big gap between the potential of integrated appraisal as an SD tool and current practice. There is an urgent need to clarify the 'first steps' along the road from conventional, and mostly separate, environmental, economic and social appraisals to fully integrated and operational SD appraisals.

Scale and uncertainty problems
The use of integrated appraisals to promote sustainable development means that it will need to be increasingly applied at more strategic levels of decision making for policies, plans and programmes. This is the least developed level of appraisal at present and its greater use raises a number of challenges:

- Scaling up and adapting methodologies, which were originally developed for environmental impact assessment, cost–benefit analysis, social impact assessment and so on at the project level, for use with smaller amounts of less detailed data in strategic appraisals of PPPs.
- Clarifying the structures of the three main subsystems (economic, social and environmental), and the linkages between them, through which SD goals are to be achieved and impacts of different development strategies are to be appraised.
- Determining how best to handle, within the framework of an integrated appraisal–decision-making framework, the pervasive uncertainties which exist in any large-scale and long-term planning and management study.

A number of responses to each of these difficulties are being developed and tested. A combination of scaling up project-level appraisal methods and adapting others previously applied in other policy and planning contexts are now being tried out (Cassios 1995; Canter and Sadler 1997; Kleinschmidt and Wagner 1998). Interdependencies between subsystems are increasingly being analysed through the linkage of economic, environmental and social system models.[4] However, many of these are still at a developmental stage. Concerns over the treatment of uncertainty are being addressed through a variety of predictive and evaluative methods (for example, scenario and probabilistic analyses) and through the use of more adaptive approaches to integrated appraisals and their use for planning and management purposes. The latter transform appraisal, planning and management into an ongoing, interactive process. Appraisals are regularly updated and plans and the management of their implementation are adjusted accordingly.

Each of these initiatives shows considerable promise but most are still in a developmental stage. Until their core essentials have been identified and the appraisal methods based on them have been sufficiently simplified, their practical use in most LDCs and CITs, will remain problematic.

Some necessary safeguards

The challenges involved in a comprehensive switch to integrated appraisal and decision making, to promote sustainable development, are substantial. This is not an argument for ignoring or rejecting them. Rather it is a case for trying to ensure that responses are set at a realistic and appropriate level. Progress can be achieved on a step-by-step basis with clearly defined priorities and appropriate assistance in supporting research, training and capacity strengthening. More specific measures to achieve this are proposed in the final section of the chapter.

Another kind of safeguard to be considered concerns the preservation of benefits that have been achieved through the more specialized appraisals in use during the past 25 years. The earlier developments, first of EIA and then of other specialist forms of appraisal, originated from the belief that the financial, economic and technical appraisals which then existed were incomplete or inadequate. Any move to integrated appraisal is accompanied by some risks that a dominant stakeholder, or lead authority, may 'capture' the appraisal process and similar kinds of deficiencies as pre-existed EIA may re-emerge. Consideration should be given to the kinds of safeguards which are needed to reduce the likelihood of this occurring.

1.5   Conclusions and recommendations

Since the first conference on this subject in 1996, there have been a number of advances in the study and understanding of integrated appraisal and decision making in the development process. However, whilst these have been occurring, the scope of the 'integration issue' has widened. Ironically, as deeper insights have been obtained, the complexities of the tasks facing the policy maker, practitioner and researcher appear to have increased. Growing acceptance of sustainable development as an overarching policy goal has re-enforced the need for integrated (economic, social and environmental) appraisal, but it has also created a need, not yet satisfactorily met, for new and broader-based criteria and indicators to use in integrated appraisal and decision making. Considerable progress has been made but substantial 'unfinished business' remains.

Additional to the more general impact assessment (IA) studies which have already been completed (see Part I), an increasing number of IA case studies have also been undertaken (see Part II for some LDC examples). The approaches which these case studies adopt to integrated appraisal are very diverse, partly reflecting the formative state of current knowledge and methodology. Nevertheless, the more detailed analyses which they contain, which are set in widely differing development contexts, are very helpful in deepening understanding of IA practice and the difficulties with which it has to deal.

In what directions should IA research and practice now develop, particularly in LDCs and CITs? Given the large scope of the 'integration issue' and an inability to deal with all of its components simultaneously, a clear ordering of priorities and a 'step-by-step' approach in dealing with these is likely to be desirable. This needs to be undertaken within the individual countries concerned but some external assistance will be needed. Based upon the findings in this overview, the following suggestions are presented for further consideration.

1. The overall scope of the 'integration issue' should be clarified and its main components and their inter-relationships identified. This will help in determining what the future priorities for follow-up work should be and how these relate to each other and the integration issue as a whole.
2. Opportunities for more effective coordination between individual appraisal procedures and with decision making should be explored, drawing upon the advice of the principal stakeholders.
3. A programme of further case studies and trial runs, which focuses upon procedural and methodological practice in integrated appraisal and decision making, should be undertaken. This should take explicit account of the appraisal–decision-making context in which the individual cases or trials occur.
4. A supporting programme of additional studies is required to address the various unresolved integration questions that have been raised in this review. These include:

   • the causes of conflicts which lead to unsatisfactory coordination between appraisals and decision making, and how the resulting difficulties might be avoided or resolved;
   • the nature of the differences between alternative paradigms of appraisal and decision making and how multiple paradigm approaches might be developed and tested;
   • how to address problems of overlap, inconsistency and so on between the different methods of appraisal currently in use;
   • how to identify and construct sets of sustainable development indicators for use in integrated appraisal and decision making at different stages in the policy, planning and project appraisal process;
   • how economic, social and environmental appraisals may be 'scaled up' from the project to the PPP level. For example, how simplified interlinking models (to address economic–social–environmental interdependencies) might be developed and how stakeholder participation might operate at more strategic levels of planning;

- how integrated appraisals would function within adaptive planning and management systems; and
- how the benefits of specialized impact appraisals may be retained within more closely coordinated or integrated appraisal systems.

5. If the above kinds of studies are to be undertaken and, more importantly, beneficial changes in practice are to result, then additional measures will be required. These include:

- raising awareness and understanding of the benefits which may result from integrated appraisal and decision making;
- increasing the number of professionals who are able and willing to cross the paradigm and discipline boundaries which often divide economic, social and environmental appraisals;
- institution-strengthening to increase the capacities of key stakeholders to participate in, and make more effective use of, integrated appraisals for decision making;
- strengthening data collection and analysis relevant to integrated economic, environmental and social appraisal; and
- preparing practical guidance (based on appropriate research, case study examples and stakeholder consultations) on undertaking and using integrated appraisals and then providing follow-up training in its use.

It is hoped that the publication of this book will encourage these and similar initiatives to be undertaken.

Notes

1. In May 1996 a conference was held at the University of Bradford to explore these issues and to identify the main challenges to the successful realization of integrated appraisal in sustainable development. Two collections of papers presented at the conference were subsequently published in a Special Issue of *Project Appraisal*, December 1996 (entitled 'Environmental Assessment and Socio-Economic Appraisal in Development') and in C. Kirkpatrick and N. Lee (eds) (1997), *Sustainable Development in a Developing World: Integrating Socio-Economic Appraisal and Environmental Assessment*, published by Edward Elgar.
2. A follow-up conference was held at the University of Manchester in October 1998. Its purpose was to review recent studies relating to integrated appraisal and decision making, and evaluate the issues which they raised, and to consider the directions in which future work should proceed. Approximately 100 delegates from 30 countries participated and 41 papers were presented. Of these, twelve are included in this publication and eight have been published in a Special Issue (May 1999) of the *Environmental Impact Assessment Review*.
3. The regulatory scope of environmental assessments varies considerably between different jurisdictions. In some cases it is confined to narrowly-defined environmental impacts; in other cases it also specifically includes socio-economic impacts; and in certain cases there

is a degree of flexibility in the types of impacts which may be included in assessments. Further details and country examples are contained in Sadler and Verheem (1997).

4. The literature on this subject is substantial and continues to grow. It relates to a variety of different types of policies, plans and programmes, including trade liberalization agreements (Potier 1997; OECD 1997), structural adjustment programmes (Munasinghe and Cruz 1995; Kessler and van Dorp 1998), sectoral policies and city-level initiatives (Oglethorpe and Sanderson 1999; Camagni et al. 1998). Integrated assessment approaches which were originally developed to analyse climate change issues are now being adapted to apply to other types of policy issues and aim to combine participatory methods with systems modelling (Tol and Vellinga 1998; Rotmans 1998; Toth and Hizsnyik 1998).

References

Bellinger, E., Lee, N., George, C. and Paduret, A. (eds) (1999 forthcoming), *Environmental Assessment in Countries in Transition*, Budapest: Central European University Press.

Birley, M.H. (1995), *The Health Impact Assessment of Development Projects*, London: HMSO.

Bourguignon, F. and Morrison, C. (1989), *External Trade and Income Distribution*, Paris: OECD.

Camagni, R., Capella, R. and Nijkamp, P. (1998), 'Towards sustainable city policy: an economic–environmental–technology nexus', *Ecological Economics*, **24**, 103–18.

Canter, L.W. (1996), *Environmental Impact Assessment*, 2nd edn, New York: McGraw-Hill.

Canter, L. (1998), 'Integration of HIA and EIA', *EIA Newsletter*, **16**, 10–12.

Canter, L. and Sadler, B. (1997), *A Tool Kit for Effective EIA Practice – Review of Methods and Perspectives on their Application*, Oklahoma: University of Oklahoma.

Cassios, C. (ed.) (1995), *Environmental Impact Assessment Methodology and Research*, Brussels: European Commission, DGXI.

Clark, R. and Canter, L. (eds) (1997), *Environmental Policy and NEPA: Past, Present and Future*, Boca Raton, FL: CRC Press.

Dalal-Clayton, B. and Sadler, B. (1998), *The Application of Strategic Environmental Assessment in Developing Countries*, London: International Institute for Environment and Development.

Devarajan, S., Squire, L. and Suthiwant-Narueput, S. (1996), 'Project appraisal in the World Bank', in Kirkpatrick, C. and Weiss, J. (eds), *Cost–Benefit Analysis and Project Appraisal in Developing Countries*, Cheltenham: Edward Elgar.

Devarajan, S., Squire, L. and Suthiwant-Narueput, S. (1997), 'Beyond rate of return: reorienting project appraisal', *World Bank Research Observer*, **12** (1), 35–46.

Donnelly, A., Dalal-Clayton, B. and Hughes, R. (1998), *A Directory of Impact Assessment Guidelines*, 2nd edn, London: International Institute for Environment and Development.

Francis, P. and Jacobs, S. (1999), 'Institutionalising social analysis in the World Bank', *Environmental Impact Assessment Review*, May, 341–57.

George, C. (1997) 'Assessing global impacts at sector and project levels', *Environmental Impact Assessment Review*, **17** (4), 227–47.

George, C. (1999 forthcoming), 'Comparative review of environmental assessment procedures and practice', in Lee, N. and George, C. (eds), *Environmental Assessment in Developing Countries and Countries in Transition*, Chichester: Wiley.

Harberger, A. (1997), 'New frontiers in project evaluation', *World Bank Research Observer*, **12** (1), 73–82.

Institute of Environmental Assessment (1995), *Guidelines for Baseline Ecological Assessment*, F.N. Spon, London.

Kanbur, R. (1990), 'Project versus policy reform', *Proceedings of the World Bank Annual Conference on Development Economics*, Washington, DC: World Bank.

Kessler, J.J. and van Dorp, M. (1998), 'Structural adjustment and the environment: the need for an analytical methodology', *Ecological Economics*, **27** (3), 267–82.

Kirkpatrick, C. and Lee, N. (eds) (1997), *Sustainable Development in a Developing World: Integrating Socio-Economic Appraisal and Environmental Assessment*, Cheltenham: Edward Elgar.

Kirkpatrick, C. and Weiss, J. (1996), 'Cost–benefit analysis for developing countries', in Kirkpatrick, C. and Weiss, J. (eds), *Cost–Benefit Analysis and Project Appraisal in Developing Countries*, Cheltenham: Edward Elgar, pp. 3–23.

Kleinschmidt, V. and Wagner, D. (eds) (1998), *Strategic Environmental Assessment in Europe*, Dordrecht: Kluwer.

Kolhoff, A.J. (1996) 'Integrating gender assessment study into environmental impact assessment', *Project Appraisal*, **11** (4), 261–6.

Lee, N. (1999 forthcoming), 'Integrating appraisals and decision making', in Lee, N. and George, C. (eds), *Environmental Assessment in Developing Countries and Countries in Transition*, Chichester: Wiley.

Lee, N. and Kirkpatrick, C. (eds) (1996), Special Issue on 'Environmental Assessment and Socio-Economic Appraisal in Development', *Project Appraisal*, **11** (4).

Lee, N. and Kirkpatrick, C. (1997), 'The relevance and consistency of EIA and CBA in project appraisal', in Kirkpatrick, C. and Lee, N. (eds), *Sustainable Development in a Developing World: Integrating Socio-Economic Appraisal and Environmental Assessment*, Cheltenham: Edward Elgar, pp. 125–38.

Lee, N. and Walsh, F. (1992), 'Strategic environmental assessment: an overview', *Project Appraisal*, **7** (3), 126–36.

Little, I.M.D. and Mirrlees, J. (1991), 'Project appraisal and planning twenty years on', *Proceedings of World Bank Annual Conference on Development Economics*, Washington, DC: World Bank.

MacGillivray, A. and Zadek, S. (1995), *Accounting for Change: Indicators for Sustainable Development*, 2 vols, London: New Economics Foundation.

Moldan, B. and Billharz, S. (eds) (1997), *Sustainability Indicators*, Chichester: Wiley.

Munasinghe, M. and Cruz, W. (1995), 'Economy-wide policies and the environment: lessons from experience', *World Bank Environment Paper*, No. 12, Washington, DC.

Mwalyosi, R. and Hughes, R. (1998), *The Performance of EIA in Tanzania: An Assessment*, London: International Institute for Environment and Development.

Niekerk, F. and Arts, J. (1996), 'Impact assessments in Dutch infrastructure planning: towards better timing and integration', *Project Appraisal*, **11** (4), 237–46.

Oglethorpe, D.R. and Sanderson, R.A. (1999), 'An ecological–economic model for agri-environmental policy analysis', *Ecological Economics*, **28**, 245–66.

Organization for Economic Cooperation and Development (OECD) (1996), *Coherence in Environmental Assessment: Practical Guidance on Development Cooperation Projects*, Paris: OECD.

Organization for Economic Cooperation and Development (OECD) (1997), *Freight and the Environment: Effects of Trade Liberalisation and Transport Sector Reforms*, Paris: OECD.

Potier, M. (1997), 'Environmental assessment of trade liberalisation: an OECD perspective', in Kirkpatrick, C. and Lee, N. (eds), *Sustainable Development in a Developing World: Integrating Socio-Economic Appraisal and Environmental Assessment*, Cheltenham: Edward Elgar, pp. 46–57.

Prest, A. and Turvey, R. (1965), 'Cost–benefit analysis: a survey', *Economic Journal*, **75**, 685–705.

Rees, C. (1999), 'Improving the effectiveness of environmental assessment in the World Bank', *Environmental Impact Assessment Review*, May, 333–9.

Rotmans, J. (1998), 'Methods for IA: the challenges and opportunities ahead', *Environmental Modeling and Assessment*, **3**, 155–79.

Sadler, B. (1996), *Environmental Assessment in a Changing World: Final Report of the International Study of the Effectiveness of Environmental Assessment*, Ottawa: Canadian Environmental Assessment Agency.

Sadler, B., Dusik, J. and Casey-Lefkowitz, S. (eds) (1998), *Strategic Environmental Assessment in Transitional Countries*, Szentendre: Regional Environmental Centre for Central and Eastern Europe.

Sadler, B. and Verheem, R. (1996), *Strategic Environmental Assessment: Status, Challenges and Future Directions*, The Hague: Ministry of Housing, Spatial Planning and the Environment.

Sadler, B. and Verheem, R. (1997), *Country Status Reports on Environmental Impact Assessment*, Utrecht, The Netherlands: Netherlands Commission for Environmental Impact Assessment.

Squire, L. (1989), 'Project evaluation in theory and practice', in Chenery, H. and Srinivasan, T.N. (eds), *Handbook of Development Economics*, 11, Amsterdam: North-Holland.

Tol, R.S.J. and Vellinga, P. (1998), 'The European Forum on integrating environmental assessment', *Environmental Modeling and Assessment*, **3**, 181–91.

Toth, F.L. and Hizsnyik, E. (1998), 'Integrated environmental assessment methods: evolution and applications', *Environmental Modeling and Assessment*, **3**, 193–207.

Vanclay, F. (1999 forthcoming), 'Social impact assessment', in Lee, N. and George, C. (eds), *Environmental Assessment in Developing Countries and Countries in Transition*, Chichester: Wiley.

Vanclay, F. and Bronstein, D.A. (eds) (1995), *Environmental and Social Impact Assessment*, Chichester: Wiley.

Wood, C. (1995), *Environmental Impact Assessment: A Comparative Review*, Harlow: Longman.

PART I

INTEGRATED APPRAISAL AND DECISION MAKING: ALTERNATIVE PERSPECTIVES AND METHODS

2 Strengthening the integrated approach for impact assessments in development cooperation

Jules Scholten and Reinoud Post

2.1 Introduction

The second environmental assessment review of the World Bank (Kjorven 1997) and unpublished evaluations of various donor agencies make clear that the thematic policies[1] for development cooperation, as defined by these agencies or by national governments, are not fully and satisfactorily reflected in the projects carried out under their auspices.

It is readily accepted that, since such policies have been formulated, project portfolios include more projects than previously that are specifically designed to get environmental, social, gender, cultural and institutional issues on the development agenda and to promote the integration of these issues in decision making on development planning. This is a consequence of the earmarking of budget components and the appointment of thematic experts within the donor agencies. However, the attention paid to thematic issues in non-thematically oriented projects and to other policy themes in thematically oriented projects is often substandard.

In some cases, the non-compliance of project design with these defined policies can be attributed to the variable degree of commitment of the various sections of the responsible agency to the thematic policy intentions. In other cases, policies are insufficiently translated into the operational guidelines to be used by project officers and field staff; implementation of these policies is left to the good intentions of the individual project officer or to the appraisal teams. In yet other cases, where guidelines do exist, project officers may circumvent their application. In general, obligations and guidelines on policy implementation and its reporting are lacking or weak and real enforcement is often absent.

2.2 Constraints on implementing thematic policies

Unequal attention to thematic issues: an historical perspective
Some twenty to thirty years ago, development projects were largely the product of engineers and economists (Rashid 1998). A combination of technical criteria and internal rates of return determined project design. Whilst the basic goal was poverty alleviation, the main focus was essentially on

increase in production, particularly in the agricultural sector, in many developing countries.

The example given in Box 2.1 illustrates the adverse impact arising from the dominance of economic and technical considerations in rural development, in the case of a project in Jamaica that was designed between 1977 and 1981.

Box 2.1   An agricultural development scheme in Jamaica

Jamaica's main food staple is rice but it is mainly imported. The idea was developed among economists that Jamaica should grow rice as an import substitute to save precious foreign currency. The engineers concluded that, as a mainly hilly country, Jamaica's only level areas that were suitable for irrigated rice production were certain coastal mangrove swamps along the north and south-west coasts of the island.

The mangrove swamps were cleared, the reclaimed land was levelled and irrigation systems including reservoirs were constructed. A farm structure was laid out. The land was then ready for the farmers to produce the rice. However, it became apparent that many Jamaicans are unwilling to become paddy rice farmers as they prefer hillside agriculture and dislike wetland agriculture for fear of waterborne diseases.

The paddy rice development project ended in failure. The farm and feeder roads that were constructed were used as landing strips for small aircraft transporting the illicit marijuana crop that is grown on small hillside plots to the USA.

Source: Personal experience and observation (Jules Scholten).

Agricultural extension services began to challenge the oversimplification of the development issue by economists and others, in cases such as these. As a consequence, in the 1970s, a number of project preparation teams came to include agronomists and experts in other agricultural specializations. Their work was intended to deepen the economic analyses that were being undertaken.

In the 1980s, social and institutional aspects did get a toehold in the thinking about project design, although gender was not yet an issue. It was only halfway through this decade that environmental impacts of project design and implementation started to attract wider attention, although environmental impact assessment (EIA) was being practised in some developed countries during the 1970s. The introduction of EIA began to pull sustainability and appraisal away from the sphere of economic analysis. EIA emphasized the existence and importance for decision making of values that cannot be expressed easily in monetary terms. The urge to take these values into account has both complicated decision making and threatened the dominance of the engineers and economists.

Budget spending as a criterion of professional performance
As a consequence of the mainly technical character of development aid in the 1960s and 1970s, growing aid budgets and limited absorption capacity of development countries, for a considerable period of time the main difficulty for the project officer has been realizing projects according to the budget schedule. This has always been a problem, even when appraisal was based only on traditional economic and financial criteria. In nearly all donor organizations there was pressure on project officers to have a significant number of projects implemented. Hence, the budget that was spent slowly became a liability factor in job evaluation. The success of the projects themselves, based on proper project preparation, was in practice less important. In most cases, the degree of success can be measured only after years of project implementation. If, as is mostly the case, the job assignment of a project officer is for a maximum period of four years, then project quality and success can rarely be used for job evaluation.

Thematic policies, of the types described above, were formulated mainly in the 1980s and the early 1990s. These policies, and the assessments they brought with them, have further complicated the job of the project officer who, in most cases, is not an expert on thematic issues. It is understandable, in these circumstances, that evasive action sometimes occurred in a situation where little specific guidance or effective enforcement was present. In more recent years, when aid budgets have been shrinking, these pressures have been eased, leaving room for a more considered approach to project preparation and appraisal.

Modifying proposals is cumbersome
In order to appreciate the complexity of the project officer's job and to identify points where quality improvement measures may be taken, it is useful to explore the process of project generation.

Little formal research has been carried out concerning how ideas for development cooperation projects are born and how they find their way into donor programmes for financing their implementation. However, informal unpublished research suggests that often these originate from personal contacts between representatives of donor agencies and recipient countries' officials. Once an idea is launched, those initially involved frequently become its 'caring parents' as it develops into a project proposal.

In order to avoid possible weaknesses and unwanted consequences of the proposal, donor agency procedures may (and often do) prescribe screening of the proposal to determine whether it should be submitted to one or more thematic assessments. For instance, Dutch procedures prescribe screening for environmental impact assessment (EIA), social impact assessment (SIA), gender assessment study (GAS), poverty assessment (PA), cost–benefit analysis (CBA) and others.

If it is clear that there is a need for one or more thematic assessments, in many cases the execution of these results is a cumbersome process of adjusting and readjusting the proposal. Sometimes additional thematic studies are required and further adjustments to the project are sought. Adaptations to proposals have then to be renegotiated with recipient country government institutions. This may threaten the personal relationships which originated the project proposal, and cause delays in project approval and inception.

Integrating thematic requirements into project design is complex
Each thematic assessment will propose its own conditions for project implementation. It is the task of the project officer or an appraisal team to translate sometimes contradictory or mutually incompatible recommendations of the individual thematic assessments into a coherent project proposal of good quality. This is virtually impossible. It is a complex and frustrating job, especially as one realizes that the outcome gives no guarantee of quality since interdependent influences between the thematic fields will have been ignored. Hence, the need for the integration of impact assessments (IAs) has arisen in order to overcome the difficulties in synthesizing the results of a number of aspect-by-aspect IAs.

2.3   Integrated approaches to impact assessments

Aspect-by-aspect versus integrated approaches
Different assessment methods have been developed over time and in relative isolation of each other, in separate specialized institutes. Donor agency assessment practices typically reveal thematic compartmentalization with specialized departments for environment, rural development, gender and economy, each stressing the importance of their specific theme in project appraisal. Thus, in most cases, the aspect-by-aspect approach is formally still the only available approach. This has revealed a number of weaknesses, mainly associated with the lack of coordination.

A first weakness relates to lack of coordination in time. Thematic assessments are often prepared at different moments in time by different groups of specialists without sufficient exchange of information (see Box 2.2).

Box 2.2   Groundwater borewell irrigation scheme in India

A GAS for this project was published in 1993. An environmental impact study was commissioned in the same year and published and reviewed in 1995. The GAS was not referred to in the environmental impact statement (EIS). It also was not made available to the EIA review team. Recommendations in the GAS, the EIS and its review were not taken into account in project approval and implementation. In 1997 an evaluation mission which studied the situation in the Nalgonda district (a pilot zone) concluded that impacts had occurred as foreseen in the EIS and were a consequence of not implementing the project set-up and mitigating measures which had been proposed. The evaluation team made the same recommendations as had previously been formulated in the GAS and EIS review findings.

Sources: Commission for EIA in the Netherlands (1995) and Ooijen et al. (1997).

A second weakness relates to the lack of coordination in the substance of assessments. Some thematic assessments consider alternative solutions that will be able to meet the project's objectives whereas other sectoral assessments consider only the preferred option which is commonly formulated when initiating the project concept. Appraisers of the sectoral assessments are then unable to compare the potential impacts of such alternatives and may discard them even though some might have been promising (see Box 2.3).

Box 2.3   Hydro-power project in Nepal

An economic assessment compared various large-scale power generation options to smaller-scale power generation options. On the basis of economic criteria it was decided to discard the small-scale options and to focus the EIA on a preferred large-scale power generation option only. An appraisal based on a combination of environmental, social and economic criteria might have resulted in the selection of one of the smaller-scale options.

Source: Commission for EIA in the Netherlands (1994).

A third weakness arises where thematic assessments, separately prepared, neglect interdependencies (due to cause–effect relationships associated with crosscutting issues) between the various thematic fields (see Box 2.4).

Box 2.4   Drinking water and sanitation project in Yemen

Although scoping highlighted the importance of the themes 'institutional capacity' and 'gender' for the overall sustainability of this project, no studies were carried out relating to these. The aid agency, having received the scoping report, was aware of the importance of these studies for project sustainability but decided to limit its studies to the environmental (biophysical) impacts. Undoubtedly, this will have an impact on the implementation of the project and the follow-up.

Sources: Commission for EIA in the Netherlands (1993, 1996).

A fourth weakness of the aspect-by-aspect approach is that the prospect of having to carry out many separate assessments may cause officers to skip one or more of these. In the current situation, some relevant thematic assessments are not carried out because of lack of funds, lack of time, failure to recognize their relevance or because further study does not fit into the agency's budget allocation agenda. Consequently, project appraisal then ignores impacts that may originate from the neglected thematic fields (see Box 2.5).

The weaknesses in the aspect-by-aspect approach relate to the risk of misjudgement of impacts and oversight of valuable alternative solutions that could have taken crosscutting issues into account (Brown 1998). Projects resulting from this approach risk failure because their formulation is biased or incomplete. When applying an integrated approach, screening and scoping should identify thematic fields in their order of relevance and see to it that they are appropriately addressed in the assessment. In a fully integrated approach, there is only one assessment process. Coordination between different thematic assessments is no longer required and the project officer is presented with an integrated overall picture, covering all of the choices that can be made.

Thinking about integrated approaches for project preparation is not new. At this moment, however, the thinking has intensified and is starting to yield results. Various development banks are working on it and some of their officials expect[2] that assessments will commonly apply an integrated approach within a time period of 5 to 10 years.

Box 2.5   Interdependencies and sustainability in Yemen

A striking example of the importance of crosscutting issues, linking economic, social and biophysical subsystems, can be gleaned from recent developments in Yemen. In this country, for more than two thousand years, agricultural production flourished on hillside terraces irrigated by runoff from the mountains during the rainy season. The traditional division of labour dictated that women work the terraced fields whereas men maintain the terraces, the irrigation structures and implement the traditional rules for water use by farms in the catchments. Then economic development in oil-rich Saudi Arabia and the Gulf States attracted many men from Yemen to work as migrant labourers in unskilled and semi-skilled jobs in those countries.

The departure of so many men led to a breakdown in the maintenance of the terraces and irrigation structures as well as to neglect of the rules for water use in the catchment and for the release of impounded runoff. The introduction of a number of donor-supported rural development projects that pump groundwater for flood irrigation on valley bottoms, plains and plateaux caused a further deterioration in the terraced and irrigated hillside agriculture. The result is that within a time span of thirty years a sustainable form of agriculture which depended on renewable natural resources has been replaced by an unsustainable form of agriculture which depletes non-renewable resources of fossil fuels and groundwater.

Source: Milroy (1990).

Assessment of crosscutting issues: towards more integration
At the 1998 annual meeting of the International Association for Impact Assessment (IAIA) in Christchurch, New Zealand, a workshop addressed the issue of integrated approaches to impact assessment (Vanclay 1998). The question was raised whether the compartmentalized approach to impact assessment is a problem that compromises the quality of projects. The workshop concluded that indeed this is the case and also that integration of impact studies is not only feasible but inevitable. Therefore it resolved the issue of necessity, but, although several examples from actual practice were presented, it did not resolve how integration should best be realized.

Varying degrees of integration can be envisaged. As a first step, procedural tuning of the various sectoral impact assessments may create sufficient overlap in the timing of assessments so that the different assessment teams have the opportunity to communicate and exchange findings. It is then the task of the project planners and donor agency officials to create the conditions for procedural synchronization in time and place.

However, whilst procedural tuning can offer a considerable improvement in the aspect-by-aspect approach, it still does not provide a guarantee that the exchange of assumptions, findings and so on will actually take place between sectoral and thematic assessment teams. Too much still depends on the willingness of individual teams to communicate with each other and to be receptive to each other's ideas and findings. Therefore, as a further step in synchronization, project planners and managers may need to develop a more comprehensive scoping approach leading to the identification of alternative solutions that take into account crosscutting issues. These alternatives then form the subjects of study in the various sectoral assessments.

The formulation of a comprehensive set of alternatives offers a solution to the integration problem that is halfway between procedural synchronization and full integration of impact assessments. If this approach is still found to offer insufficient guarantee for the full consideration of crosscutting issues and impacts, a single impact assessment should be carried out that covers all cross-sectoral aspects throughout the procedure from problem identification through project formulation to its implementation. Consequently, one team carries out the assessment and the team leader has the task of liaising between all team members and balancing all thematic and crosscutting issues.

The goal of such an integrated impact assessment is described in Post et al. (1997):

> It aspires to describe – from the perspective of an identified problem or a proposed project – the relations between the human communities concerned, their economic organization and their actual resource base. It qualifies, quantifies and, as far as possible, values the effects of proposed and alternative interventions on the three (economic, social and natural) subsystems and their inter-system relations. It attempts to identify beneficial interventions and to fully expose unavoidable trade-offs. (p. 50)

The theoretical basis of the conceptual framework for integrated impact assessment is the system-analytical model used by Dalal Clayton (1992) to define sustainability. In this model, the world is seen as a system comprising three subsystems which support human existence: economic, social, and natural or biophysical. It cannot (yet) be determined whether it is each separate subsystem, or the overall system, which is required to function sustainably. However, interventions may be made in the functioning of each subsystem that will result in increased sustainability. Criteria with which such interventions are to comply should be set in the social and environmental (that is, thematic) policies. Decreasing the sustainability of the functioning of each subsystem implies the long-term non-viability of the system as a whole. Sustainability of the overall system can probably be reached only by improving the sustainability of each of the three subsystems.

As yet there is no generally accepted conceptual framework available for integrating thematic assessments. So, the question arises as to how crosscutting issues can be better addressed and how integration can be facilitated.

In 1997, the Netherlands Commission for EIA reported on a possible conceptual framework and on some experimental work relating to the integration of assessments (Post et al. 1997). Further experimental work is needed and the Commission sees good prospects for practical cases to be undertaken in the near future as donor agencies, with the environmental department of the World Bank as front runner, acknowledge the limitations of the aspect-by-aspect approach and the advantages of integrating thematic assessments.

In 1998, the Netherlands Development Agency requested the Netherlands Commission for EIA to study the usefulness of the various forms of impact assessment that have been developed for project appraisal by the Agency. The Commission for EIA carried out this task (Commission for EIA in the Netherlands 1999) and, additionally, presented recommendations on the perceived need for integration as noted by the IAIA workshop in Christchurch, New Zealand. The Commission recommends the full integration of assessment instruments for policy and programme planning and continued use of thematic assessment instruments at the project level. The latter, however, should be restructured to include assessments for other neglected thematic fields of interest. At the project level, it also proposes integrated screening to determine the 'leading' theme and to identify contributing thematic issues of importance. The instrument assessing best the impacts on the leading theme would then be used and adopted to include the other contributory issues.

2.4 Conclusions

Development cooperation has resulted, so far, in less than optimal project quality. Initially, development cooperation targeted only economic and technical goals. In the 1970s and 1980s, awareness grew that development should be more broadly based. Policy themes relating to culture, equity, gender, environment and institutional capacity emerged. These, to varying degrees, were successfully promoted by thematic experts who managed to develop their own strongholds within the aid agencies. The result was a thematically compartmentalized structure within many aid agencies and, in many cases, an obligation for project officers to implement an aspect-by-aspect appraisal of project proposals. The need to consider these themes in project formulation was often laid down in formal thematic policies. The aspect-by-aspect appraisal of proposals has serious weaknesses that may lead to suboptimally formulated projects. For project officers it has seriously complicated their work, and, as enforcement of thematic policy is generally weak, there has been a tendency to ignore or bypass some thematic assessments.

An integrated approach could overcome the weaknesses of the aspect-by-aspect appraisal. This would lead to more optimal project formulation and would greatly simplify project officers' work. The thinking about integrated approaches to impact assessment and project appraisal is developing and it is increasingly recognized that the use of integrated approaches is inevitable in the near future. An analysis of available instruments carried out by the Commission for EIA in the Netherlands for the Netherlands development cooperation programme suggests that for appraisal of policies, plans and programmes a fully integrated instrument should be developed from the best assessment instruments currently available, taking one of them as the core instrument. For project appraisal, the analysis suggests that a 'leading theme' and other themes of importance (contributory issues) be identified, that the assessment instrument developed for the leading theme be applied and that assessment of the contributory issues be incorporated in that instrument.

Notes

1. Thematic policies address issues that in pursuing the leading goal of development cooperation – that is, economic development – tend to be overlooked but that are considered relevant for all development efforts. Most aid agencies have formulated (thematic) policies on culture, equity, gender, environment and institutional capacity.
2. Oral communication at the workshop on 'Developing an integrated approach to impact assessment' at the Eighteenth Annual Meeting of the International Association for Impact Assessment, Christchurch, New Zealand, 23 April 1998.

References

Brown, L. (1998), 'EA of development assistance should include all crosscutting issues', paper presented at the workshop on 'Developing an integrated approach to impact assessment' at the Eighteenth Annual Meeting of the International Association for Impact Assessment, Christchurch, New Zealand, 23 April 1998.

Commission for EIA in the Netherlands (1993), 'Advice on the specifications for the content of the EIS on the water supply, sanitation and waste water disposal projects for Ataq, Wadi Jirdan, Nisab and Beihan areas, Shabwah Governorate, Republic of Yemen', Advice submitted to Netherlands Development Agency, ISBN 90-5237-587-9.

Commission for EIA in the Netherlands (1994), 'Advisory review of the environmental impact statement of the Arun III hydroelectric project, Nepal', Advice submitted to NEDA, ISBN 90-5237-698-0.

Commission for EIA in the Netherlands (1995), 'Advisory review of the environmental impact statement Andhra Pradesh groundwater bore well irrigation schemes (Apwell) and recommendations for the Inception Report of the Apwell project, India', Advice submitted to Netherlands Development Agency, ISBN 90-5237-896-7.

Commission for EIA in the Netherlands (1996), 'Advisory review of the environmental impact statement/feasibility study Shabwah: water and sanitation and recommendations for project identification, Yemen', Advice submitted to Netherlands Development Agency, ISBN 90-5237-993-9.

Commission for EIA in the Netherlands (1999), 'Review of thematic instruments for appraisal of development initiatives, their compatibility and possibilities for integration', Advice submitted to Netherlands Development Agency, ISBN 90-421-0494-5.

Dalal Clayton, B. (1992), 'Modified EIA and indicators of sustainability: first steps towards sustainability analysis', paper presented to the Twelfth Annual Meeting of the International Association for Impact Assessment, Washington, DC, 19–22 August.

Kjorven, O. (1997), *The Impact of Environmental Assessment: A Review of World Bank's Experience*, World Bank, Technical Paper No. 363, Washington, DC.

Milroy, A. (1990), 'The hanging gardens of Yemen', Film produced for the Television Trust for Environment, the British Overseas Development Administration (Foreign and Commonwealth Office), the Dutch Development Cooperation Programme and the Yemen Arab Ministries of Agriculture, Information and Foreign Affairs.

Ooijen, R., Uil, H., Chatterji, S., Hanumantha Rao, T. and Reddy, T.N. (1997), 'Andhra Pradesh ground water bore well irrigation schemes (APWELL)', mid-term review mission report, Netherlands Economic Institute, Rotterdam, The Netherlands.

Post, R.A.M., Kolhoff, A.J. and Velthuyse, B.J.A.M. (1997), 'Towards integration of assessments, with reference to integrated water management in third world countries', *Impact Assessment and Project Appraisal*, **16** (1), p. 50.

Rashid, H.E. (1998), 'Impact assessment of projects – then and now', paper prepared for the workshop on 'Developing an integrated approach to impact assessment' at the Eighteenth Annual Meeting of the International Association for Impact Assessment, Christchurch, New Zealand, 23 April 1998 (not published, available from the author).

Vanclay, F. (1998), Report on the workshop on 'Developing an integrated approach to impact assessment' at the Eighteenth Annual Meeting of the International Association for Impact Assessment, Christchurch, New Zealand, 23 April 1998 (not published, available from the author).

3 Integrating crosscutting issues in the environmental assessment of development assistance projects

A. Lex Brown

3.1 Introduction

This chapter concerns international development assistance, or international cooperation, and the desire amongst countries and agencies providing this assistance to ensure that its outcomes are sustainable, that activities promoted by the assistance result in minimal environmental damage, preferably environmental improvement, that its benefits are fairly distributed, including across gender, and that it contributes to sustainable livelihoods in the recipient country. Within the headquarters of the major development assistance agencies, whether international or bilateral, these matters are likely to be official policy. Also there are staff in the country offices of these agencies who are strongly committed to these policies. But there are equally a range of pressures within the country offices of the agencies to pay little more than lip service to these issues, and to 'get on with the essential job of development' – the issues being seen as impediments, and peripheral, to the core activity of designing and implementing projects and programmes.

This chapter arises from experience of working with project and programme appraisal across a wide range of countries and a wide range of projects. It represents an informed opinion – not based on specific data collection but instead on lessons, taught by those who are working in-country, in designing, appraising and implementing development cooperation programmes. The chapter is not concerned directly with the well-developed environmental impact assessment (EIA) procedures for large infrastructure projects, though much of it is relevant there too, but instead with the much greater range of soft development assistance projects which today constitute the vast majority of the activities of multilateral and bilateral donors.

In summary, this chapter argues that:

- Government compartmentalizes activity and expertise into line agencies with well-defined areas of responsibility.
- Development assistance programmes tend to mirror this model because international and bilateral development agencies tend to negotiate and implement their support at line agency level (though

within the larger framework of a national development assistance programme).

- There is a growing understanding that mainstreaming of crosscutting issues such as gender, environment, poverty, sustainability and sustainable livelihoods is impeded where programme formulation is compartmentalized.
- Most countries already have considerable experience in appraisals of projects/programmes on one crosscutting issue, environment, through their environmental (impact) assessment procedures.
- The dynamics of development assistance project/programme formulation are such that there is no opportunity to have 'several bites at the apple' in the form of different appraisal tools for different crosscutting issues.
- There is a need to extend the current environmental assessment processes (EIA, strategic environmental assessment (SEA) and so on) to include the full range of crosscutting issues.
- Such a conceptual leap is hardest for professionals steeped in Western environmental assessment (EA) modalities and traditions; but it is quite natural for, even anticipated by, those working at the coalface in development.

3.2 Compartmentalization

The complexity of modern government results in administrative compartmentalization of activity, budgets and expertise into line agencies with specific, but limited responsibilities – agriculture, transport, education, health, industry, trade and so on. Line agency activities are coordinated through national budgets and national development strategies by finance departments, planning departments, prime minister's departments, or similar, but only at the broad level of setting frameworks and budgets in which the individual line agencies operate.

Development assistance programmes tend to follow this model, with the detailed formulation of programmes, and their implementation, being handled at line agency level. This is generally true, whether the development assistance is through a bilateral arrangement, international organizations, or multilateral banks. Compartmentalization in government ensures that the necessary disciplinary expertise and implementation skills are brought to bear on specific development activities. But it also restricts the range of perspectives and disciplinary skills that can contribute to the formulation of that particular development activity. Understanding the limitation that this imposes on project/programme formulation is crucial to understanding how to address the problem.

3.3 Crosscutting issues

All development assistance agencies – bilateral and international agencies, and multilateral banks – now require that their programmes address not only economic development issues, but also a range of issues such as environment, sustainability, gender disparity, and perhaps poverty alleviation or sustainable livelihoods.

Environment

That environmental issues and development issues are inextricably linked through the interdependencies that exist between people and natural resources is familiar to all who work in the environmental field. Environmental change occurs through the application of development models, practices and life-styles, and any modification of the natural and physical environment has important socio-economic consequences that affect the quality of life. Environmental issues span global, national and local concerns. They include consideration of renewable use of natural resources such as water, forests and land, and use of non-renewable resources such as minerals and fossil fuels. They include the use of the environment as a sink for solid, liquid and gaseous wastes, and the assimilative capacity of oceans, airsheds, land and inland water bodies for these wastes. They also concern the maintenance of biological diversity through ensuring that sustainable yield from natural re-source use is not exceeded, and through conservation reserves and other forms of protection. Environmental issues cut across all development activi-ties, and their successful management requires a wide range of actions. Equally their management requires an understanding of the functioning of the whole of the biophysical and socio-economic system in which develop-ment occurs, and of how these systems respond to the growth of populations and economies. Traditional practice in land husbandry, and traditional cul-tural and religious perspectives of land and environment, are important considerations.

Gender in development

Women and men are inescapably linked to each other and their societies through relationships, attitudes, roles and responsibilities. It is through a full understanding of these linkages that we can identify dynamic and innovative ways of enhancing the development potential of women and men. All devel-opment initiatives are gendered: they will impact men and women differently. Gender mainstreaming means taking account of the social, cultural, eco-nomic and political differences between and among women and men in all programming activities. It comprises being informed of the gender character-istics of the population and setting, taking full account of this in the development of policy and programmes, and appraising all programmes in terms of potential gender disparities. Areas of focus for the advancement of women include fostering enabling environments for this advancement, and empowering women in issues such as social and economic assets and resources, income-generating activities, gender-sensitive legal and policy frameworks, and education and training.

Poverty and sustainable livelihoods
The concept of sustainable livelihoods has emerged in response to the challenges of development in today's world and to the need for new approaches that are integrative, can accommodate diverse realities, and do not attempt to be so all-encompassing as to be vague and ineffective in leading to action. Sustainable livelihoods are people's capacity to access options and resources and use them to make a living in such a way as not to foreclose options for others to make a living, either now or in the future. Agenda 21 used the term 'livelihoods' in the context of combating poverty, and its objectives include providing all persons urgently with the opportunities to earn sustainable livelihoods. Livelihoods of disadvantaged groups and resource-poor populations in both urban and rural areas need to be targeted for improvement. This approach to sustainable livelihoods requires building on aspects of communities' existing or potential livelihoods, adaptive strategies, knowledge, and natural resources base, understanding what these are through participatory learning and action research, and by investing in and building on these by development interventions in areas such as governance, policy, technology and capital availability. Sustainable livelihoods is an integrative construct which brings together all economic activities relevant to employment, as well as the social dimensions of sustainability and equity. The concept can, if well developed to reflect the country-specific heterogeneity of livelihood types and aspirations, bring a new synthesis to the ecological and economic sides of human activity, while addressing equity as a central principle.

It is useful to describe these issues collectively as 'crosscutting'. They manifest themselves in nearly all types of development activities and generally are not the planned outcomes of the particular development intervention. They cut across all government responsibilities as they are not the province of any single line agency, or at least not the province of any single line agency with any real power (environment departments, for example, are exceptionally weak in most governments). Implementation of a particular programme may achieve its intended outcomes, but at the same time may result in unintended externalities, say, in adverse effects on income distribution or increases in environmental degradation or non-sustainable resource use. Development interventions may also appear to be beneficial when observed from the perspective of the proponent, but far less beneficial when observed from other perspectives. An employment-generating programme may produce more jobs, but achieve very little in terms of alleviating poverty or in overcoming existing gender disparity in access to sustainable livelihoods.

Mechanisms have to be developed to tackle crosscutting issues of this type in development programming. However, there is a growing understanding that these issues are not easily mainstreamed when faced with the compartmentalization of programme formulation and implementation as described above. Their appropriate consideration can be achieved only by appraising projects and programmes using much wider skills and perspectives than those available in the narrower disciplinary positions dominant in implementing line agencies.

3.4   Environmental assessment and development assistance

Most developing countries already have experience, many considerable experience, at bringing these wider skills and perspectives to bear on development problems through their EIA activities. However, historically, these experiences have tended to focus on only one set of crosscutting issues – the environmental ones.

Most of this experience, too, has had a project-based focus, with the EIA directed at the appraisal of hardware projects such as dams, roads, mines and industrial developments. In addition, project-based EIA appraisals have often tended to emphasize the biological and physical environmental effects of development, more so than the social effects – and in this there has been considerable confusion foisted on developing countries depending on which developed country has had the most influence on the EIA processes there – with a narrow biophysical definition of 'environment' adopted by some European countries (for example, the Netherlands and the United Kingdom) but a broader biophysical and socio-cultural definition of the term adopted by others (such as Australia).

Multinational and bilateral aid agencies and banks have been particularly interested in the extension of project-based EIA-type approaches upstream from project-level activities to the strategic levels of planning and decision making (World Bank 1993, 1996). Increasingly, both developed and developing countries alike are giving consideration to extending environmental appraisals upstream from *projects* to *plans, policies and programmes* (the PPPs) through strategic environmental assessment (SEA) (UNEP 1996; Verheem 1992; Partidario 1996). The appropriate form, or forms, of SEA appraisal to adopt in particular circumstances are undergoing rapid evolution and remain the subject of ongoing debate. Both project-based EIA, and SEA, are examples of crosscutting appraisals, albeit confined at the moment to the range of issues normally considered in EIA.

Whereas aid in the past has often been in forms amenable to project-based EIA, most aid today is 'softer'. It is not project based. It may be programmatic – a range of inter-related activities under a single theme. It may provide wide-ranging support to a sector or subsector of government. Moreover, it is likely to focus primarily on in-country capacity building, both through human development and institution building, over a wide range of governmental and non-governmental activities. Programmes such as *developing the capacity to privatize state-run enterprises*, or *technical assistance to develop a fishing industry*, or *promotion of export growth*, or *capacity development for land-use planning*, are common in development assistance. These types of aid projects deal with activities which occur upstream in the project cycle. They deal with whole programmes, even whole government sectors. Often in their capacity-building focus they are part of policy development. Projects and programmes like this need to be subject to EIA/SEA procedures as they can have large environmental consequences, and wide-ranging consequences across the other crosscutting issues described above.

3.5 Extending environmental assessment to include all crosscutting issues

Approaches which rely on a simple checklist are common in attempts to ensure development assistance considers crosscutting issues: 'Does the project have any effect on poverty?' or 'Have women's issues been considered in formulating this project?'. However, simple box ticking like this is mere lip service. At best it achieves little. At worst it relieves individual and corporate consciences on these matters and creates the impression of concern and action. Checklist approaches cannot be effective. Roe et al. (1995) and other commentators note that there are many examples where crosscutting assessments of aid projects have turned into meaningless efforts only to satisfy procedural requirements.

There are no examples of tools, other than checklists, for the considerations of non-environmental crosscutting issues, which have the same widespread acceptance for project and programme appraisal, as does EIA. Even if there were the sound development of such tools, the dynamics of project/programme formulation in development assistance are such that there would be extreme reluctance to subject activities to a sequence of different appraisals. Despite directives in most bilateral and international development agencies for cognisance of these matters, at the level of field officers at the development interface, any such appraisals are often perceived to complicate and delay the processes of programme formulation, and similar views would be held within the counterpart line agencies.

If conventional EIA can mainstream the consideration of environmental issues in project-based appraisals, and SEA can do the same in policy and programme appraisals, why can they not also be adapted to mainstream the consideration of, say, gender and poverty? The simple answer is that they can, and should. There are at least three compelling reasons why EIA and SEA are suitable vehicles for achieving this.

First, consideration of any crosscutting issue requires that there be a clear understanding of the biophysical and social systems in which the development will occur and the complexity of interlinkages between the different parts of the system. Despite many other failings, the underlying strength of EIA processes has been that they have encouraged their practitioners to think in this holistic manner.

Second, in environmental assessment processes, it is the norm to consider need and alternatives, positive and negative impacts, and mitigation strategies – all essential to proper consideration of all crosscutting issues. EIA is also starting to move beyond reactive assessment towards proactive consideration of opportunities within development proposals, and it is in finding opportunities that the greatest gains will be made in addressing crosscutting issues. The distinction between *positive impacts* and *opportunities* is a useful one. *Positive impacts* include those things that will happen deliberately as part of a programme, say an increase in employment resulting from a development assistance programme to increase the magnitude of the tourism sector in a country. *Opportunities*, on the other hand, are those additional things that could be incorporated into a programme to achieve wider objectives. An example would be the potential, in the same tourism sector programme, to include a gender equity component to ensure that both sexes benefited from the increased employment. Identifying opportunities as part of appraisal provides the chance for lateral thinking in development aid programming, and a way to contribute creatively to programme formulation.

Third, in most development contexts, particularly amongst those who work at the coalface, the boundaries between environment, sustainable livelihoods, economic development, poverty, quality of life and gender are blurred. They all interact in most situations. This author's experience is that there is a far greater understanding of how all of these things are inter-related than there is in the developed world. The concepts and the absolute necessity of sustainability in development are paramount. In working alongside national development professionals in a wide range of countries, experience has been that their understanding (read 'scoping' in EIA parlance) of what needed to be considered in particular programme appraisals encompassed all the crosscutting issues described above. One would have had to impose 'Western' limits on what should 'properly' be considered in an 'environmental' appraisal to prevent the group involved from considering *all* the elements in the system in which the development intervention was to occur.

There is a conceptual leap required, but no methodological leap, to extend the current environmental assessment processes (EIA, SEA and so on) beyond Western-defined 'environmental issues' and to ensure that they consider the full range of crosscutting issues relevant to each particular development context. Such an extension is readily accommodated in development. However, it appears that this may be difficult, through inertia, for professionals steeped in Western EA modalities and traditions.

It is useful to examine how an environmental appraisal tool can be extended to consider all crosscutting issues. While it is recognized that the example below represents a very particular form of appraisal, and a particular set of circumstances, it does provide lessons and, in part, a model, for a more holistic use of current environmental assessment tools.

3.6 An example

Brown (1997a, 1997b and 1998) has described the application of a rapid environmental appraisal tool, the 'environmental overview' for use in the formulation stages of development assistance projects and programmes. It is a coarse, but effective, tool, taking its basic philosophy from accepted SEA concepts. The environmental overview uses a participatory procedure involving development agency officers, counterpart officers from government, non-governmental organizations (NGOs), and other stakeholders. The underlying philosophy is that a structured, participatory activity at the earliest stages of programme formulation is an efficient and effective means of tapping into the broad range of knowledge and perspectives required in appraising a programme's environmental soundness.

The environmental overview (see Brown (1997a) for a full description) asks its participants to collectively address a set of questions related to the draft of a proposed development assistance project (or programme) usually of 'soft' aid of the type described earlier. The questions are similar to those asked in conventional project-based EIA, but with different players and within a very different time frame. They also have additional emphases on pre-existing environmental issues in the area of the proposal, on the economic forces that prevail, and on relevant management capabilities and practices.

The first set of questions concerns the baseline conditions for the project/programme:

- What are the biophysical and social characteristics of the programme area?
- What are the major environmental and social issues that currently exist in the programme area?
- What are the economic forces that are currently operating in the programme area?
- What are the current management practices and capabilities in the programme area?

It should be noted that the term 'area', for different programmes, may refer to a *geographical area* or, more likely with soft aid, a *sectoral area* – agriculture, for example.

Next are questions concerning the programme impacts and opportunities, followed by how the draft programme can be redrafted in an operational strategy to take these, and the baseline conditions, into account:

- What are the major natural and socio-economic impacts and opportunities associated with the implementation of the programme?
- What modifications/alternatives are there for programme design?
- What operational strategy can be put in place within the programme to address these?

In the environmental overview, a group works interactively and sequentially through these questions in a highly structured way. The interactive group technique is a critical element of the procedure, and its participants must represent a broad mix of specialists and others. The mix, from different line agencies, from different disciplinary backgrounds and, where possible, from stakeholder interests, provides the diverse range of perspectives and knowledge bases required to set the original proposal in the context of its environmental and social systems. The bulk of the environmental overview can be completed with considerable speed, perhaps in a single day.

For effectiveness, the development proposal should desirably be in its draft formulation stages at the time of the environmental overview. Further, the process must extend, past mere analysis and critique, to develop modifications to the original proposal as an integral part of the appraisal. The environmental overview must be perceived and operated as a creative process in programme formulation and not as a static procedure which simply results in the preparation of just another document. The value is in the process of conducting the environmental overview, not in the additional words on paper.

Project documents pass through many drafts in their progress from raw concept to final proposal ready to be submitted for funding. It is during this drafting and redrafting – preferably as early as possible in the process – that the environmental overview can prove most effective, allowing the proposed development intervention to be appraised, and reformulated where necessary.

The tool has been applied, albeit in a training context, by development professionals in a range of countries to a variety of substantive development assistance proposals. This has included programmes such as planning for the resettlement of tsetse-fly cleared areas, institutional support for the implementation of a national shelter strategy, achieving international competitiveness through technology transfer and development, and employment generation through the development of small, medium and micro enterprises. It is instructive to the central argument of this chapter to look at the outcome of the environmental overview of one such programme – *building human capacity to develop and manage tourism at a national level* – in a South-east Asian country.

The original programme was focused on developing government and private capacity to identify major tourism destinations, capacity to market the country's tourism potential, and capacity to plan the necessary transport and other services essential for tourism. The aid was to be used to provide foreign expertise to assist and guide the capacity building, to plan structural changes in the government and private tourism sectors, and to provide overseas and national training. When the draft proposal was appraised using the environmental overview tool, its participants soon recognized that the original programme had ignored important environmental constraints to the successful sustainable development of large-scale tourism in the country (limitations on coastal resort development, limited capacity in government to request and assess EIA of overseas-funded resort proposals, for example). They were also able to suggest alterations to the draft proposal: modifying the terms of reference for foreign personnel, inserting new modules in the national training programmes and so on, to ensure that issues like these were addressed as an integral part of the development assistance programme.

But beyond recognizing the 'environmental' shortcomings in the original proposal, because of the diversity of disciplines and sectoral interests of the participants, the environmental overview simultaneously turned up shortcomings across other crosscutting issues. These, too, were recognized to be fundamental omissions in the original draft programme. For example, the failure of much tourism activity in developing countries to significantly uplift sustainable livelihoods in local populations, gender disparity in employment opportunities within new tourism developments and, most damning of all, total oversight in the original proposal of the need to develop the in-country capacity in health education and health services to accompany the massive increase in foreign tourism visits promoted by the proposal. This was despite common knowledge of the huge social and economic costs of sexually transmitted diseases and other health effects inflicted on neighbouring countries that had 'succesfully' developed their tourism potential. Again, participants were able to recommend quite small changes to the objectives and to the terms of reference of components of the original proposal to make sure that these critical issues would be given appropriate resources in the implementation of the capacity building to be provided within the development assistance programme.

The experiences reported in this example were repeated in nearly every country, and in nearly every development assistance project, which was appraised by the environmental overview tool. Participants in these environmental

overviews were not foreign experts, but were typical of development specialists involved at the coalface of development assistance programming that one
finds in every country in the world. The obvious conclusion is that when one
provides the opportunity and the correct milieu for a holistic, and systematic,
appraisal of a development activity – and this is what 'environmental' appraisal techniques generally do provide – one simultaneously provides the
opportunity for the full consideration of a wide range of 'non-environmental'
crosscutting issues.

The environmental overview tool was formulated originally as an environmental appraisal tool, but based on some five years of experience, the current
author has modified it to give equal weight to other dominant development
themes: gender, poverty and sustainable livelihoods. This has harnessed the
reality that good development practitioners in the field consider all components of the system in which the development is to occur. The modification
was simple, and the tool is easily recognized to be identical in form, content
and process to the environmental overview, but with an expanded focus. In
recognition of this expanded focus, and also because of its fit to many of the
principles of strategic environmental assessment, the new tool has tentatively
been renamed the 'strategic overview'.

3.7   Conclusions

This *strategic overview* is a response to the need for holistic approaches to
programme formulation in the complex social and biophysical systems in
which development interventions occur. The strategic overview identifies the
scope of environmental and social issues associated with the programmes
being formulated, recognizes where there may be environmental and social
opportunities, and forces the consideration of options, alternatives and modifications to the programme design. Once the strategic overview has identified
potential issues, one can then build their consideration into a reformulated
programme. In accordance with growing experience in best practice in SEA,
the strategic overview is not intended as a stand-alone assessment of an
already formulated proposal, but as a planning tool to be integrated into the
early stages of project and programme formulation. Underpinning the strategic overview is the belief that most of the knowledge and skills essential at
least *to recognize* (not necessarily *to solve*) potential gender, poverty, environmental and other crosscutting issues and opportunities in development
proposals, resides in-country. This knowledge and skill is best tapped through
an interactive participatory activity involving a range of government line
agencies, NGOs, the universities, community stakeholders and international
organizations. The strategic overview provides both structure and process by
which this expertise can be harvested practically and efficiently in a participatory group process with the programme formulators.

The strategic overview will work at all levels – project, programme or country. It is applicable to soft projects such as capacity building and is even applicable to the assessment of policies. While the tool has evolved within the context of an international agency programme, and its origins were in meeting requirements for environmental appraisal of development assistance programmes, experience in developing countries suggests that it will prove a versatile tool to appraise programmes on all crosscutting issues, and a model that governments themselves can adopt and adapt as appropriate to their own internal development planning procedures.

Acknowledgement
Some of the descriptions of environment, of gender and of sustainable liveli-hoods were compiled from a range of agency leaflets and various oral and written personal communications. Their unattributable sources are gratefully acknowledged.

References

Brown, A.L. (1997a), 'The environmental overview in development project formulation', *Impact Assessment*, **15** (1), 73–88.

Brown, A.L. (1997b), 'Further developments of the environmental overview as a strategic environmental assessment tool in development assistance', International Association of Impact Assessment 17th Annual Meeting, New Orleans, 28–31 May, p. 12.

Brown, A.L. (1998), 'The environmental overview as a realistic approach to strategic environmental assessment in developing countries', in Porter, A. and Fittipaldi, J. (eds), *Environmental Methods Review: Retooling Impact Assessment for the New Century*, Fargo: Army Environmental Policy Institute and International Association for Impact Assessment, pp. 127–34.

Partidario, M.R. (1996), 'Strategic environmental assessment: key issues emerging from recent practice', *Environmental Impact Assessment Review*, **16** (1), 31–55.

Roe, D., Dalal-Clayton, B. and Hughes, R. (1995), *A Directory of Impact Assessment Guidelines*, London: Environmental Planning Group, International Institute for Environment and Development.

United Nations Environment Programme (1996), *Environmental Impact Assessment: Issues, Trends and Practice*, New York: UNEP Environment and Economics Unit.

Verheem, R. (1992), 'Environmental assessment at the strategic level in the Netherlands', *Project Appraisal*, **7** (3), 150–56.

World Bank (1993), *Sectoral Environmental Assessment*, Environmental Assessment Sourcebook Update, No. 4.

World Bank (1996), *Regional Environmental Assessment*, Environmental Assessment Sourcebook Update, No. 15.

4 Environmental cost–benefit analysis and sustainability

Michael Common

4.1 Environmental impact assessment and economic cost–benefit analysis

Environmental impact assessment (EIA) and environmental cost–benefit analysis (ECBA) are about the appraisal of projects with environmental impacts, where the term 'project' covers policy changes and programmes as well as discrete investments in plant and equipment or infrastructure. However, it will simplify matters here to mainly have in mind a project as normally understood, and to consider initially what is, in terms of its environmental impacts, a very simple project in that it directly affects just one environmental indicator. It will also help to make a sharp distinction between EIA on the one hand and ECBA and alternatives to it on the other, treating EIA as the business of assessing the environmental impacts and ECBA and alternatives to it as being about social decision making on the basis of the EIA.

In Figure 4.1, panel (a) shows the time profile of the net benefit results from a standard commercial appraisal of the project, in discounted present value terms. Date t_1 is when the project comes on-stream, date t_2 is the end of its economic life. Given that area 2 is larger than area 1, the project would be assessed as commercially viable. We have net present value $(NPV) = (2 - 1) > 0$. We shall assume that, apart from the environmental impact, all of the project inputs and outputs are traded in competitive markets. In that case, leaving aside the environmental impact, there is no 'market failure', and a commercial appraisal and a properly conducted cost–benefit analysis (CBA) would give the same result for NPV. Going ahead with the project would be consistent with the requirements for efficiency in allocation. The argument for using efficiency criteria is that the inputs to projects are scarce – there are 'resource constraints' – and that using such criteria ensures that the inputs are not wasted by being used for poorly performing projects.

In panels (b) and (c), the vertical axis is the level of some environmental indicator E, where a lower level of E goes with more environmental damage. NP is the trajectory for E in the absence of the project, and P is the trajectory if the project goes ahead. The two panels show alternative outcomes in terms of whether or not P involves E crossing some threshold, shown as T. EIA is the business of figuring out NP and P for the project. Given that is done, the

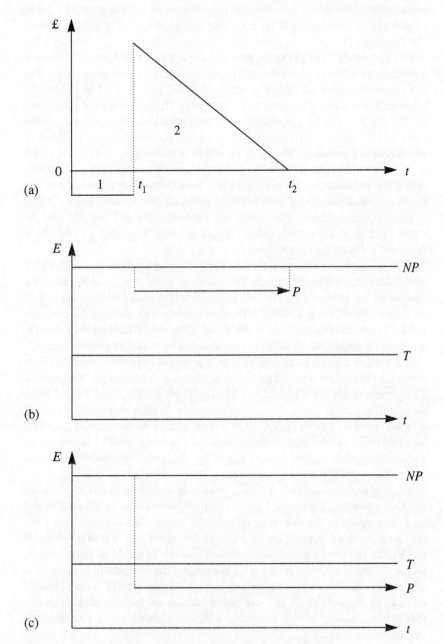

Figure 4.1   Alternative environmental impacts for a project

question remains as to whether the project should go ahead or not. This entails a prior question: *how* should society decide whether or not the project should proceed?

The economist's answer to the procedural question, which does not involve a distinction between panel (b) and panel (c) type EIA outcomes, is ECBA. An essential feature of ECBA is 'environmental valuation'. The difference between *P* and *NP* is expressed as a (discounted present value) sum of money *M*. If *NPV* > *M* the project should go ahead, otherwise it should not. While there is a large, and often esoterically technical, literature on ECBA and environmental valuation, the basic idea here is really quite simple. *M* is the amount of money that those affected would be willing to accept as compensation for experiencing *P* rather than *NP*. If *NPV* is greater than *M* and the project goes ahead, those to whom the project's net benefits accrue could fully compensate those who suffer the environmental effects and still be better off than if the project did not go ahead. Hence, society as a whole is better off if the project goes ahead.

This amounts to bringing environmental impact within the domain of application of efficiency criteria. The test 'is *NPV* > *M*?' is a particular version of the potential Pareto improvement test, which has been subject to criticisms which have nothing particularly to do with the natural environment.[1] Two such criticisms are worth mentioning here. Although they have, at the level of principle, no necessary connection with matters environmental, they are often argued, in fact, to be highly pertinent to projects with environmental impacts. The first is that compensation is potential rather than actual. The project of Figure 4.1 would, if *NPV* > *M*, get the go ahead even if there were to be put in place absolutely no compensating payments to those affected by *P* rather than *NP*. The second is that no account is taken of inequalities of income and wealth across, and between, project beneficiaries and sufferers. A benefit of £*x* accruing to the rich would be treated as equivalent to a cost of £*x* impacting on the poor.

In principle the second of these problems could be dealt with in an ECBA by assigning 'distributional' or 'equity' weights to £s of benefits and costs according to the affluence of those to whom they accrue.[2] However, this is rarely done in practice. One reason for this is that it is often difficult to identify the winners and losers closely enough to establish their income levels. There is also the problem of specifying the weights to be used. An alternative that has been suggested is to give the project some kind of qualitative equity rating and use some variant of multi-criteria analysis (MCA) to consider jointly economic efficiency, equity and environmental impact.[3]

4.2 Sustainability

Since the publication of the 'Brundtland Report' (World Commission on Environment and Development 1987) much ink has been spilt over the definition, and feasibility, of 'sustainable development'. It is, in my view, more useful to think about the issues subsumed under the rubric of sustainable development in terms of the global sustainability problem. That problem is to manage human affairs so as to address the problems of poverty and inequality while minimizing threats to ecological sustainability. Such threats arise from the interdependence of human and natural systems and the current level of activity in human systems. A threat to ecological stability arises when a system is driven to the point where it lacks resilience, the ability to maintain its structure and patterns of behaviour in the face of disturbance.[4]

Sustainability is a system property, the presence or absence of which can be determined only with hindsight by observation of its behaviour in the face of disturbance. An important question is whether there are indicators of resilience, such that by monitoring them it would be possible to say prior to a disturbance whether or not the system would prove resilient. At present there do not appear to be any generally agreed resilience indicators. A system that has proved resilient to one type or size of disturbance may not prove resilient in the face of a shock of different type or size.

Whereas economics largely ignores it, the new interdisciplinary field of ecological economics starts from an appreciation of the interdependence of economic and natural systems.[5] Perrings et al. (1995) define ecological economics as 'the study of interdependent economic and ecological systems' and note several 'distinct but related strands in the development of ecological economic models'(p. 8) of interdependence:

1. ... the realisation that not just the economy and its environment are jointly determined systems, but that the scale of economic activity is now such that this matters.
2. ... the perception that the dynamics of the jointly determined system are characterised by discontinuous change around critical threshold levels both for biotic and abiotic resources, and for ecosystem functions ...
3. ... path-dependence means that system history is relevant to current and future opportunities.
4. ... recognition that the stability of the jointly determined system depends less on the stability of individual resources, than on the resilience of the system – or the ability of the system to sustain its self-organisation in the face of stress and shock.

The sustainability problem is the central problem of ecological economics.

CBA and ECBA are essentially about correcting market failure so as to realize a state of allocative efficiency. Common and Perrings (1992) have shown that market failure correction is not sufficient for sustainability. In the absence of market failure, consumer sovereignty determines the allocation of resources and economic activity reflects individuals' preferences over the domain of feasible alternatives. Individuals' preferences may be such that economic activity is consistent with the integrity of natural systems, but they may not be. If the latter is the case, correcting market failure will not guarantee sustainability. A meaningful commitment to sustainability as a policy objective would imply a willingness to override the dictates of consumer sovereignty. ECBA privileges consumer sovereignty, and environmental valuation methods are all about revealing consumers' preferences, which are taken as given. One implication of the Common and Perrings result is that a society committed to sustainability could legitimately seek to 'educate' its members so that their preferences would be more likely to be consistent with sustainability. Economics takes it that individuals' preferences are given and sacrosanct. For economists, preference shaping is illegitimate – although, in fact, socially organized education involves it, and private agents spend lots of money on it.

4.3   Sustainability and project appraisal

One way to begin to think about project appraisal in relation to sustainability is in terms of thresholds. Panels (b) and (c) in Figure 4.1 show different situations for the project introduced in Section 4.1 according to whether or not the impact involves E crossing some threshold, T.

In panel (b), the threshold is not crossed. In such circumstances we might, notwithstanding a commitment to sustainability as a policy objective, be content to use ECBA and determine the project's fate by weighing NPV against M. As noted above, some have argued that an MCA approach involving efficiency, equity and environmental impact would actually be more useful.[6] Whatever the merits of this argument, the important point is that with both ECBA and MCA we are dealing with a situation where it is considered admissible to, in one way or another, decide the project's fate by comparing the economic gains with the environment impact. Economic gains and environmental impact can be traded off against each other.

The situation is different in panel (c). In this case the threshold is crossed, and given a commitment to sustainability, it could be argued that we should reject the project whatever the relative sizes of NPV and M. In terms of the project appraisal procedure, if an EIA revealed a panel (c) situation, some would argue that there would be no ECBA/environmental valuation stage as there would be no need to know M. This approach would elevate the avoidance of threats to sustainability, of crossing thresholds, to an overriding and binding constraint in project appraisal. *Any* project that an EIA revealed as sustainability threatening would not be allowed to go ahead.

This argument involves two, related, problems. First, economists would note that following it could involve forgoing a very large economic gain –

NPV – in order to avoid an environmental problem which had small *economic* implications, *M*. The natural system that collapses might be of little interest to humans, or the human interest that it serves might, at low cost, be served by some human-made system. The second problem is uncertainty, in the strict sense. The joint economy–environment system is complex and evolving and the future is inherently unknowable (Perrings 1987). For many projects, particularly those involving genuine innovation, the decision problem is characterized by uncertainty rather than risk. Where the EIA can say 'the immediate environmental implications of going ahead with this project are either as in panel (b) with a probability of *p* or as in panel (c) with probability $1 - p$' we are dealing with risk. Uncertainty is where probabilities cannot be attached to future possible states, or where the EIA cannot even enumerate possible future states – 'going ahead with this project may involve crossing some threshold level for *E*'. Further, the wider environmental implications of threshold crossing will also generally be unknown, as will, therefore, the economic implications.[7]

This kind of uncertainty was used 30 years ago (Ciriacy-Wantrup 1968) to argue for an approach to nature conservation, or biodiversity conservation as we would now call it, which would dispense with the environmental valuation step involved in ECBA. As developed by Bishop (1978) the argument for a 'safe minimum standard' (SMS) approach to biodiversity conservation goes as follows. Species extinction involves an irreversible reduction in the stock of potentially useful resources which is currently existing biodiversity. There is no way of knowing how large the future value to humans of any of the existing species will turn out to be. There are two kinds of ignorance. First, there is social ignorance – we cannot now know future preferences and technologies. Second, there is scientific ignorance – we cannot now know how the characteristics of any currently existing species would relate to future preferences and technologies. The loss of any species now could therefore involve very large future losses.

In situations of uncertainty, as opposed to risk, decision making cannot be axiomatized. Various rules have been proposed on the basis of treating the decision-making problem as a game against nature, where conjectured possible outcomes are specified as conditional on the state of nature. Essentially, the SMS approach involves the conjecture that the costs of species extinction, *M*, will be so large as to dominate any conceivable net economic benefits, *NPV*, and adopting a decision rule (minimax regret) that focuses on avoiding large costs. SMS would reject any project that could entail species loss.[8]

While originally developed in the context of 'nature conservation', the SMS has been advocated as a more generally applicable approach to setting environmental standards and appraising projects.[9] It faces the first of the problems noted above in regard to dealing with threshold crossing – while it may avoid very large losses, it may entail forgoing very large gains. Imagine a project offering the prospect of an inexhaustible low-cost environmentally benign substitute for the fossil fuels which could entail the extinction of some species not currently understood to be of any significance for human interests – the SMS would stop it. A 'modified SMS' has been proposed whereby a project that entailed the possibility of species extinction, or the crossing of some threshold, would be rejected unless the costs of rejection were unacceptable to society. This leaves to be answered the question of what, in any particular case, represents an unacceptably large cost. The modified SMS takes us back, that is, from thinking in terms of overriding and binding constraints towards thinking about making trade-offs. In terms of Figure 4.1, the matter of determining whether forgoing *NPV* is a price it is worth society paying to avoid the possibility of a panel (c) type situation has a lot in common with comparing *NPV* with *M* as in an ECBA.

4.4   Environmental performance bonds

Environmental performance bonds have recently been suggested in the ecological economics literature (Perrings 1989; Costanza and Perrings 1990; Shogren et al. 1993) as a means for dealing with uncertainty in project appraisal. Assume that there is in existence an environmental protection agency (EPA), without permission from which the firm cannot go ahead with the project. The EPA takes independent expert advice on the project, and comes to a view about the worst conceivable environmental outcome of the project going ahead. Approval of the project is then conditional on the firm depositing with the EPA a bond of £*x*, where this is the estimate of the social cost of the worst conceivable outcome. The bond is fully or partially returned to the firm at the end of the project's lifetime, defined by the longest-lasting conceived consequence of the project, not by the date at which it ceases to produce output, according to the damage actually occurring over the lifetime. Thus, if there is no damage the firm gets back £*x*, plus some proportion of the interest. The withheld proportion of the interest is to cover EPA administration costs and to finance EPA research. If the damage actually occurring is £*y*, the firm gets back £*x* – £*y*, with appropriate interest adjustment. For *x* equal to *y*, the firm gets nothing back, forfeiting the full value of the bond. It is, of course, possible that *y* will turn out to be greater than *x*, in which case also the firm gets back £0.

The advantages claimed for such an instrument are in terms of the incentives it creates for the firm to undertake research to investigate environmental impact and means to reduce it, as well as in terms of stopping projects. Taking the latter point first, suppose that the EPA decides on £*x* as the size of the bond, and that the firm assesses NPV as £(*x* – 1), and accepts that *x* is the appropriate estimate of actual damage to arise. Then it will not wish to go ahead with the project. If, however, the firm took the view that actual damage would be £$(x-2)$ or less, it would wish to go ahead with the project. The firm has, then, an incentive to itself assess the damage that the project could cause, and to research means to reduce that damage. Further, if it does undertake the project it has an ongoing incentive to seek damage-minimizing methods of operation, so as to increase the eventual size of the sum returned to it, £x – £y. This incentive effect could be enhanced by having the size of the bond posted periodically adjustable. Thus, if the firm could at any point in time in the life of the project, on the basis of its research, convince the EPA that the worst conceivable lifetime damage was less than £x, the original bond could be returned and a new one for an amount less than £x could be posted.

At the end of the project lifetime, the burden of proof as to the magnitude of actual damage would rest with the firm, not with the EPA. The presumption would be, that is, that the bond was not returnable. It would be up to the firm to convince the EPA that actual damage was less than £x if it wished to get any of its money back. This would generate incentives for the firm to monitor damage in convincing ways, as well as to research means to minimize damage. In the event that damage up to the amount of the bond, £x, occurred, society, represented by the EPA, would have received compensation. If damage in excess of £x had occurred, society would not receive full compensation. Recall that £x is to be set at the largest amount of damage seen as conceivable by the EPA at the outset. A socially responsible EPA would have an incentive to take a cautious view of the available evidence, implying a high figure for x, so that society would not find itself uncompensated. This, it is argued, would coincide with the selfish motivations of EPA staff, since a higher x would mean more funding available for EPA administration and research.

Environmental performance bonds are clearly an interesting idea for an addition to the range of instruments for environmental protection, given the pervasiveness of uncertainty and the need for research addressed to reducing it. In the form discussed here, they do not appear to be in use anywhere.[10] Clearly further consideration of the details of their possible implementation is warranted. To date, the proponents of this type of bond have not been explicit about how the EPA would go from its assessment of the worst conceivable environmental outcome to a figure for £x, the size of the bond. Given this, one assumes that they envisage use of the standard methods of environmental valuation.

4.5 Environmental valuation and its critics
ECBA and environmental valuation have in economics a history of some 30 years. Economists now claim to have a range of methodologies that can provide monetary valuations of the services provided by the natural environment of sufficient reliability that they can be used in social decision making

generally, and project appraisal particularly.[11] Here I shall concentrate on the contingent valuation method (CVM) for five reasons:

1. It is the most widely used of the methods that can deal with what economists call 'non-use value' – that is, the value that individuals place on an environmental service over and above any direct consumptive use of the service. It is generally understood that it is non-use values that are most relevant to sustainability issues.
2. In terms of the underlying basis for environmental valuation methods, it is the most transparent. The defining characteristic of CVM is asking a random sample of the affected population direct questions about their willingness to accept compensation for, or make payments for, some hypothetical change with environmental implications.
3. Perhaps because of this transparency, it is the method that has attracted most criticism from non-economists concerned about social decision making and the natural environment. CVM is also controversial within the economics profession, though for different reasons.
4. It is a flexible method. Although generally seen as being about determining non-use values, it can be used for use values, that is, values arising from direct consumptive use of the environment such as recreation.
5. Following on from this, while CVM cannot do what is claimed for it – value environmental services for incorporation into ECBA – it appears to me that, given a proper appreciation of what it actually does, it is capable of providing useful inputs to social decision making about some environmental matters, as discussed below.

There is now a substantial literature which argues that ECBA with environmental valuation is not the proper way to make social decisions on projects with environmental implications.

First, from outside of economics, there are 'ethical arguments'. The ethical basis for market solutions, and hence ECBA solutions, to social allocation problems is a particular form of utilitarianism which some critics refer to as 'preference satisfaction' (perhaps a more precise terminology than 'consumer sovereignty'). Many philosophers, and others, have argued that, particularly where there are environmental implications, this is an ethically incorrect basis for social choice. Sagoff (1988, 1994, 1998), for example, argues that environmental services and ordinary commodities should be treated as incommensurable, and that in such contexts decisions should be taken by deliberative 'citizens' rather than on the basis of some aggregation over the preferences of 'consumers'. There is evidence that some respondents to CVM questioning do in fact respond as citizens rather than as consumers: see, for example, Blamey et al. (1995), Common et al. (1997).

A second class of arguments concerns what is achievable by environmental valuation methods, leaving aside ethical issues and using economists' own criteria. Economists are divided on the extent to which the CVM can generate useful inputs to ECBA. One assessment is that there is the prospect, at some cost, of refining such methods so that useful results can be forthcoming: see, for example, Arrow et al. (1993), discussed below. Others take the position that the problems identified in relation to such methods are insurmountable: see, for example, contributions in Hausman (1993).

Beckerman and Pasek (1997) review some aspects of the 'ethical' critique of ECBA, noting that the proposed alternative in that literature is some kind of 'public debate and discussion of the merits' of the projects in question. They argue that while such debate and discussion may be appropriate for such matters as 'the morality of abortion', 'voluntary euthanasia', or 'which person would make the best Prime Minister', they are unsuitable for dealing with the environmental impacts of projects, or with environmental policy, as these involve, as the former examples do not, 'resource constraints'. They identify the existence of such constraints as a distinguishing characteristic of environmental policy/management questions, and argue that any satisfactory process for addressing such questions must observe the relevant constraints. A similar point is frequently made in order to differentiate CVM surveys from public opinion polling, and to argue for the superiority of the former. Beckerman and Pasek observe that while:

> there is a vast literature on the efficacy of various political institutions for reaching complex decisions of different kinds, the special problem of how to incorporate the need for public debate about environmental issues into any representative political institutions is relatively new. It raises difficult practical problems as well as difficulties in political and social choice theory. (1997, p. 80)

4.6 Recent developments in CVM practice
Experience with CVM over a couple of decades has resulted in an emerging consensus over what constitutes 'best practice' in the design and administration of CVM surveys. While CVM advocates and practitioners generally continue to claim that it is about putting values on environmental services for use in conventional ECBA, it is actually clear that the results from best-practice CVM studies are not doing this. It could be claimed with some justification, however, that they are generating information which could be useful for policy making and project appraisal. If the status of the results from best-practice CVM were more widely and clearly understood, if economists ceased to claim that they were 'valuing the environment', then there would be a lot less controversy, and perhaps the basis for a more constructive approach to public involvement in social decision making on the basis of EIAs.

The following is an example of what is involved. In an Australian application (Resource Assessment Commission 1991) it was found that Australians were willing to pay some A$500 million to prevent mining in a small part of the Kakadu national park. Given the claim that CVM was about environmental valuation, this result was widely reported as meaning that 'clapped out buffalo country' was being valued at several times the price per acre for Manhattan real estate, and widely derided. The CVM study appears to have been entirely disregarded in reaching a decision on the mining project – which was that it should not go ahead. The NPV for the mine, the cost of not allowing it to go ahead, was A$80 million, so that a more useful interpretation of the survey result would have been that Australians were willing to bear the cost in order to avoid the damage that the mine could entail.

An exhaustive account of how experience with CVM led to the current understanding of what constitutes 'best practice' is beyond the scope of this chapter.[12] However, three aspects can be usefully, if somewhat superficially, discussed here. First, in Section 4.1, above, reference was made to compensation for environmental damage as the basis for figuring M. It is generally agreed that CVM should, for ECBA purposes where a project involves environmental damage, ask individuals about their willingness to accept compensation for a postulated damage scenario. However, experience with asking 'willingness to accept' questions has been taken to indicate that many individuals find such questions difficult to deal with – they refuse an answer or ask for huge amounts of compensation. The best-practice position is that, while compensation acceptance is the theoretically correct basis for valuation, getting useful responses requires actually asking people about what they would be willing to pay to avoid the damage, and treating the answer as a lower bound on the theoretically correct number.

Second, early CVM applications would typically ask about compensation or payment in an open-ended way – simply outlining the scenario and then saying 'please tell me the maximum amount that you would be willing to pay to avoid this'. This tended to produce a high incidence of protest responses – refusal to give any answer – and a highly skewed distribution of usable responses. It is now understood that such problems can be mitigated by asking a respondent a yes/no question – 'would you be willing to pay £x to avoid this, answer yes or no please'. The £x figure is varied across different subsamples, and statistical modelling used to convert the yes/no responses to different £x figures into some kind, usually the median, of average willingness to pay.

Third, experience showed that response patterns were sensitive to the 'payment vehicle' used in the survey. The scenario has to specify how payment will be made. Early CVM applications would often refer to something like 'higher prices for the commodities that you regularly purchase'. It is now seen as best practice to use taxation as the payment vehicle, with the willingness to pay question being along the lines of: a programme to avoid the damage described would require a government-financed programme which would raise your annual tax bill by £*x*, would you vote for the programme?

The upshot of all this is that according to a high-level US inquiry into CVM (Arrow et al. 1993), where best practice is followed, the answer to the question 'what are CVM results about?' is that: 'The simplest way to approach the problem is to consider the CV survey as essentially a self-contained referendum in which respondents vote on whether to tax themselves or not for a particular purpose' (p. 4606). This inquiry identified 'a number of stringent guidelines for the conduct of CV studies', what has been referred to here as 'best practice', concluding that:

> *under those conditions* ... CV studies convey useful information. We think it is fair to describe such information as reliable by the standards that seem to be implicit in similar contexts, like market analysis for new and innovative products and the assessment of other damages normally allowed in court proceedings. (p. 4610, emphasis added)

The reference to 'court proceedings' here reveals the US provenance. The convening of this inquiry was closely connected with the aftermath of the Exxon Valdez oil spill, when the state of Alaska commissioned a CVM study to assess the monetary value of the environmental damage due to that spill. In all essentials, the CVM exercise conformed to the conditions specified by the inquiry and followed best practice. The form that it took was as follows.[13] After being asked about their knowledge of the Exxon Valdez incident, respondents were presented with information about Prince William Sound, the port of Valdez, the spill and its environmental effects, and a programme to prevent damage from another spill. The programme would involve two Coast Guard vessels escorting each loaded tanker on its passage through Prince William Sound. These vessels would have two functions. First, reducing the likelihood of a grounding or collision. Second, should an accident occur, they would keep the spill from spreading beyond the tanker. It was then stated that the programme would be funded by a once-off tax on oil companies using the port of Valdez and that all households would also pay a once-off tax levy. Respondents were then asked whether or not they would vote for the programme, given that the once-off household tax would be an amount US$*x*, with US$*x* varying across subsamples.

This CVM exercise was widely interpreted and reported as putting a value on the environmental damage done by the oil spill, or in some cases as valuing the Alaskan marine environment. A more appropriate interpretation is that it provides an estimate of what the US population would be willing to pay in additional taxes for a specific programme to reduce the probability of future oil spills in Prince William Sound, and reduce the impact should one occur. This interpretation is perhaps less appealing to the ambitions of many economists, but would seem likely to encourage others to engage in debate about how the survey results might be used in policy making. In this CVM exercise, the total willingness to pay of US citizens was estimated as US\$2.75 billion.

One member of the team that carried out this application was Richard Carson, a leading CVM theorist and practitioner. In 1998, Carson published a paper reflecting on how CVM might be applied to the global issue of tropical deforestation. The title is 'Valuation of tropical rainforests: philosophical and practical issues in the use of contingent valuation', and the article embeds discussion of a number of generic issues in the specific context of tropical rainforest. This is an important paper because notwithstanding the title, Carson makes it clear that as far as he is concerned it is policies/programmes/projects that get 'valued', in willingness-to-pay terms, rather than environmental amenities or ecosystem services *per se*. He judges that while CVM can provide useful information, it cannot 'provide the definitive answer to any major policy question'(p. 20). Many non-economists would see this as a reasonable perspective on ECBA. Carson also states: 'The legitimacy of a role for public preferences in democratic public policy making seems difficult to deny'(p. 20). Many critics of ECBA and environmental valuation would disagree with this. However, I am not aware that any would object to the statement: 'The legitimacy of a role for public input to, and involvement in, the processes by which public policy on matters affecting the environment is determined seems difficult to deny'. What critics would object to in the first of these statements is the explicit reference to 'preferences' and the implicit reference to consumers. They would see the information needed as being about the results of the deliberations of citizens.

4.7 Alternative models for public input
In recent years some political scientists/philosophers and public administration analysts have become interested in institutions for citizen deliberation, and the use of the results arising as input to the decision-making processes of representative democracy. While experience in designing and using such institutions is still rather limited, it suggests that they could be of considerable interest and promise in regard to the problems of making decisions based on EIA reports.[14]

Deliberative polling involves running an opinion poll then asking respondents to attend a meeting at which they will collectively consider the issues, by hearing and questioning expert witnesses and debating amongst themselves. At the end of this process, the participants are asked to again respond to the original survey instrument. As reported in Fishkin (1997) the results, in regard to the movement of opinion between the first poll and that conducted after deliberation, are often striking. Of particular interest here are some of the results from three such exercises conducted in Texas in 1996. In Texas, regulated public utilities are required to consult the public as part of their integrated resource planning, and three chose to use deliberative polling to do this in regard to electricity supply planning. Respondents were asked to specify their first choice for the provision of additional power from four alternatives: renewable sources, fossil fuel sources, energy conservation, and buying in electricity. Between the two polls, respondents attended meetings at which they were provided with, *inter alia*, cost data on these four alternatives. In all three exercises there was the same pattern of response variation between the before and after polls. As first choice, renewable fell from 67 to 16 per cent, 71 to 35 per cent, and 67 to 28 per cent, while conservation rose from 11 to 46 per cent, 7 to 31 per cent, and 16 to 50 per cent. The cost data showed conservation to be less expensive than renewable sources.

This suggests that information provision and deliberation are very important to public views. This is consistent with CVM experience, where it is well documented that the results obtained are heavily influenced by the information provided to respondents. There is, of course, no deliberation involved in CVM. It would be interesting to investigate the relative contributions to the sort of outcome reported above of the acquisition of additional information between the two polls and the deliberations that took place. This would be expensive. Indeed, the principal problem with deliberative polling itself is that it is very costly. The idea is to poll a random sample of sufficient size to produce results up to the standard normal in opinion polling. This may mean hundreds of people, which makes the information provision and deliberative parts of the exercise expensive, especially where the population of interest covers a large geographical area. As practised to date, deliberative polling has usually involved opinions on somewhat broadbrush issues of interest to large media organizations (prepared to spend money to get, for example, one or more TV programmes). However, as exemplified by the example from Texas noted above, the general strategy could, given funding, be applied to more narrowly defined decision problems, with respondents being required to consider resource constraints and their implications.

A citizens' jury exercise is less expensive than deliberative polling. In a report on experience with citizens' juries in the UK, Coote and Lenaghan (1997) describe what is involved as follows:

> Citizens' juries involve the public in their capacity as ordinary citizens with no special axe to grind. They are usually commissioned by an organisation which has power to act on their recommendations. Between 12 and 16 jurors are recruited, using a combination of random and stratified sampling, to be broadly representative of their community. Their task is to address an important question about policy or planning. They are brought together for four days, with a team of two

moderators. They are fully briefed about the background to the question, through written information and evidence from witnesses. Jurors scrutinise the information, cross examine the witnesses and discuss different aspects of the question in small groups and plenary sessions. Their conclusions are compiled in a report which is returned to the jurors for their approval before being submitted to the commissioning authority. The jury's verdict need not be unanimous, nor is it binding. However, the commissioning authority is required to publicise the jury and its findings, to respond within a set time and either to follow its recommendations or to explain publicly why not. (p. ii)

Obviously the particulars described here are not immutable, and there could be considerable variation consistent with the underlying rationale. In the environmental context, for example, it would likely often prove necessary to provide access to appropriate modelling facilities. There is no reason why the jury cannot be required to observe appropriate resource constraints.

In regard to underlying rationale, Coote and Lenaghan put it as follows: 'Compared with other models, citizens' juries offer a unique combination of *information, time, scrutiny, deliberation and independence*' (p. ii, original emphasis). Note that deliberation is absent from CVM, while there are necessary and often severe limitations on the information provided and the time available for its assimilation.[15] Coote and Lenaghan report positively on the citizens' jury process. Of particular interest here, they judge that 'Jurors readily adopt a community perspective', that most 'accept that resources are finite and were willing to participate in decisions about priority setting', and that 'a substantial minority of jurors said they had changed their minds in the course of the session'. It should also be noted that a number of the participating jurors expressed 'strong doubts about the jury's capacity to influence the commissioning authority'.

Experience in using citizens' juries in relation to decisions concerning the natural environment is limited.[16] In the USA, the Jefferson Center has conducted four projects dealing with agriculture and water quality, hog farming, environmental risks, and electricity generation. These exercises were reported in a paper tabled at a July 1997 conference in London organized by the Institute for Public Policy Research, where it was stated that they will be described in Sexton and Burkhardt (forthcoming). In the UK it appears that just one exercise has been completed. Aldred and Jacobs (1997) report on a citizens' jury conducted in Ely which was asked to discuss the question: what priority, if any, should be given to the creation of wetlands in the Fens? I am aware of an exercise under way in Scotland which is concerned with a floodplain restoration project, where there is also being conducted a CVM exercise and MCA type exercise.[17] In Australia a research project is about to start which will involve two comparisons of the citizens' jury approach to decision making with ECBA and conventional environmental valuation methods. The contexts are the allocation of water between irrigation and feeding an important wetland, and the control of weeds in protected areas.[18]

4.8 Future directions?

Sagoff (1998) argues that CVM can only take into account, as it should, individuals' 'principled views of the public interest not private preferences about their own consumption' (p. 213) if it 'moves toward a deliberative, discursive, jury-like research method emphasising informed discussion leading toward a consensus' (p. 213). While I agree with this at the level of principle and in substance, it seems unlikely that the costs of deliberation would be seen as tolerable across the whole range of projects with environmental impacts. However, I think it can be argued that deliberative procedures are of particular relevance to the problem of deciding what to do on the basis of an EIA which suggests that there may be threats to sustainability involved in going ahead with the project, and that in that context the costs are worth bearing.

Deliberative procedures for public input could be a suitable way of addressing the question involved in implementing the question raised by the modified SMS. And, in terms of the question, they would not actually involve all that large a departure from what has been noted here as the proper understanding of what best-practice CVM actually does, except in that citizens' deliberation would replace consumers' preference revelation as the basis for an answer. A citizens' jury could, for example, be asked to consider the following sort of question: Company X wants to proceed with a project the EIA for which indicates the following environmental impacts ... which could be threats to sustainability in that ... . If the project does not go ahead, the costs to society would be ... . Should the project be allowed to proceed?

In Section 4.4 above, proposals for environmental performance bonds were noted which address the problem of uncertainty attending threats to sustainability. A key feature of such proposals, which does not appear to have been addressed, is the appropriate method for fixing the size of the bond. This would appear to be a very good question to put to a citizens' jury.

Even where it is not considered that threats to sustainability are involved, securing and using 'public input' is a crosscutting issue in discussions of integrated environmental and social impact assessment, and some of the recent developments discussed here could be of interest to practitioners in those fields.

Notes

1. The test is also known as the Hicks–Kaldor test. The 'welfare foundations' of CBA are discussed in numerous texts: see, for example, Pearce and Nash (1981). Hanley and Spash (1993) provide a brief overview of CBA then review environmental valuation methods and report applications. Common (1996) discusses an illustrative ECBA which exposes

some popular misconceptions – such as the idea that lowering the discount rate always works in favour of environmental protection.

2. An analysis using distributional weights is sometimes described as a 'social' CBA. Pearce and Nash (1981) discuss the pros and cons of using distributional weights and the difficulties.

3. See, for examples, Van Pelt (1993), Munda et al. (1994) and Joubert et al. (1997).

4. This view, the basis for it, and the arising implications for policy are discussed at length in Common (1995).

5. The journal *Ecological Economics* has been running since 1989. A useful entry to the ecological economics literature is Costanza et al. (1997b).

6. See, for example, Van Pelt (1993) where it is suggested that sustainability considerations could be handled within an MCA framework.

7. Faucheux and Froger (1995) take uncertainty to be the defining characteristic of sustainability and consider procedural rationality in such a context, advocating an approach to social decision making founded in MCA.

8. The minimax route to SMS is discussed in Chapter 7 of Common (1995).

9. See, for example, Randall and Farmer (1995). The SMS approach has obvious affinities with the precautionary principle which has been endorsed, at least rhetorically, by a number of national governments and international agreements.

10. There are a number of types of environmental bonds in use, but not involving the features discussed here. Returnable deposits on drink containers can, for example, be seen as an environmental bond.

11. Hanley and Spash (1993) provide an overview of the various methods. While originally seen as providing inputs to ECBA, environmental valuation is now seen also as having (in the USA) a role in the assessment of compensation payable for damage done, and as a tool for adjusting national income measurement so that it reflects environmental costs. In Chapter 8 of Common (1995) I argue that meaningful measurement of 'green national income' is impossible. However, the idea that in order to influence policy in the direction of sustainability it is necessary to put money values on environmental services is widespread and powerful, as exemplified by the publication in *Nature* (Costanza et al. 1997a), of an estimate of the total value of global ecosystem services as US$33 trillion per year. This paper has attracted a lot of attention and comment, much of it favourable. It is clear that if this exercise has any value at all, it is, notwithstanding where the results were published, political rather than scientific.

12. Mitchell and Carson (1989) is a comprehensive account of the theory and practice of CVM, but is now somewhat dated and should be supplemented with, for example, Arrow et al. (1993).

13. See Carson et al. (1995).

14. For an overview of some models for public participation in environmental decisions, and a proposed framework for evaluating alternative approaches, see Beierle (1998), which does not, however, consider deliberative polling. This paper can be accessed at http://www.rff.org.

15. It could be argued that an element of deliberation is involved in 'best-practice' CVM in so far as it involves, as described in Carson et al. (1995) for the Exxon Valdez application, the use of focus groups to design the scenario to be used in the survey.

16. The Public Involvement Programme is run by the Institute for Public Policy Research and one of its aims is to 'Provide a clearing house for the exchange of information ideas and practical experience relating to new models of public involvement'. The models include deliberative polling and citizens' juries. The Programme's website, address http://www.pip.org.uk/, includes links to the sites of other organizations working in the area.

17. For further information contact the email address w.kenyon@ed.sac.ac.uk.

18. For further information contact either blameyra@emnw2.arts.adfa.oz.au or rfjames@cres.anu.edu.au.

References

Aldred, J. and Jacobs, M. (1997), *Citizens and Wetlands: Report of the Ely Citizens' Jury*, University of Lancaster: Centre for the Study of Environmental Change.
Arrow, K., Solow, R., Leamer, E., Portney, P., Radner, R. and Schuman, H. (1993), *Report of the NOAA Panel on Contingent Valuation*, Federal Register, 58, 10, Washington, DC, pp. 4601–14.
Beckerman, W. and Pasek, J. (1997), 'Plural values and environmental valuation', *Environmental Values*, **6**, 65–86.
Beierle, T.C. (1998), *Public Participation in Environmental Decisions: An Evaluation Framework Using Social Goals*, Discussion Paper 99-06, Washington, DC: Resources for the Future.
Bishop, R.C. (1978), 'Economics of a safe minimum standard', *American Journal of Agricultural Economics*, **57**, 10–18.
Blamey, R., Common, M. and Quiggin, J. (1995), 'Respondents to contingent valuation surveys: consumers or citizens?', *Australian Journal of Agricultural Economics*, **39**, 263–88.
Carson, R.T. (1998), 'Valuation of tropical rainforests: philosophical and practical issues in the use of contingent valuation', *Ecological Economics*, **24**, 15–30.
Carson, R.T., Mitchell, R.C., Hanemann, M., Kopp, R.J., Presser, S. and Rudd, P.A. (1995), *Contingent Valuation and Lost Passive Use: Damages from the Exxon Valdez*, Discussion Paper 95-02, Department of Economics, University of California, San Diego, January.
Ciriacy-Wantrup, S.V. (1968), *Resource Conservation: Economics and Politics*, Los Angeles, CA: University of California Press.
Common, M.S. (1995), *Sustainability and Policy: Limits to Economics*, Melbourne: Cambridge University Press.
Common, M.S. (1996), *Environmental and Resource Economics: An Introduction*, 2nd edn, Harlow: Longman.
Common, M.S. and Perrings, C. (1992), 'Towards an ecological economics of sustainability', *Ecological Economics*, **6**, 7–34.
Common, M., Reid, I. and Blamey, R. (1997), 'Do existence values for cost benefit analysis exist?', *Environmental and Resource Economics*, **9**, 225–38.
Coote, A. and Lenaghan, J. (1997), *Citizens' Juries: Theory and Practice*, London: Institute for Public Policy Research.
Costanza, R. and Perrings, C. (1990), 'A flexible assurance bonding system for improved environmental management', *Ecological Economics*, **2**, 57–75.
Costanza, R., d'Arge, R., de Groot, R., Farber, S., Grasso, M., Hannon, B., Limburg, K., Naeem, S., O'Neill, R., Paruelo, J., Raskin, R., Sutton, P. and van den Belt, M. (1997a), 'The value of the world's ecosystem services and natural capital', *Nature*, **387**, 253–60.
Costanza, R., Perrings, C. and Cleveland, C.J. (eds) (1997b), *The Development of Ecological Economics*, International Library of Critical Writings in Ecological Economics, Cheltenham: Edward Elgar.
Faucheux, S. and Froger, G. (1995), 'Decision making under environmental uncertainty', *Ecological Economics*, **15**, 29–42.
Fishkin, J.S. (1997), *Voice of the People*, New Haven, CT: Yale University Press.
Hanley, N. and Spash, C.L. (1993), *Cost Benefit Analysis and the Environment*, Cheltenham: Edward Elgar.
Hausman, J.A. (ed.) (1993), *Contingent Valuation: A Critical Assessment*, Amsterdam: North-Holland.
Joubert, A.R., Leiman, A., de Klerk, H.M., Katua, S. and Aggenbach, J.C. (1997), 'Fynbos (fine bush) vegetation and the supply of water: a comparison of multi-criteria decision analysis and cost–benefit analysis', *Ecological Economics*, **22**, 123–40.
Mitchell, R. and Carson, R. (1989), *Using Surveys to Value Public Goods: the Contingent Valuation Method*, Washington, DC: Resources for the Future.
Munda, G., Nijkamp, P. and Rietveld, P. (1994), 'Qualitative multicriteria evaluation for environmental management', *Ecological Economics*, **10**, 97–112.
Pearce, D.W. and Nash, C.A. (1981), *The Social Appraisal of Projects: A Text in Cost Benefit Analysis*, London: Macmillan.

Perrings, C. (1987), *Economy and Environment: A Theoretical Essay on the Interdependence of Economic and Environmental Systems*, Cambridge: Cambridge University Press.

Perrings, C. (1989), 'Environmental bonds and environmental research in innovative activities', *Ecological Economics*, **1**, 95–115.

Perrings, C., Turner, R.K. and Folke, C. (1995), *Ecological Economics: The Study of Interdependent Economic and Ecological Systems*, Discussion Papers in Environmental and Economics and Environmental Management No. 9501, University of York.

Randall, A. and Farmer, M. (1995), 'Benefits, costs, and the safe minimum standard of conservation', in D.W. Bromley (ed.), *The Handbook of Environmental Economics*, Oxford: Blackwell, pp. 26–44.

Resource Assessment Commission (1991), *Kakadu Conservation Zone Inquiry: Final Report*, Canberra: Australian Government Publishing Service.

Sagoff, M. (1988), *The Economy of the Earth*, Cambridge: Cambridge University Press.

Sagoff, M. (1994), 'Should preferences count?', *Land Economics*, **70**, 127–44.

Sagoff, M. (1998), 'Aggregation and deliberation in valuing environmental public goods: a look beyond contingent pricing', *Ecological Economics*, **24**, 213–30.

Sexton, K and Burkhardt, T.D. (forthcoming), *Better Environmental Decisions: Strategies for Governments, Businesses and Communities*, Publisher unknown.

Shogren, J.F., Herriges, J.A. and Govindasamy, R. (1993), 'Limits to environmental bonds', *Ecological Economics*, **8**, 109–33.

Van Pelt, M.J.F. (1993), 'Ecologically sustainable development and project appraisal in developing countries', *Ecological Economics*, **7**, 19–42.

World Commission on Environment and Development (1987), *Our Common Future*, Oxford: Oxford University Press.

φol Q2o
022 (UKjLDC's)

5   Sustainability assessment through integration of environmental assessment with other forms of appraisal: differences in approach for industrial and developing countries

Clive George

5.1   Environmental assessment and sustainable development

In principle, because of its position at the heart of the development decision-making process, environmental assessment (EA) should provide one of the most powerful tools for achieving sustainable development. If sustainable development can be defined, then it should in principle be possible, through environmental assessment, to test any proposed development for whether it is or is not sustainable development.

The potential value of environmental assessment as a tool for sustainability assurance was recognized (Jacobs and Sadler 1989) soon after publication of the Brundtland Report, *Our Common Future* (WCED 1987). At the Rio Earth Summit of 1992 this potential was given powerful backing in Principle 17 of the Rio Declaration, calling on all states to introduce EA as part of the conference's overall sustainable development objectives (United Nations 1992). Subsequently, the International Study of the Effectiveness of Environmental Assessment identified a number of actions through which EA might be given sharper focus as a sustainability instrument (Sadler 1996). These included:

- further guidance on the use of sustainability principles in EA;
- incorporating relevant criteria and indicators;
- identifying 'environmental bottom lines' such as precautionary-based thresholds and capacities;
- specifying requirements for in-kind compensation of residual impacts;
- addressing uncertainty and irreversibility; and
- the integration of EA with other forms of impact assessment.

This chapter addresses all of these, beginning with the first, and moving on to the second via the others. All are shown to be important components in implementing sustainability principles, including integration.

5.2   Fundamental principles of sustainable development
The first action recommended by the Effectiveness Study, the application of sustainability principles, is fundamental to all the others. Before environmental assessment can be used as a test for sustainable development, sustainable development must first be defined with some precision. The phrase itself is open to widely differing interpretations, each of which can lead to different and possibly conflicting criteria or indicators. The interpretation which is used here is that employed at the Rio conference, and in particular in the Rio Declaration on Environment and Development. The criteria which are developed for use in EA are intended specifically as an instrument for realizing the goal of sustainable development as elaborated at Rio, and not for any other interpretation of the concept.

Principle 3 of the Rio Declaration implicitly defines sustainable development as 'to equitably meet developmental and environmental needs of present and future generations'. This definition is an extension of that derived from the Brundtland Report, as development which 'meets the needs of the present without compromising the ability of future generations to meet their own needs'. This widely used definition has established the principle of inter-generational equity as a fundamental pillar of the sustainable development concept, but in doing so it does not do full justice to the Brundtland Report itself. In its discussion of the development process, the report placed as much emphasis on equity within generations as it did on equity between them. By applying the word 'equitably' to both present and future generations, the Rio definition more fully reflects the ideas presented in *Our Common Future*. It establishes the twin principles of inter-generational and intra-generational equity as the two fundamental pillars of sustainable development, as envisaged by the Rio conference (see Box 5.1).

Box 5.1   The twin pillars of sustainable development

inter-generational equity
    a necessary condition for sustainability

intra-generational equity
    a necessary condition for development

The inclusion of intra-generational equity as one of these twin pillars results from the Rio, and Brundtland, interpretations of the word 'development'.

Development that is not equitable within the current generation, and hence within future ones, is commonplace. It can also be made sustainable, simply by restricting the numbers of people who benefit from it. However, that was not the form of development envisaged by either Brundtland or Rio. Their aim was to make development both sustainable and equitable at the same time, in the face of global environmental constraints.

The Rio definition also goes beyond the one derived from Brundtland by making specific mention of the environment, but still strictly as a human need. This follows from Principle 1 of the Rio Declaration, which proclaims that 'human beings are at the centre of concerns for sustainable development'. This anthropocentric approach is rejected by many environmentalists, prompting other competing definitions of sustainable development. It is, however, the basis of the Rio definition.

5.3 Testing for sustainable development

Following the Rio definition, only two tests are needed for whether or not a proposed development is sustainable development: is the development equitable for future generations, and is it equitable for the present generation? Neither question is straightforward, however, and both need expansion.

Some of this necessary expansion is provided by the other principles of the Rio Declaration. As part of demonstrating that a proposed development is sustainable development, in Rio's terms, an EA must demonstrate that the proposal complies with all 27 of the Rio Declaration's principles, or at least that it does not violate any of them. Some of these principles are better implemented by other instruments, but several are particularly relevant to EA, notably

- the participation principle (Principle 10);
- the precautionary principle (Principle 15); and
- the polluter pays principle (Principle 16).

As well as being based on fundamental equity principles, all three are closely associated with established principles of environmental assessment. In particular, the polluter pays principle ('the polluter should, in principle, bear the cost of pollution ...') is built into EA's requirements for mitigation of adverse impacts, by the developer. However, further elaboration of the equity principles is needed in order to decide whether the proposed mitigation is adequate.

Figure 5.1 shows schematically how the two equity principles may be expanded. Following this approach, a set of detailed implementation criteria has been derived for use in environmental assessment (George 1999). These are listed in Tables 5.1 and 5.2a, as applicable in industrial countries. Table

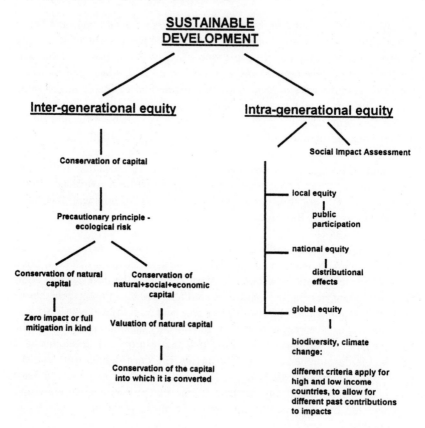

Figure 5.1   Expansion of the equity principles

5.2b lists modified criteria for application in developing countries. To be classified as sustainable development, a proposal must satisfy all the criteria, the derivation of which is discussed below.

Intra-generational equity, social impact assessment and public participation
The first step towards satisfying intra-generational equity (criterion 1 of Table 5.1) is to attempt to demonstrate, within the EA itself, that the principle is satisfied, for example through a social impact assessment (Interorganizational Committee 1994; Vanclay and Bronstein 1995). However, a more stringent test is to allow the public themselves to decide whether or not the proposal is equitable (criteria 2 and 3). These two criteria, which are generally regarded as good EA practice, are necessary for complying with Rio's participation principle ('environmental issues are best handled with the participation of all concerned citizens ... each individual shall have appropriate access to

Table 5.1 Assessment criteria for sustainable development (general criteria)

Principles		Criteria
Intra-generational equity (local/national)	1	Have all groups or individuals affected by the project been identified, and have the impacts on them been assessed, using a full social impact assessment where appropriate?
	2	Will the EIA report be published and made readily available to all members of the public?
	3	Will all members of the public have the opportunity to comment on the proposals, and will their views be taken into account before a decision is made?
	4	If indigenous peoples or other minority groups are affected, have suitable provisions been made for their participation in project decisions?
Intra-generational equity (transnational)	5	Have transboundary impacts been properly assessed, where appropriate, with the participation of the affected public?
Inter-generational equity (preliminary)	6	Have any potentially critical ecosystem factors that may be affected been identified?
	7	Has the risk of serious or irreversible damage arising from any such impact been satisfactorily assessed, using risk assessment techniques if appropriate?
Inter-generational equity (strong sustainability)	8	If the risk of serious or irreversible damage is significant, or if the project adds to a risk that is already significant, will the impact be fully mitigated, in kind, such that there will be no significant adverse residual impact?
Inter-generational equity (weak sustainability)	9	Have any specific groups or individuals adversely affected by an impact expressed satisfaction with the compensation offered, or has any dispute been satisfactorily arbitrated?
	10	Has the natural capital, which the project will convert into other forms of capital, been identified?
	11	Has an appropriate socio-economic appraisal been carried out?
	12	Does this socio-economic appraisal demonstrate that total capital will be conserved?

information concerning the environment ... and the opportunity to participate in decision-making processes').

Criterion 4 is necessary in order to allow for equity for minority groups, whose interests may otherwise be overridden by the majority. This too is part of established EA practice (for example, World Bank 1993), and follows Rio's Principle 22 ('indigenous people and their communities, and other local communities, have a vital role in environmental management and development ... states should ... enable their effective participation in the achievement of sustainable development'). Principle 20 ('women have a vital role in environmental management and development ... their full participation is therefore essential') must also be satisfied in applying all four of these criteria for intra-generational equity.

The first four criteria in Table 5.1 test for intra-generational equity at the local or national level, but not at the international or global levels. Principle 2 of the Rio Declaration lays down that 'states have ... the responsibility to ensure that activities within their jurisdiction or control do not cause damage to the environment of other states or of areas beyond the limits of national jurisdiction'. Global issues are particularly important for sustainable development, and are covered by separate criteria. More limited transnational impacts are dealt with specifically in Principle 19 of the Declaration and are covered by criterion 5. Arrangements for implementation have been set out in the Espoo Convention on EIA in a transboundary context (UNECE 1991).

Inter-generational equity and the conservation of capital
The principle of inter-generational equity can be re-stated as the principle of conservation of capital (Pearce et al. 1989). If the capital, natural or human-made, which future generations inherit is no less than the current capital stock, then development is equitable inter-generationally. In implementing this alternative statement of the principle, a decision has to be made on whether natural capital will itself be conserved (strong sustainability), or whether it may be converted into some other form (weak sustainability).

The precautionary principle and integration with risk assessment
This decision can be based on Rio's precautionary principle ('where there are threats of serious or irreversible damage, lack of full scientific certainty shall not be used as a reason for postponing cost-effective measures to prevent environmental degradation'). Rio's wording of the principle was aimed particularly at eliciting a response to hotly contested concerns over global impacts, but its implication is that the strong sustainability condition should apply whenever there is a threat of serious or irreversible environmental damage. In order to make the decision, it is necessary to identify any potentially critical ecosystem factors that may be affected, and to assess the risk of serious or

irreversible damage arising from any impact on them (criteria 6 and 7). For some types of development these may be particularly difficult tasks, but various techniques for addressing them within EA have already been developed (for example, CAG Consultants and Land Use Consultants 1997; Carpenter 1995; Gabocy and Ross 1998).

5.4   Strong and weak sustainability

Strong sustainability and full mitigation in kind
Criterion 8 marks the first major diversion from established EA practice. Whenever the precautionary principle shows that the strong sustainability condition should be applied, it is not sufficient to argue that any adverse residual impact is insignificant. It must be zero. This is important in dealing with cumulative impacts, and is required by Principle 15, which does not refer to the significance or otherwise of environmental degradation, but to preventing it. It is also part of the definition of strong sustainability. Natural capital will not be conserved if even the smallest fragment of it is lost or converted to some other form. This requirement for full mitigation in kind is particularly important for biodiversity conservation, where it is dealt with under global impacts (criteria 14 to 16).

Weak sustainability and the valuation of natural capital
When there is no significant risk of serious or irreversible damage, natural capital may be converted into some other form, but its value must not decrease in the conversion. The value of the natural capital must therefore be compared in some way with the value of the social or economic capital that will replace it. This entails a value judgement which, according to the principle of intra-generational equity, must be made by the people who will be affected by the capital conversion. The judgement must be made on behalf of future generations, but only the present generation can make it.

When it is specific groups or individuals who will be affected, those people must be satisfied with whatever transaction takes place in the conversion (criterion 9). The value of the environmental effect is then determined by direct negotiation between polluter and polluted.

When it is the public as a whole who are affected by the capital conversion, the public as a whole must make the necessary value judgement. When publicly owned natural capital is sold to the developer, the value can again be determined by direct negotiation, between the polluter and representatives of the polluted (that is, the government). In other cases there is no such transaction, and so other means are required for making the value judgement.

Weak sustainability and the integration of environmental, social and economic appraisal

Criteria 10, 11 and 12 mark the next major diversion from established EA practice. In general, EA systems tend to address the environmental issues of development in isolation from its social and economic implications. This may be well suited to testing for strong sustainability, but weak sustainability requires some form of integrated assessment, so that environmental factors may be weighed against social and economic ones. The extent of the natural capital that is to be converted must be defined (criterion 10), and also the extent of the corresponding socio-economic benefit (criterion 11). A demonstration must then be made that capital is conserved in the conversion, and not frittered away on short-term benefits (criterion 12). It is not within the remit of EA to carry out a full socio-economic appraisal, or to assess what is or is not a sound capital investment. EA can, however, perform the integration, by requiring that these other appraisals be performed, and by drawing together their results in its public participation processes. This integration may or may not include assessing the value of environmental impacts in economic terms, but it should include putting all of the relevant information before the public, so that they can make the necessary value judgement themselves.

5.5   Global sustainable development

When a development has global impacts, the affected public is the entire world's population. All of the criteria derived above should then be applied on behalf of present and future generations of the global public. Existing environmental assessment and economic appraisal processes do not directly allow for this. Public participation is normally restricted to the local or national public, except perhaps in the case of transboundary impacts. The conservation of environmental and other forms of capital is generally considered only in local or national terms. In order to achieve intra- and inter-generational equity globally, within existing EA processes, additional criteria must be defined. These are presented in Tables 5.2a and 5.2b, for industrial and developing countries, respectively. Criterion 13 is included in both tables because assessments very often ignore global impacts (McCold and Holman 1995; George 1997). Criteria 14 to 17 deal with the two global impacts of greatest concern, biodiversity loss and climate change. Criterion 18 deals with any other global impacts.

For both biodiversity loss and climate change, environmental damage is threatened which is both serious and irreversible, and so the strong sustainability condition should apply. No loss of natural capital should be permissible. No development which increases the concentration of greenhouse gases in the atmosphere should be permitted, nor any which reduces the area of a natural habitat that is important for species conservation.

Table 5.2a   Assessment criteria for global impacts (industrial countries)

Principles	Criteria	
Inter- and intra-generational equity (global)	13	Have all potential global impacts been considered?
biodiversity	14	Does the assessment quantify any natural habitat that will be lost which is important for species conservation?
	15a	Is an equivalent area set aside for replacement/regeneration?
	16a	Has a satisfactory justification been made for the habitat area lost through the project, as a proportion of the total area of this type of habitat, in such a way that the overall rate of loss will not exceed the equilibrium regeneration rate?
greenhouse gases	17a	If the project produces greenhouse gas emissions, is it shown to make an appropriate contribution to reducing emissions in accordance with the Kyoto agreement?
other global impacts	18	Has a satisfactory justification been made for any other global impact, in terms of a compensating global benefit that is acceptable?

Table 5.2b   Assessment criteria for global impacts (developing countries)

Principles	Criteria	
Inter- and intra-generational equity (global)	13	Have all potential global impacts been considered?
biodiversity	14	Does the assessment quantify any natural habitat that will be lost which is important for species conservation?
	15b	Is this consistent with a national plan which will prevent the area of natural habitat falling below industrial country levels before development has reached industrial country levels?
	16b	Is the project shown to make a contribution to development that is consistent with the share that it will take of planned habitat loss?
greenhouse gases	17b	If the project produces greenhouse gas emissions, and may still be operational when per capita emissions reach industrial country levels, is its greenhouse gas efficiency shown to be adequate?
other global impacts	18	Has a satisfactory justification been made for any other global impact, in terms of a compensating global benefit that is acceptable?

If these constraints were applied uniformly to all development activities, in both industrial and developing countries, this would violate the principle of intra-generational equity. This is implied by Principle 7 of the Rio Declaration, under which 'the developed countries acknowledge the responsibility that they bear in the international pursuit of sustainable development in view of the pressures their societies place on the global environment'. The past and present impacts of industrial countries on both global biodiversity and climate change greatly exceed those of developing countries to date, and this must be accommodated in the criteria.

Carrying capacity and time-limited weak sustainability
Additionally, if the constraints were applied immediately, this could cause considerable upheaval in the development process. To avoid this, the concept of carrying capacity can be brought into play, following the alternative definition of sustainable development proposed by the World Conservation Union, the United Nations Environment Programme and the World Wide Fund for Nature as 'improving the quality of human life while living within the carrying capacity of supporting ecosystems' (IUCN/UNEP/WWF 1991). This offers the possibility of postponing action to halt global environmental degradation, until carrying capacity is in immediate danger of being exceeded. Although the strong sustainability condition should ideally be applied, and must be applied at some time in the future, inter-generational equity can still be achieved by applying the weak sustainability condition instead, for a limited time only.

Criteria for loss of natural habitat in industrial countries
Industrial countries have already converted a major proportion of their species-rich habitats to intensive human use, as part of their own development process. Global equity requires that there be no barrier to developing countries doing the same as industrial countries. Unless some other agreement is made, strong sustainability cannot be imposed until the proportion of land area devoted to natural habitat in developing countries has fallen to that in industrial countries. If the associated risks from biodiversity loss are considered too great, the alternatives are for industrial countries to embark on extensive habitat regeneration, or to fund conservation in developing countries. Some steps in these directions have already been taken, through Rio's Biodiversity Convention, national biodiversity action plans such as in the UK (Department of the Environment 1994) and the World Bank's Global Environment Facility. As yet, however, these steps fall far short of what is required to have major effect (Pearce and Moran 1994). Currently, the most stringent criterion that can reasonably be applied is that industrial countries will not reduce their own areas of natural habitat any further, while corresponding losses remain permissible in developing countries.

The resulting industrial country requirement for no net loss of natural habitat is applied through criteria 14, 15a and 16a. All three can be applied at the project level as well as at the strategic level of policies or plans (George 1997). However, criterion 16a requires some form of overall monitoring, and preferably planning, to ensure that loss and regeneration remain in balance. More sophisticated techniques (CAG Consultants and Land Use Consultants 1997) may be used to expand on these simple criteria, but it should be borne in mind that they may still result in major global environmental degradation, as a result of unchecked habitat loss in developing countries. The criteria are true sustainable development criteria only to the extent that the associated risk is globally acceptable.

Criteria for loss of natural habitat in developing countries
The corresponding requirement for developing countries can be derived (George 1997) from the weak sustainability condition that any natural capital consumed in the development must be converted into social or economic capital of equivalent value, together with an appropriate limit beyond which strong sustainability must be applied. Criteria 14, 15b and 16b are based on this approach. Conversion up to the levels of industrial countries may be permitted, on the assumption that this will help to enable development in standards of living up to those in industrial countries. The total permissible reduction in area of natural habitat in any country can be defined by comparison with industrial countries, and the total increase in standards of living that needs to be achieved as a result can similarly be defined. The reduction that is permissible for any individual development proposal can then be calculated pro rata according to the contribution the development is expected to make to the overall objective.

This justification of habitat loss in developing countries requires support by some form of long-term national development plan, which places strict limits on the total area of natural habitat that will ultimately be converted in the course of achieving industrial country levels of development. The calculation of how much can be converted in an individual development should ideally be based on a full socio-economic appraisal, particularly for large-scale activities such as forest clearance. For less significant activities, simpler approaches may suffice, for example based on measures and forecasts of capital investment (ibid.). However, it remains essential in all cases to demonstrate that the natural capital is indeed converted into social or economic capital of equivalent value, and that the benefits accruing from the conversion are equitably distributed (criteria 1 to 4 and 9 to 12).

Major global environmental degradation may still result from applying these criteria. If the risk is considered too great, more stringent criteria can be applied only through global agreements which are more stringent and which also preserve global equity.

The 'bottom lines' represented by these criteria are based on the assumption that developing countries will choose to follow the same pattern of development as industrial ones. Alternative patterns which may be less environmentally damaging remain a matter of choice for individual countries. They may become a more frequent choice if biodiversity attains a higher economic value, but they should not be imposed without appropriate global agreements which place equivalent demands on industrial countries.

Criteria for greenhouse gas emissions in industrial countries
Considerations for climate change are similar to those for biodiversity, except that in this case industrial countries still contribute the major proportion of the current effect, as well as having contributed most of the cumulative impact to date. Under Rio's Climate Convention, these countries agreed not to increase their greenhouse gas emissions any further (returning them to 1990 levels by 2000), and under the 1997 Kyoto Protocol they undertook to begin reducing them. For global equity, there should be no barrier to developing countries increasing their per capita emissions to whatever level industrial countries reduce theirs (and possibly further, to allow for the differences in cumulative contribution). In order to stabilize the atmospheric concentration, as developing countries increase their emissions to equal those in industrial countries, the latter will need to reduce theirs by at least a factor of four, and more probably a factor of eight or more, depending on population growth rates (Brown 1996). If the rates of reduction agreed at Kyoto (ENDS 1997) are achieved and continue linearly, a factor of eight reduction will take about two hundred years. This is the currently agreed time limit on weak sustainability, after which strong sustainability may be presumed to apply. If, during that time, predictions of climate change reach a level where the risk of serious or irreversible damage becomes globally unacceptable, the rate of reduction will need to be increased. In the meantime, the current level of risk has been judged to be acceptable, under the Kyoto agreement.

The requirement to comply with the Kyoto Protocol is applied through criterion 17a. This may be satisfied by compliance with an appropriate national plan for meeting Kyoto commitments, or in the absence of such a plan, by demonstrating that the proposal itself makes a suitable contribution to the overall reduction target (George 1997, 1999).

Criteria for greenhouse gas emissions in developing countries
On equity grounds, no overall constraint can be placed on emissions in developing countries until they reach those in industrial countries. However, some constraint is needed if per capita emission levels are to be prevented from exceeding those in industrial countries.

When per capita income levels in developing countries reach those in industrial countries, the average greenhouse gas efficiency at that time (for example, MW per tonne of CO_2) should be no lower than in industrial countries. In countries that are developing reasonably rapidly, many of the investments currently being made in transport and energy (the greatest contributors to greenhouse gas emissions) will still be operational at that time. Ideally therefore, investments being made now should have a similar efficiency to those currently being made in industrial countries. Some allowance can be made for the different age distribution of the technologies that are likely to be in place (George 1997), and perhaps also for different contributions to the cumulative effect. However, a demonstration should be made that the project will not create later difficulties in keeping national emissions within industrial country per capita levels (criterion 17b).

5.6 Applying the criteria in industrial and developing countries

Industrial countries
The criteria given in Tables 5.1 and 5.2a have been applied in a review of the contents of the environmental statements for six typical UK projects (George 1999). The following conclusions were drawn:

1. a fuller integration of environmental, social and economic assessment is necessary in order to demonstrate clearly that a project can be classed as sustainable development;
2. the existing environmental assessment process as applied in the UK is reasonably effective in testing for sustainable development in respect of impacts that are strictly local or national;
3. the existing environmental assessment process is reasonably effective in containing any further contribution to global biodiversity loss from UK projects, and could be made fully effective with little difficulty;
4. some minor changes to project design and mitigation measures would be necessary in order to meet fully the sustainable development criteria for local and national impacts and global biodiversity, but these are unlikely to be costly;
5. power generation projects typical of those currently being undertaken in the UK are likely to meet the sustainable development criteria for the global impact of greenhouse gas emissions, as derived from the Kyoto agreement; and
6. many road schemes and airport developments are likely to fail the test for sustainable development, in the absence of a national plan for compensating their contributions to greenhouse gas emissions.

In all of the examples, the decision on whether or not to mitigate fully potential impacts was based on a fairly rudimentary or non-existent assessment of environmental risks. However, for local and national impacts, a reasonable degree of caution was demonstrated in the environmental statements. In some cases, greater caution would have entailed fuller mitigation to achieve zero adverse impact, but the cost of this was judged to be relatively low.

In other industrial countries similar conclusions are expected to apply, except where oil and coal are used in power generation. The two UK power generation projects examined both used natural gas as the fuel source, replacing generating capacity with considerably higher greenhouse gas emissions. For oil or coal, the conclusions are likely to be similar to those reached above for UK road and airport schemes.

Developing countries
The EIA systems in existence in developing countries vary widely from country to country, as do the types of development being undertaken. The relevant criteria need to be applied to a large number of environmental statements covering this spectrum before any firm conclusions can be drawn. However, from an initial examination of reasonably typical statements, and from the analysis of EIA systems in different countries (Lee and George 1999 forthcoming), the following tentative conclusions are drawn:

1. as concluded in the UK review, a fuller integration of environmental, social and economic assessment is necessary in order to demonstrate clearly that a project can be classed as sustainable development;
2. as in the UK, existing EA processes are likely to be reasonably effective in dealing with local or national impacts, except in respect of public participation;
3. the public participation provisions in many countries' EIA systems are inadequate to meet several of the criteria; for some projects, compliance may result in significantly higher mitigation costs or costly changes to project design;
4. for some projects in some countries, transboundary impacts may not be dealt with adequately; compliance with the criteria could in some cases have a significant effect on project costs;
5. most projects are likely to be capable of meeting the criteria for global biodiversity loss, although to do so it would be necessary to elaborate a national plan defining an upper limit to loss of habitat; and
6. most projects generating greenhouse gases are likely to meet the criteria; for some projects such as coal-fuelled electricity generation, in some countries there may be long-term problems in keeping per capita emissions within industrial country limits.

5.7   Conclusions

The sustainable development criteria which have been developed for use in environmental assessment require some changes in EA practice, including a fuller integration of environmental assessment with other forms of appraisal.

These changes in practice are likely to result in some modifications to project design or mitigation measures, in order to satisfy the criteria. For many projects however, these changes are not expected to be costly.

In industrial countries, the types of project which would present the greatest difficulty in demonstrating that they can be classified as consistent with sustainable development are road schemes, airport developments, and power generation projects using oil or coal. However, such projects could pass the test if they were required to comply with a national plan for compensating their contributions to greenhouse gas emissions.

In developing countries, the types of project most likely to present difficulties are those for which the introduction of a greater degree of public participation in the EIA process could result in requirements for costly changes to design or mitigation measures.

Some of the criteria which have been developed are dependent on the appropriateness of existing global agreements relating to climate change and biodiversity loss. They have the disadvantage of classifying developments as consistent with sustainable development even though, if these global agreements are themselves inadequate, the projects may still contribute to significant risks of serious global environmental damage. The criteria do, however, focus attention on the fundamental principles of sustainable development, and help to ensure that development proposals do at least comply with currently negotiated 'bottom lines'.

References

Brown, L. (ed.) (1996), *State of the World 1996*, London: Earthscan.
CAG Consultants and Land Use Consultants (1997), *Environmental Capital: A New Approach*, Cheltenham: Countryside Commission.
Carpenter, R.A. (1995), 'Risk assessment', *Impact Assessment*, **13** (2), 153–87.
Department of the Environment (1994), *Biodiversity: The UK Action Plan*, London: HMSO.
ENDS (1997), *The Unfinished Climate Business after Kyoto*, ENDS Report 275, 16–20.
Gabocy, T. and Ross, T. (1998), 'Ecological risk asssessment: a guideline comparison and review', in Porter, A.L. and Fittipaldi, J. (eds), *Environmental Methods Review: Retooling Impact Asssessment for the New Century*, Fargo, USA: AEPI/IAIA/The Press Club, Ch. 23.
George, C. (1997), 'Assessing global impacts at sector and project levels', *Environmental Impact Assessment Review*, **17** (4), 227–47.
George, C. (1999), 'Testing for sustainable development through environmental assessment', *Environmental Impact Assessment Review*, **19**, 175–200.
Interorganizational Committee on Guidelines and Principles for Social Impact Assessment (1994), *Guidelines and Principles for Social Impact Assessment*, US Department of Commerce, National Oceanographic and Atmospheric Administration Technical Memorandum NMFS-F/SPO-16.
IUCN/UNEP/WWF (1991), *Caring for the Earth: A Strategy for Sustainable Living*, Switzerland: Gland.

Jacobs, P. and Sadler, B. (eds) (1989), *Sustainable Development and Environmental Assessment: Perspectives on Planning for a Common Future*, Quebec: Canadian Environmental Assessment Research Council.

Lee, N. and George, C. (eds) (1999 forthcoming), *Environmental Assessment in Developing Countries and Countries in Transition*, Chichester: John Wiley and Sons.

McCold, L. and Holman, J. (1995), 'Cumulative impacts in environmental assessments: how well are they considered?', *Environmental Professional*, **17** (1), 2–8.

Pearce, D., Markandya, A. and Barbier, E. (1989), *Blueprint for a Green Economy*, London: Earthscan.

Pearce, D. and Moran, D. (1994), *The Economic Value of Biodiversity*, London: Earthscan.

Sadler, B. (1996), *Environmental Assessment in a Changing World: Final Report of the International Study of the Effectiveness of Environmental Assessment*, Ottawa: Canadian Environmental Assessment Agency.

United Nations (1992), *Report of the United Nations Conference on Environment and Development*, UNCED Report A/CONF.151/5/Rev.1, 13 June.

United Nations Economic Commission for Europe (1991), *Convention on Environmental Impact Assessment in a Transboundary Context*, Geneva: UNECE.

Vanclay, F. and Bronstein, D.A. (eds) (1995), *Environmental and Social Impact Assessment*, Chichester: John Wiley & Sons.

World Bank (1993), *Environmental Assessment Sourcebook Update No. 5 – Public Involvement in Environmental Assessment: Requirements, Opportunities and Issues*, Washington, DC: Environment Department, World Bank.

World Commission on Environment and Development (WCED) (1987), *Our Common Future*, Oxford: Oxford University Press.

6 Integrating environmental, economic and social appraisal in the real world: from impact assessment to adaptive management

David Hulme and Russell Taylor

6.1 Introduction[1]

Despite concerted efforts to integrate environmental, economic and social analyses in the *ex-ante* appraisal (and *ex-post* evaluation) of development policies, programmes and projects the majority of 'integrated appraisals' remain informed guesswork parading around as objective technical analysis. Often such work is as likely to damage the livelihoods of those that interventions seek to help as it is to benefit them. There are many good reasons for this sorry state of affairs but this chapter focuses on only two of them. First, the failure of those involved in appraisal to devote sufficient attention to integrating different paradigms of how knowledge is created. Second, the failure of those involved in appraisal to consider 'who' should be involved in appraisal work and in what ways. Too much effort has gone into top-down and technocratic discussions about how to integrate environmental science, economic science and social science, often with a focus on 'big projects'. Too little effort has gone into looking at how we can integrate the three different paradigms of knowledge creation – scientific, humanities and participatory approaches – and the different stakeholders in development action, into appraisal and management processes.

This chapter does not focus purely on criticisms of what is done under the banner of 'integrated appraisal'. Examples of better practice are emerging. One of these examples, a case study of wildlife management in Zimbabwe, is used to illustrate the direction that integrated appraisals might take in the future.

6.2 Paradigms of appraisal: science, the humanities and participation

The major conceptual problem that confronts any appraisal exercise is the assessment of the ways in which a development intervention will lead to attributable impacts (environmental, economic and social). From the vast literature on appraisal it is possible to draw out three very different ways by which analysts have sought to appraise impacts.

The first is the conventional scientific method with its origins in the natural sciences and its focus on scientifically proven links between cause and effect.

The second has its roots in the humanities (particularly history, geography and anthropology) and focuses on making a reasoned argument supported by theory and specific pieces of evidence. Although the former originally dominated discussions about appraisal, especially when 'environment' was the focus, the latter tradition is now being used increasingly. The third part of this section explores a recent entrant to the field – participatory learning and action (PLA) – which offers a radical challenge to both conventional appraisal and to 'science' itself. Although these three approaches can be separated for analytical purposes, in good practice elements of all three approaches are woven together.

Scientific method

Scientific method seeks to ensure that effects can be attributed to causes through experimentation.[2] A particular stimulus to a particular object in a rigorously controlled environment is judged to be the cause of the observed effect. The experimental approach is rarely feasible for environmental appraisal and virtually infeasible for economic and social appraisal because of the nature of the subject matter, and so the approach is usually adapted into quasi-experiments (Casley and Lury 1982). Quasi-experiments seek to compare the outcomes of an intervention with a simulation of what the outcomes would be if there was no intervention. For physical processes this can be done by simulation with models. For economic processes multiple regression can be used, but this is rarely done because of its enormous demands for data on other possible causal factors and its assumptions (Mosley 1997, pp. 2–3). A second approach is the *control group* method which is widely used in agricultural and microfinance projects. This requires a before and after comparison of a population that receives a specific treatment (for example, a microfinance programme) and an identical population (or as near as possible) that did not receive the treatment. These results can then be used to predict impacts at a macro level. While this idea is elegantly simple a number of 'elephant traps' may befall its user. In particular problems of sample selection bias, mis-specification of underlying causal relationships and respondent motivation must be overcome (for a discussion of these problems, see Hulme 1999 forthcoming).

The humanities tradition[3]

The broad set of approaches that fall under this head have their roots in the humanities. Originally history, human geography and rural sociology were the 'lead' subjects, but over the last 20 years anthropology has become the hearth. Its main features are an inductive approach to appraisal, a focus on key informants, recording by notes or image, and the data analyst is usually directly and heavily involved in data collection. This tradition does not try to appraise impact within statistically definable limits of probability. Rather, it seeks to provide an interpretation of the processes involved in intervention and of predicted impacts that have a high level of plausibility. It recognizes that there are usually different, and often conflicting, accounts of what will happen and what will be achieved by a programme. The validity of appraisals adopting this approach has to be judged by the reader on the basis of (i) the logical consistency of the arguments and materials presented; (ii) the strength and quality of the evidence provided; (iii) the degree of triangulation used to cross-check evidence; (iv) the quality of the methodology; and (v) the reputation of the researcher(s). Commonly the bulk of data generated by such an approach is 'qualitative', although at later stages of analysis such work often quantifies some data. The main types of methods used are rapid appraisal, participant observation and case studies.

Although such work has been common in development studies for decades, it is only recently that its relevance for appraisal has been recognized.[4] This recognition has arisen partly because of the potential contribution of qualitative approaches (especially in understanding beneficiary perceptions of impact, changes in social relations) and partly because of the widespread recognition that much survey-based appraisal work was based on inaccurate information collected by ill-designed questionnaires from biased samples (Chambers 1993). Low-budget and low-rigour appraisals adopting the scientific method were at best pseudo-science, but more often simply bad science, applying sophisticated analytical tools to very poor data.

Participatory learning and action (PLA)
In the last five years, participatory approaches to development planning and management have moved from being a fringe activity to centre stage. While many donor agencies have simply added a bit of PLA to their existing procedures, it can be argued that this is inappropriate as conceptually participatory approaches challenge the validity and utility of the scientific method as applied to developmental problems (Chambers 1997). According to this line of argument the scientific method fails because it ignores the complexity, diversity and contingency of winning a livelihood; it reduces causality to simple unidirectional chains, rather than complex webs; it measures the irrelevant or pretends to measure the immeasurable; and it empowers professionals, policy makers and elites, thus reinforcing the *status quo* and directly retarding the achievement of a programme's economic and social goals. At heart, PLA theorists do not agree that ultimately there is one objective reality that must be understood. Rather, there are multiple realities and before any analysis or action is taken the individuals concerned must ask themselves, 'whose reality counts?' (ibid.). The answer must be that the perceived reality of the poor must take pride of place as, if development is about 'empowering the poor' or 'empowering women' (as virtually all development agencies now

say), then the first step towards empowerment is ensuring that 'the poor' or 'women' take the lead in knowledge creation and problem analysis.[5]

For impact assessment, the purist PLA line is damning: 'conventional baseline surveys are virtually useless for impact assessments ... The question now is how widely local people can be enabled to identify their own indicators, establish their own participatory baselines, monitor change, and evaluate causality' (ibid. p. 123). By this means two objectives may be achieved (i) better impact assessments, and (ii) intended beneficiaries will be 'empower[ed] through the research process itself' (Mayoux 1997, p. 2).

The reliability of participatory methods varies enormously, as with 'scientific' surveys, depending 'largely on the motivation and skills of facilitators and those investigated and the ways in which informants' perceptions of the consequences of research are addressed' (ibid., pp. 12–13). Nevertheless, it is argued that 'a number of rigorous comparative studies have shown that, when well-conducted, participatory methods can be more reliable than conventional surveys' (ibid., and see Chambers 1997, pp. 141–6).

From a scientific perspective PLA has grave problems because of the subjectivity of its conceptualizations of impact; the subjectivity of the data used to assess impact; because the variables and measures used vary from case to case and do not permit comparison; and because its pluralist approach may lead to a number of mutually conflicting accounts being generated about causality. From the perspective of a 'new professional' (Chambers 1997), then, such a set of accounts is unproblematic, as it reflects the complexity and contingency of causality in the real world. In addition, PLA, it can be argued, contributes to programme goals (perhaps particularly in terms of empowering women (Mayoux 1997) and the poor) by not facilitating the continued dominance of target groups by powerful outsiders. Why dwell on issues of attribution when efforts to overcome such problems require the adoption of methods that will undermine the attainment of programme goals?

Competition or integration
There are two main ways in which appraisal exercises can respond to the choices that these three paradigms present. One is to treat them as 'competing' and thus to evaluate them and choose the optimal paradigm. For natural scientists and quantitative economists this has meant the selection of the scientific method because of its inherent rigour and the 'fact' that humanities and participatory approaches are based on 'anecdote'. At the other extreme, for the increasingly voluble group of appraisers who have become committed to participatory approaches (amongst them large numbers of non-governmental organizations) then participatory approaches are the only valid means of appraisal as the other methods are extractive and, directly or indirectly, reinforce the structures of power that are the root cause of poverty.

An alternative is the integration of these paradigms into a pluralist appraisal process that uses data generated by all three approaches. In this way the advantages of each can be combined and the weaknesses offset (see Hulme 1999 forthcoming and Montgomery et al. 1996 for detailed examinations of strengths and weaknesses). This can be done by having a multi-paradigm, multi-disciplinary team run the appraisal exercise, as has happened in World Bank poverty assessments. However, while such a strategy follows the conventional top-down, planning model and while it gives intended beneficiaries 'voice' it does not give them decision-making power. Indeed, work on Bank participatory poverty assessment questions whether the information generated has influenced policy and practice (Robb 1997). A more radical way forward – and the strategy favoured by this chapter – is to devolve decision-making authority to the unit that will ultimately manage the intervention, that is, to adopt a bottom-up approach that provides managers with appraisal data and makes them a central part of the appraisal process. For many projects' programmes and policies this will mean giving the lead role in the assessment and appraisal process to intended beneficiaries – villagers, slum dwellers and so on. This proposition can be best illustrated through an example that shows the way in which a pluralist approach to appraisal allied to devolved decision making can work.

6.3 Wildlife utilization programmes: the conventional approach

Plans to permit the offtake of wildlife by human populations inevitably entail environmental, economic and social analysis – environmental analysis to assess what the wildlife resource can sustainably yield and to consider wider impacts on the environment; economic analysis to assess whether offtake plans are viable and the need for loans or grants; and social analysis to examine 'who' benefits from a programme, whether there is an institutional framework that can support the programme and how well the design 'fits' the socio-cultural context. However, attempts to appraise wildlife utilization programmes by conventional means have rarely proved effective (Adams and McShane 1992; Bonner 1993; IIED 1994).[6]

Environmental science, including wildlife management, deals with systems about which we know little, but yet want to manage or exploit. Moreover, there are severe limitations in our ability to experimentally manipulate, in a scientific sense, these systems and thereby gain the knowledge thought to be needed for the appraisal of wildlife utilization (Macnab 1983; Hilborn and Ludwig 1993). Failure to recognize that the appraisal process is itself an experiment reflects many a lost opportunity (Macnab 1983). Adaptive management (Holling 1978) has a pre-eminent role to play in the integration of environmental economic and social analysis into resource use.

Here we highlight the limitations of conventional wildlife management methodologies for large mammal census and the establishment of harvest rates. These are fundamentally flawed, ecologically and institutionally. As a consequence, either underutilization or overuse of resources results, with potentially adverse impacts for the environment, economic efficiency and the livelihoods of poor people. Invariably, such approaches are centralized, non-participatory, expensive and usually remote from the resource user or manager. They are unlikely to provide sustainability (environmental, financial or institutional), and intended beneficiaries are largely passive recipients of decisions flowing from inappropriate policy formulation. Alternative and innovative approaches which reverse the role of local communities and resource managers to that of active participants in appraisal and management are described below. The Zimbabwean example of CAMPFIRE and trophy hunting is used but the approach has a much wider applicability, both to resource management and community participation, in Africa and elsewhere. Following a brief description of the CAMPFIRE programme we review the conventional approach to appraising wildlife utilization and then an integrated approach.

6.4   Appraising wildlife utilization for the CAMPFIRE programme

Background to CAMPFIRE
Throughout pre-independent southern Africa, conservation policy and practice, based on centralized and racial lines, alienated most rural people from their wildlife resources. Over the past decade, however, a number of initiatives have sought to return rights of access to these natural resources to local residents. In Zimbabwe, the CAMPFIRE programme (Communal Areas Management Programme for Indigenous Resources) is an innovative example that seeks to place the proprietorship of natural resources, especially wildlife, with the people living most closely with them (Martin 1986). The legal and administrative framework for CAMPFIRE evolved out of the successful devolution of user rights over wildlife to large-scale commercial farmers, provided for in the Parks and Wild Life Act (1975). This Act was amended in 1982 to give Rural District Councils (RDCs) in the communal lands of Zimbabwe (where the bulk of the black, rural population lives) similar rights, known as 'appropriate authority'. Such authority allows districts to manage and benefit from wildlife resources occurring in them and these districts constitute the CAMPFIRE programme. This decentralization of authority (Figure 6.1), although not yet complete reflects a crucially important step in the institutional reform necessary for the effective appraisal and management of wildlife resources.

In Zimbabwe, internationally marketed sport hunting for trophies is an important form of wildlife use (Cumming 1989) and particularly so in the

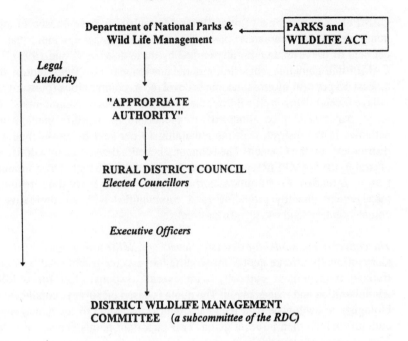

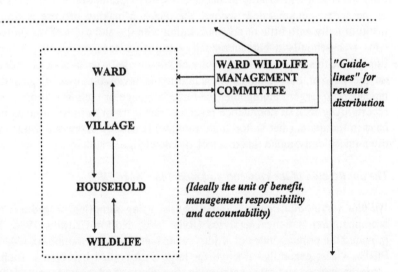

Figure 6.1   The legal and administrative framework for CAMPFIRE in Zimbabwe

CAMPFIRE programme (Taylor 1994). Most districts have chosen to lease hunting rights to commercial partners and such use generates more than 90 per cent of the revenue presently earned by these districts (Bond 1994). The CAMPFIRE guidelines for wildlife-derived revenue (Child 1995) require that at least 50 per cent of gross income is devolved to communities (outward and village levels) living with wildlife, the so-called 'producer communities'. Up to 35 per cent can be allocated to expenditure on wildlife management activities in the district, with the remaining 15 per cent being retained as a district levy by the Council. The economic benefits derived from wildlife are central to the CAMPFIRE programme. Access to these benefits by communities is intended to stimulate both collective and individual resource management, thereby providing rural communities with an alternative or complementary land use to agro-pastoralism.

The conventional model for assessing levels of wildlife utilization
Conventionally offtake quotas for wildlife harvests are established by a centralized management authority with overall responsibility for wildlife administration and management. The quota is based on surveys conducted by biologists or ecologists who feed back their information to the management authority which then issues a quota. Two important points should be noted. First, surveys are invariably inadequate – spatially, temporally and in respect of the species enumerated; second, the decision-making process is limited institutionally with little or no consultation with the end users of the quota in what is essentially a bureaucratically-dominated decision-making process. Implicit in this approach is a paucity of knowledge. Any lack of confidence on the part of the management authority is invariably well disguised in bureaucratic jargon, ambiguous scientific language or technical footnotes to reports. Any lack of confidence resource managers or conservationists may have in the quota (that is, too high, too low) is usually expressed loudly and often uncritically, again due to a lack of knowledge.

The application of the conventional model to CAMPFIRE

Wildlife survey and census   Aerial census using sampling procedures and accompanying statistical analyses (Jolly 1969; Norton-Griffiths 1978) has provided the primary index of wildlife abundance and distribution for CAMPFIRE. Whilst generally effective for large dark-bodied herbivores, such as elephant, buffalo and sable antelope in Zimbabwe (Taylor and Mackie 1997), such censuses are inefficient for most smaller-bodied antelope and predators. This is especially pronounced in heavily bushed and wooded savannas where sampling and observer biases are particularly problematic (Caughley 1977). Whilst reasonably satisfactory and very cost effective for the objectives of protected area management at a coarse scale of resolution (1000–10 000 km^2), the method is unsuited for the purpose of estimating animal abundance at a finer scale (<1000 km^2). Apart from the fact that harvestable species may remain undetected, the error associated with the estimate of population size for most species is invariably greater than their likely growth rate so as to make the detection of population trend almost impossible, at least on an annual basis, if not longer. The high variability associated with population size estimates over relatively small areas, typical of CAMPFIRE districts and wards, is exacerbated by the mobility of herbivores, such as elephant and buffalo, which function spatially at a scale larger than the average size of a ward or census stratum. Aerial surveys and wildlife censuses in CAMPFIRE districts are undertaken by, or on behalf of, the Department of National Parks and Wildlife Management (DNP&WLM). Conducted annually during the dry season in Zimbabwe, these surveys are technologically sophisticated, centrally managed and directed, expensive and remote from resource managers and wildlife producer communities. Recent aerial surveys for the CAMP-FIRE programme have all been undertaken with donor support, which brings into question their longer-term sustainability.

Decision-making process   In Zimbabwe, management decisions, especially those involving the killing of large mammals, are determined within the country's wildlife legal and administrative framework (Cumming 1983). Whilst the decision-making process relates mostly to protected areas, DNP&WLM also has responsibility for the conservation and use of wildlife outside of the core protected area system. Consequently, overall offtake quotas for sport hunting, and other management activities, are established centrally by a departmental management committee comprising senior research, management and administrative personnel. Offtake quotas for CAMPFIRE districts, until very recently, have been established at this level, as well as decisions relating to other wildlife matters such as problem animal control.

There is no formal involvement of resource managers or users outside of DNP&WLM in this decision-making process, although occasional informal discussion may take place, for example with RDC staff or safari operators marketing communal wildlife tourism. Once the quota is established, this is issued to the RDC which then allocates the quota for different uses, primarily sport hunting but which may also include cropping, culling and capture and translocation. The sport, or trophy-hunting quota, is marketed through a commercial safari operator who has leased the hunting rights from the RDC. Revenue thus earned accrues to the RDC which then distributes the revenue according to the CAMPFIRE guidelines (Figure 6.2). While this represents a devolution of benefits it does not bring together ownership, management, cost and benefit of wildlife in one unit (Murphree 1994). In this model,

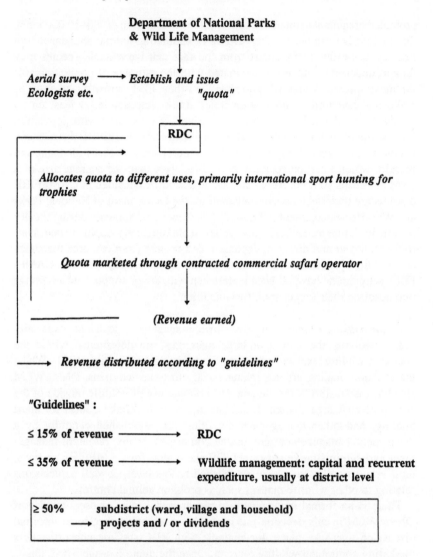

Figure 6.2   The conventional approach to establishing offtake quotas for large mammals in Zimbabwe's CAMPFIRE programme

communities are largely passive recipients of an essentially imposed wildlife management regime which is now at district rather than national level (Murombedzi 1992; Gibson and Marks 1994).

The alternative: an integrated model of appraisal and management
The fugitive nature of wildlife and the multiple stakeholders involved in its utilization indicate that a participatory management approach is necessary. In the conventional model, the role of the producer communities in CAMPFIRE was restricted to that of passive recipients of wildlife revenue: DNP&WLM set and allocated sport-hunting quotas; the private sector leased the use rights (tourism and sport hunting) from RDCs and the RDCs controlled the financial benefits from wildlife. Under such conditions wildlife utilization as a long-term sustainable land-use option can be considered unlikely unless two important changes are implemented. First, a stronger and more clearly defined enabling environment for the use of wildlife is required, namely that appropriate authority status, or some such similar instrument, be devolved from district to ward level. This is discussed in Taylor (1999).

Second, participatory resource appraisal and management methodologies have to be developed to allow community wildlife producers to participate more meaningfully in wildlife management activities and optimize their role in a wider decision-making framework. Such changes would provide incentives for the development of common property management regimes, collective and individual, for wildlife and wildland. Underpinning the development of these methodologies is their use as tools which involve local communities as active participants, rather than passive recipients, in natural resource management. Participatory technology development (PTD) (Sutherland et al. 1998) brings together technical specialists, in this case ecologists or biologists, and local communities, represented by ward wildlife management committee (WWMC) members, to design, implement, test, monitor and refine locally applied and management methods.

Wildlife survey and census   The development of participatory methodologies builds on local community knowledge and assessments of wildlife resources which are both simple and robust. To ensure that census principles of rigour, standardization and repeatability are met, however, it is necessary to classify census techniques (Table 6.1) and establish criteria for their selection (Collinson 1985). This important first step is all too often missed or ignored in our haste to implement a technique (Caughley 1977). The most important criterion is the objective of a wildlife census and its goals.

In the case of trophy hunting, the objective is sustained yield harvesting of high-quality trophy animals. Ideally, if hunting quotas are to be based on census data alone, then the goal of the census is an absolute estimate of population size. Important properties of the estimate would be moderate accuracy, a high level of precision and a high level of repeatability over time. (Despite wildlife biologists having yet to achieve this goal in many instances, trophy hunting is a recognized and ongoing management activity worldwide.)

Table 6.1   Participatory census: classification and selection of techniques

Classification	Options	Activity/Comments
Set of objects		
animals		Direct; highly appropriate
animal sign	dung, spoor	Indirect; unsuccessful
Tactics for location		
ground or air		Ground-day-mobile
day or night		Static placement, e.g.
static or mobile		waterhole count an option
Tools and/or instruments		
mobility	vehicle, aircraft, horse, boat, **foot**	Walked patrols, transects
enumeration	binoculars, scanners, global	Use eyes for sightings
measurement	positioning system (GPS), **eyes**	Visual sightings recorded
analysis	camera, video, tape, **visual**	Time is recorded (catch/
	rangefinder, compass, **watch**	effort)
	calculator, computer, **pencil &**	Pencil & paper for
	paper	calculations
Estimation strategies		Greatest potential
numerous		difficulty; measurement of
sampling	area, **time**, ratio/regression total	area problematic; use time as
non-sampling	count	unit of measurement
Survey design		Obligatory &/or
obligatory		representative design to
random		begin with; refinements can
systematic		follow
representative		

Note: Options in **bold** type are those most likely to be appropriate for the development of community-based census methods.

Source: Adapted from Collinson (1985).

Since an appropriate participatory technique meeting these requirements is unlikely, PTD is used to design a first approximation as an intermediate step. In this way different participatory approaches to ground-based census methods have been developed with producer communities and include annual censuses, 'random walks' (see below) and fixed transect counts (Mackie, C. 1993). The goal of these methods has been an index of population abundance where accuracy is less important, but a high level of repeatability is, and precision improves with that repeatability. Because measurement of distance, commonly used in ground census methods (Buckland et al. 1993), has proved difficult to apply, time has provided the unit of measurement for the indicator of wildlife abundance in the methods used (Marks 1994). Generally, and because they do not know where the animals are, biologists stratify and systematically count the census area across ecological gradients. Local residents find this difficult to understand and tend to sample only where they know animals to occur (ibid.), a form of obligatory sampling (Collinson 1985) not well appreciated by many biologists who undertake road strip counts, for example, in the belief that their sampling is at least representative if not random. Nevertheless, this form of sampling has been adapted to produce the 'random walk' sample count over which there is no technical control other than the recording of wildlife sightings. When compared with abundance indices from standard transect counts in the same area, there was little or no difference (Taylor unpubublished data). Participants either analyse records immediately following the census (in the case of annual counts) or quarterly for those counts undertaken more frequently. Counts over three seasons have yielded consistent results, that is, within the same orders of magnitude, providing usable indices of abundance and trend for those large mammal species important to management (ibid.). These results can be and are being used, together with other trend indices, by WWMCs and RDC officials to establish offtake quotas for trophy hunting (see below).

Undertaken by community members themselves, the application of these census methods reflect local perspectives and adaptations to site-specific requirements and conditions, rather than the development of a standard methodology. PTD cannot be hurried and time is needed to develop workable and sustainable methodologies. The needs and abilities of people must take precedence over the method and its results. Long sessions of repetitive observations are avoided, as is undue physical discomfort and undertaking work at inconvenient times. Whilst intellectual ability must be taken into account, it should not be assumed that local people have no knowledge of the subject. Simple and robust methods which minimize subjective decisions are preferable to those which are highly sensitive to violations of underlying assumptions. Furthermore, methods that rely on highly accurate measurement, sophisticated technology and complicated analyses should be avoided. Census must be seen as a means to an end, that is, the establishment of a sustainable high-quality trophy offtake which attracts a lucrative market, not as an end in itself. Thus, data collection, storage and analysis are undertaken locally by community members, either ward-employed appointees (game guards, wildlife monitors) or, in the case of annual counts, volunteers. The knowledge created is locally owned, provides learning and develops local capacities. WWMCs are provided with feedback by their community members or employees which can then feed into subsequent management decisions and action.

The decision-making process   The participatory quota-setting methodology
brings together all the key stakeholders involved in the establishment of the
quota at a workshop. It recognizes the importance of the data, information and
knowledge that each stakeholder group brings to a decision-making framework. Thus aerial census data, participatory ground counting results and trophy
quality measurements, together with the local DNP&WLM warden's opinions,
safari operator's 'catch-effort' and community perceptions (for example, the
level of illegal offtakes) provide a set of indices which are triangulated and
combined in a matrix used to adapt the previous season's quota (Figure 6.3).
The methodology makes use of data (kill date, location, trophy size) provided
by official hunt return forms undertaken during previous and past seasons.
Trend data are assembled by participants, graphically represented for each
species and entered into the matrix. The existing quota is assessed against the
available data and information and the proposed quota adaptively determined

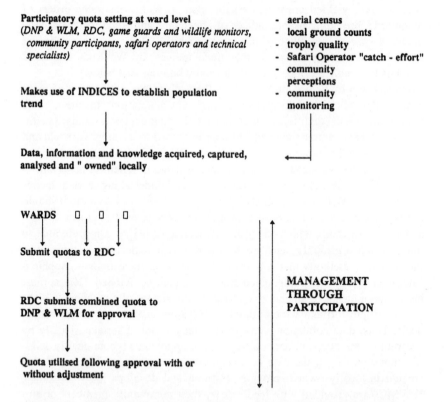

*Figure 6.3   The participatory approach to establishing offtake quotas for
large mammals in Zimbabwe's CAMPFIRE programme*

using the full set of indices. The method does not seek to measure the actual size of a population. Rather, it seeks to determine whether the population is decreasing, stable or increasing and adjust the offtake quota accordingly.

Crucially, the information and data are collated and analysed in a highly visual, interactive manner, thereby allowing full participation by all stakeholders. Built into the workshop methodology is a training component based on a series of participatory exercises (games, simulations, role plays) which provides greater understanding and simplifies data analyses. These inform producer community representatives, allowing them to participate actively in determining the quota (Table 6.2). The completed matrix and quotas thus produced are forwarded through the RDC to DNP&WLM as a recommendation for final consideration.[7]

At this stage, the proposed quota can be reviewed by departmental ecologists, taking into account, where necessary, the population dynamics of each species, permissible offtake rates and ecological relationships between the district and/or ward and adjacent protected areas, for example, cross-boundary animal population movement. Following final approval, the quota is returned to the RDC for use in the coming hunting season by the contracted safari operator. Hunting during the season is monitored by RDCs and/or WWMCs using community game guards and wildlife monitors. Compliance with the Parks and Wild Life Act and regulations by safari operators and professional hunters continues to be the responsibility of DNP&WLM while the CAMPFIRE Association ensures that hunt return forms are completed for each hunt by safari operators and RDCs. The hunt return form allows the key variables to be captured for input into the national database and provides further feedback for subsequent quota-setting exercises.

The practice of an integrated approach

This integrated approach to appraisal and management (termed 'participatory natural resource management' in Zimbabwe) has been developed over several years in pilot districts and is now being diffused throughout the CAMPFIRE programme. Initial assessments by DNP and WLM, the CAMPFIRE Association and WWF indicate positive impacts. Offtake quotas are being adjusted, both up and down, rather than remaining 'same as last year' as had become an operational norm. The likelihood of 'panic policies' to achieve environmental goals (that is, the stopping of all offtake or large-scale culling) has been reduced, helping to make the flow of economic and social benefits more stable. Community members are taking a much greater interest in the active management of local wildlife, in terms of both cropping and conserving and local institutional capacity is strengthening. In the longer term, the prospect for a more dynamic public debate about wildlife policies and use is being fostered (Taylor 1999).

Table 6.2 The type of information that is presented at a quota-setting workshop

Species	This year's quota	Aerial survey trends	Community ground count trends	Trophy quality trends	Input from Safari Operator	Community estimates	Proposed quota for next year
Elephant (M)	7	⇔	⇔	⇔	⇒	⇐	7
Buffalo (M)	20	⇔⇒	⇔	⇐	⇔	⇐	20
Lion	3	X	X	⇔	⇔	⇔	3

Key:

⇐ Indicator shows a general population increase.
⇒ Indicator shows a general population decrease.
⇒⇒ Indicator shows a medium decrease in population.
⇔ Indicator shows a stable population.
⇔⇐ Indicator shows stable but increasing population.
⇔⇒ Indicator shows stable but decreasing population.
X Information not available or irrelevant.

The management authorities (DNP&WLM and RDCs) are beginning to accept the strengths of the participatory census and quota-setting methodologies, rather than focus on their weaknesses, which indeed, there must be with any novel development. The local resource managers at a community level are becoming empowered through learning and gaining knowledge by action and the resource user (safari operator) is intimately involved and a committed participant, contributing market information linked to sustainable benefit.

6.5   Conclusions

Through a discussion of the three main paradigms of appraisal – scientific, humanities and participatory – and the examination of a specific experiment that combines these paradigms and permits a full range of stakeholders to participate in decision making we conclude that effective appraisal is about much more than multi-disciplinarity or cross-disciplinary coordination.

For the planning and management of development interventions to be more effective 'integration' is required in four differing but related dimensions (Figure 6.4).

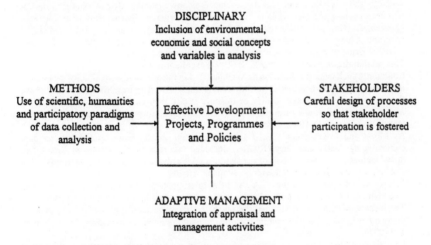

Figure 6.4   The four dimensions of integration

1. A multi-disciplinary approach is required that examines key environmental, economic and social variables.
2. A multi-method approach is required that mixes scientific, humanities and participatory methods.
3. The role of all primary stakeholders in assessment processes must be considered and, for resource-use initiatives, resource users should have a central role.

4.   The idea that 'appraisal' and 'management' are distinct functions to be carried out by different actors must be abandoned. An adaptive management approach, in which 'managers' take a central role in an iterative planning process and 'planners' work closely with managers, is needed.

This may sound like a complex prescription but, as the case study indicates, the difficulties are not insurmountable and such an approach offers the possibility of true sustainability – strong and deeply embedded institutions that are socially inclusive, have local and central level legitimacy and that can adapt to changes in their context over time.

Notes

1.   This chapter was prepared from two pre-existing papers. The first, 'Impact assessment methodologies for microfinance: a review' at a virtual meeting (7 April to 19 April 1997) of the Consultative Group to Assist the Poorest (CGAP) Impact Assessment Working Group. The original paper, and others on the topic, are available on the website of Management Systems International (MSI) at http://www.mip.org. The second paper, 'Participatory natural resource management: implications for conservation' was presented at a Workshop on 'Community conservation in Africa' at Lake Kariba, Zimbabwe (20–24 July 1998) convened by the Universities of Manchester and Zimbabwe and the African Wildlife Fund. It will be appearing as a chapter in D. Hulme and M. Murphree, *African Wildlife and African Livelihoods* (Oxford: James Currey, 2000). Numerous participants in the CAMPFIRE programme have contributed to innovations in census and quota-setting. Particular mention might be made of Ivan Bond, Charles Mackie and Norman Rigova.
2.   This section draws heavily on Mosley's (1997) excellent paper.
3.   Commonly such work is referred to as 'qualitative', but the quantitative/qualitative dichotomy is a false one. Most quantitative studies extract qualitative data from the respondent, have the interviewer immediately codify or quantify it and then use only numerical analysis. Many 'qualitative' studies transform their data into quantities at later stages of analysis (Moris and Copestake 1993, p. 4).
4.   As Moris and Copestake (1993, p. 1) point out 'the much recommended text on data collection by Casley and Lury (1982) ... included two cursory paragraphs on "quick and dirty" techniques ... almost half of the World Bank's publication that superseded it (Casley and Kumar 1988) is concerned with qualitative methods'.
5.   The reader wishing to explore PLA and PRA (participatory rural appraisal) is referred to Chambers (1997) as there is not space to explore these ideas in this chapter more fully.
6.   The history of plans to manage natural resources is replete with spectacular failures from many other fields – fisheries and forests in particular. For a wider discussion, see Ludwig et al. (1993).
7.   Over time and with further experience and confidence, quotas from a number of subdistrict wards or villages can be pooled for the district as a whole.

References

Adams, J.S. and McShane, T.O. (1992). *The Myth of Wild Africa: Conservation Without Illusion*, New York: Norton.
Bond, I. (1994), 'The importance of sport-hunted African elephants to CAMPFIRE in Zimbabwe', *Traffic Bulletin*, **14**, 117–19.
Bonner, R. (1993), *At the Hand of Man: Peril and Hope for Africa's Wildlife*, New York: Knopf.
Buckland, S.T., Anderson, D.R., Burnham, K.P. and Laake, J.L. (1993), *Distance Sampling: Estimating Abundance of Biological Populations*, London: Chapman & Hall.

Casley, D. and Kumar, K. (1988), *The Collection, Analysis and Use of Monitoring and Evaluation Data*, Baltimore: Johns Hopkins University Press.

Casley, D. and Lury, D.A. (1982), *Monitoring and Evaluation of Agricultural and Rural Development Projects*, Baltimore: Johns Hopkins University Press.

Caughley, G. (1977), *Analysis of Vertebrate Populations*, New York: Wiley-Interscience.

Chambers, R. (1993), *Challenging the Professions: Frontiers for Rural Development*, London: IT Publications.

Chambers, R. (1997), *Whose Reality Counts? Putting the First Last*, London: IT Publications.

Child, B. (1995), *Guidelines for Managing Communal Lands Wildlife Revenue in Accordance with Policy for Wildlife, Zimbabwe*, CAMPFIRE Coordination Unit, Department of National Parks and Wildlife Management, Harare.

Collinson, R. (1985), *Selecting Wildlife Census Techniques*, Monograph 6, Institute of Natural Resources, University of Natal.

Cumming, D.H.M. (1983), 'The decision-making framework with regard to the culling of large mammals in Zimbabwe', in R.N. Owen-Smith (ed.), *Management of Large Mammals in African Conservation Areas*, Pretoria: Haum, pp. 98–112.

Cumming, D.H.M. (1989), 'Commercial and safari hunting in Zimbabwe', in R.J. Hudson et al. (eds), *Wildlife Production Systems: Economic Utilisation of Wild Ungulates*, WWF, Harare, pp. 32–44.

Gibson, C.C. and Marks, S.A. (1994), 'Transforming rural hunters into conservationists? An assessment of community-based wildlife management programmes in Africa', *World Development*, **22**, 1063–83.

Hilborn, R. and Ludwig, D. (1993), 'The limits of applied ecological research', *Ecological Applications*, **3**, 550–52.

Holling, C.S. (ed.) (1978), *Adaptive Environmental Assessment and Management*, London: Wiley.

Hulme, D. (2000 forthcoming), 'Impact assessment methodologies for microfinance: theory, experience and better practice', *World Development*.

International Institute for Environment and Development (IIED) (1994), *Whose Eden? An Overview of Community Approaches to Wildlife Management*, London: IIED.

Jolly, G.M. (1969), 'Sampling methods for aerial censuses of wildlife populations', *East African Agriculture and Forestry Journal* (Special Issue), 46–9.

Ludwig, D., Hilborn, R. and Walters, C. (1993), 'Uncertainty, resource exploitation and conservation: lessons from history', *Science*, **260**, 17–36.

Mackie, C. (1993), 'Participatory wildlife census techniqiues: a preliminary attempt in North Gokwe', Unpublished report, World Wide Fund for Nature Multispecies Project, Harare.

Macnab, J. (1983), 'Wildlife management as scientific experimentation', *Wildlife Society Bulletin*, **11**, 397–401.

Marks, S.A. (1994), 'Local hunters and wildlife surveys: a design to enhance participation', *African Journal of Ecology*, **32**, 233–54.

Martin, R.B. (1986), *Communal Areas Management Programme for Indigenous Resources (CAMPFIRE)*, Branch of Terrestrial Ecology, Department of National Parks and Wildlife Management, Harare.

Mayoux, Linda (1997), *Impact Assessment and Women's Empowerment in Micro-Finance Programmes: Issues for a Participatory Action and Learning Approach*, London: Overseas Development Administration.

Montgomery, R. et al. (1996), *Guidance Materials for Improved Project Monitoring and Impact Review Systems in India*, New Delhi: Department for International Development.

Moris, J. and Copestake, J. (1993), *Qualitative Enquiry for Rural Development: A Review*, London: IT Publications.

Mosley, Paul (1997), *The Use of Control Groups in Impact Assessment for Microfinance*, London: International Labour Office.

Murombedzi, J.C. (1992), *Decentralisation or Recentralisation? Implementing CAMPFIRE in the Omay Communal Lands of Nyaminyami District*, Centre for Applied Social Sciences, University of Zimbabwe, Harare.

Murphree, M.W. (1994), 'The evolution of Zimbabwe's community-based wildlife use and management programme', Mimeo, Community Conservation Workshop, Tanzania, 8–11 February.

Norton-Griffiths, M. (1978), *Counting Animals*, Handbooks on techniques currently used in African wildlife ecology, No. 1, J.J.R. Grimsdell (ed.), African Wildlife Leadership Foundation, Nairobi.

Robb, C. (1997), 'PPAs: a review of the World Bank experience', in J. Holland and J. Blackburn (eds), *Whose Voice? Participatory Research and Policy Change*, London: IT Publications, pp. 131–48.

Sutherland, A., Martin, A. and Salmon, J. (1998), 'Recent experiences with participatory technology development in Africa: practitioners' review', *Natural Resource Perspectives*, No. 25, London: Overseas Development Institute.

Taylor, R.D. (1994), 'Wildlife management and utilisation in a Zimbabwean communal land: A preliminary evaluation in Nyaminyami District, Kariba', in W. van Hoven, H. Ebedes and A. Conroy (eds), *Wildlife Ranching: A Celebration of Diversity*, Pretoria: Promedia, pp. 210–22.

Taylor, R.D. (1996), 'Wilderness and the CAMPFIRE programme: The value of wildlands and wildlife to local communities in Zimbabwe', Paper presented at the Wilderness Symposium, Waterberg Plateau Park, Namibia, 24–27 June.

Taylor, R.D. (forthcoming), *African Wildlife and African Livelihoods: The Promise and Performance of Community Conservation*, Oxford: James Currey.

Taylor, R.D. and Mackie, C. (1997), *Aerial Census Results for Elephant and Buffalo in Selected CAMPFIRE Areas*, CAMPFIRE Association Publication Series 4, 4–11.

7 Integrating environmental appraisals of planned developments into decision making in countries in transition

Aleg Cherp

7.1 Introduction

The environmental impacts of the former socialist economies have been viewed as a major regional and even global threat. The present political, social and economic changes affect these impacts by influencing the scale and nature of economic activities, modifying environmental regulatory mechanisms, and reshaping other institutions with environmental implications. Transitional societies need to ensure that the current reforms will resolve, not intensify, the environmental problems accumulated in the past. At the same time, these countries face the challenge of achieving economic development not entailing unacceptable social costs. This can be done if decision making is guided by appraisals of proposed activities which judge their conformity to environmental, economic and social objectives.

Appraisals of planned developments are not completely new to countries in transition (CITs). In the past they were used to ensure consistency of top-down socialist planning systems. Now the role of appraisals is somewhat different: they should function in a bottom-up scheme, alerting decision makers to consequences of actions proposed by independent economic actors. This major reform of appraisal systems in transitional societies is particularly challenging because the context in which they operate is undergoing a significant transformation. Different approaches to reforming appraisal systems in CITs is the focus of this chapter.

Environmental Assessment (EA)[1] is used here as an example of a form of appraisal, because it is the most widely used formal appraisal procedure in CITs. Some of the countries in transition introduced certain forms of environmental assessment in the early 1980s, while most had enacted formal EA legislation by the early 1990s (see Table 7A.1 in the appendix to this chapter). All in all, more than a hundred EA laws, regulations and guidelines – a considerable number inspired by Western analogues – have been adopted in CITs over the last decade. Hundreds of thousands, if not millions, of activities have been subject to some form of EA. However, the question of whether these developments resulted in the expected outcomes remains largely unanswered.

EA systems can be considered effective if their utilization results in environmental improvements without posing undue obstacles to economic development. This study suggests a set of basic criteria which may be used in evaluating the effectiveness of EA systems. The proposed criteria are applied to the two main types of EA systems in CITs: the system based on the Western model of EIA/SEA and the so-called state environmental expert review (SER) system. This analysis is preceded by a brief overview of the environmental assessment in the region. In the concluding section, the chapter considers the relationship between EA systems and their changing social and economic contexts in transitional societies.[2]

7.2   EA systems in CITs: environmental assessment and ecological expertise

This chapter uses the term 'countries in transition' for the 28 former socialist countries in Europe and Asia which started reforming their political and economic systems during the last decade. CITs include the 12 countries[3] of the former Soviet Union, now referred to as the Newly Independent States (NIS), the 15 countries[4] in Central and Eastern Europe (CEE), including the three Baltic states,[5] and Mongolia.

Between 1990 and 1998, more than 100 EA laws and regulations were passed in CITs. Thus, EA has become, probably, the most widely used environmental appraisal and protection tool in the region. Having originated at approximately the same time and under similar socio-economic circumstances, EA systems in CITs share many common features. At the same time, there are a number of significant variations – the most noteworthy being a distinction between EA systems in the NIS and those in CEE.

EA systems in the NIS have their common roots in the so-called system of *state environmental expert reviews* (SERs),[6] introduced in the USSR in the late 1980s. SERs are conceptually similar to traditional *expertizas* (reviews of proposed plans and projects by expert committees) which served as a coordination and control mechanism of the Soviet centrally planned economy. SER is a process of reviewing documentation on proposed activities by environmental authorities, or expert committees appointed by authorities, in order to determine their environmental acceptability. The outcome of an SER is a resolution legally binding for developers, investors and permitting authorities. In most NIS, the laws necessitate the mandatory SER of all proposed activities independent of their size and nature.

In order to facilitate the process of SER, developers have been required to include a description of environmental aspects of proposed activities in documents submitted to SER. Such descriptions, which can be viewed as prototypes of environmental impact statements (EISs), were called '*OVOS*[7] volumes'. The Soviet and similar EIA systems are often called SER systems (see Cherp and Lee (1997) for more details on the origin and specific features of SER in the USSR and Russia).

The evolution of EA systems in many countries in CEE started from a similar point but proceeded in a different direction. Due to the larger degree of economic liberalization, the intention to join the European Union, and more radical reform of their political systems, the development of EA systems in CEE was mainly in the direction of approximating to the scheme established by the EU directives on EIA (EC 1985, 1997). The Baltic states, which originally inherited the Soviet SER system, are still in the process of switching to the Western EA model. Environmental assessment procedures in CEE will be called 'Western-style EA systems' or simply 'EA systems' in the rest of this chapter.

Integration of environmental considerations into decisions on development activities occurs differently in the EA and SER systems. A typical example of the former is the Slovak Republic which has thoroughly adopted the Western-style environmental assessment model (George and Kozova 1999 forthcoming). The EA system in Slovakia is oriented towards bringing the potential environmental consequences of proposed activities to the attention of the developer, the interested parties and decision makers (the 'permitting authorities'). The EA findings are accompanied by a 'Final Record' issued by the Ministry of Environment, reflecting the official standpoint on the adequacy of the EA procedure and documentation. The permitting authorities' decision takes account of the EA findings and the Final Record (which only has the status of a recommendation), but is also based on other considerations.

In contrast, a typical SER system can be found in the Republic of Belarus where the description of a project is submitted to competent environmental authorities, which decide whether and under what conditions it can go ahead. A decision of the competent authorities is reflected in a binding resolution. Socio-economic considerations are, in principle, not a part of such decisions since the Ministry of Environment has neither the expertise nor the mandate to take account of them (Cherp 1999 forthcoming). At the same time, socio-economic considerations are introduced into decision making through sectoral permit procedures similar to SER (such as the 'expert review' of the State Construction Committee).

Thus, CEE and NIS countries adopted two radically different approaches to environmental assessment, summarized in Table 7.1. The effectiveness of these approaches in finding the right balance between environmental and developmental objectives will be compared in the rest of the chapter. Belarus and Slovakia will mainly be used as case-studies,[8] but the experience of other CITs will also be considered.

Table 7.1 The main differences between SER systems in the NIS and EA systems in the CEE

	Environmental assessment systems in CEE	State environmental expert review systems in the NIS
Prototype	EU EIA Directives 85/337 and 97/11 and EA procedures in Western countries	Traditional expert reviews as used in the socialist planning + elements of Western-style EIA
Scope	Types of project-level activities selected through a screening process Policies, plans and programmes are not usually subject to EA	Formally, SER applies to all activities; in practice mostly to project-level activities In some NIS only selected activities require OVOS
Focus	The *process* of identifying and investigating environmental impacts and taking them into account in making decisions on the proposed activity	The *outcome*, i.e. determination of the environmental acceptability of a proposed activity through expert review
Participation	Open process encouraging participation of affected parties	Technocratic process often discouraging participation of non-experts
Decision making	In a majority of countries in the CEE the findings of EAs are in the form of recommendations and decision makers use them along with other considerations	SER resolutions issued by environmental authorities based on the analysis of the project documentation are of a binding nature; EA (OVOS) findings are not used in other decision-making procedures

7.3 Comparing the effectiveness of EA systems

Suggested criteria
An effective appraisal system and the related decision making should result in decisions which will maximize and more equitably distribute total (economic + environmental) social capital. In this way the appraisal system can facilitate sustainable development (George 1999 forthcoming). However, this

criterion may be too general for practical evaluation of EA systems. The following three more specific criteria are suggested instead:

- *The EA system should be able to protect the environment* through minimizing environmental costs and maximizing environmental benefits of proposed activities. No irreversible environmental impacts should be allowed.
- *The system should, to the extent possible, balance economic and environmental costs and benefits of the proposed development.* It should not pose undue obstacles to economic development (in particular, insignificant environmental impacts should not result in abandoning economically beneficial development proposals). Environmental optimization should be achieved in the most cost-effective manner.
- *The system should facilitate the equitable distribution of economic and environmental costs and benefits of the proposed development.* Distribution effects of proposed activities should be investigated and the views of affected parties, especially minority groups, taken into account.

Criterion 1: Environmental protection   Although SER legislation usually defines its purpose quite broadly as 'determining the environmental acceptability of proposed developments' (see, for example, *Law of the Russian Federation on State Environmental Expert Review* (1995), in Russia), in practice, the main objective of SER is to check the compliance of the proposed activity to environmental standards (understood as purely technical standards for technological processes, environmental quality and siting). There are several reasons for this reductionist approach:

- The lack of time and resources of SER competent authorities to investigate the proposed activities in more detail because of the large number of projects being reviewed. The SER procedure is applied to *all* developments without discrimination. For example, the number of SERs conducted in Belarus in 1997 was 4660 (about 450 per million of population), while the number of EAs conducted in Slovakia in the same year was 99 (about 20 per million of population). This wide application of SER naturally requires a simplified procedure which can only be, in most cases, limited to checking compliance with standards.
- The legacy of the Soviet central planning system from where the present Belarusian and other NIS SER systems originate. All economic projects in the USSR were highly standardized and appraised using standard criteria which worked relatively well in a society that lacked dynamics and innovation.

- SER experts are put in the situation where they have to decide on the environmental acceptability of a proposed development without explicit reference to its social and economic benefits and without clear public participation and consultation mechanisms. The only way to avoid purely subjective judgements in such a situation is to compare the predicted environmental impacts to 'objectively' determined norms and standards.

Since SER is focused on checking compliance with technical standards, the developers naturally limit their mitigation measures to meeting standard requirements. The main result of this system is rejecting those proposals that do not meet environmental standards. Thus, in Belarus, 480 projects (10 per cent of all considered) were rejected in 1997 as a result of SER.[9] The main substantive ground for rejecting projects was the violation of either technological or siting standards.

Conversely, EA procedures usually allow for a more thorough investigation and discussion of environmental impacts of proposed major developments. The EA system is oriented towards facilitating an environmentally conscious and publicly accountable selection between the alternatives and design of mitigation measures by the developer. Slovak experts indicate that, in 5–10 per cent of the cases, modification of projects occurs at the design stage as a result of the EA process.

At the same time, there seems to be no systematic evidence that the Slovak EA system and its analogues in CEE have a significant impact when making decisions on proposed activities. EA findings and the Final Record issued by the Ministry of Environment (an analogue of the SER resolution) in Slovakia have only a recommendation character, and decision makers seem to give more weight to economic considerations. There were only one or two cases in 1997 when a negative decision was issued as a result of EIA in Slovakia. A Hungarian EIA expert commented on this phenomenon that to expect a non-environmental public authority to voluntarily make its decision on environmental grounds is equivalent to 'entrusting a goat to guard the cabbage'.

Criterion 2: Balancing economic and environmental costs and benefits
Legally, socio-economic aspects of the proposed development are outside the scope of the SER because they are beyond the mandate and expertise of the environmental authorities who carry out SER. Thus, formally, SERs are not designed to balance environmental costs and benefits of the proposed development with any other considerations.

In practice, however, socio-economic interests clearly influence resolutions of the state environmental expert committees. This occurs implicitly and informally, often in the course of non-transparent communications within the government. For example, an interviewed official from an NIS country explained that when the SER of a certain development of strategic national importance started, the authorities made it clear that the SER resolution should be only positive. An experienced colleague explained: 'the SER is not about whether this project *may* go ahead; this has already been decided at a higher level; the review is only about how to make it happen in the way which least damages the environment'. Such an approach does not encourage the development of an objective methodology of balancing socio-economic costs and benefits against environmental ones.

Integration of socio-economic and environmental aspects in the development project is further complicated because the SER system does not encourage the developer to consider environmental issues at early stages of planning. The whole purpose of 'environmental assessment' conducted by the developer at pre-SER stages of the process is to ensure that the project is designed in accordance with standards and that sufficient proof of this is presented to the SER committee. Such an approach unnecessarily increases the costs of mitigation measures if they are required by SER only at the latest stage of the design process. Additionally, universal standards are not always the most cost-effective way of controlling environmental quality.

The EA approach seemingly provides more mechanisms for integrating environmental and socio-economic considerations. For example, in Slovakia, the decisions based on EIA are made by authorities accountable for socio-economic development, not just for environmental protection. This may have encouraged them to integrate environmental and socio-economic considerations in a more explicit and justifiable manner. Additionally, the Western-style environmental assessment is, in principle, initiated early in the planning process, thus encouraging the developer to combine socio-economic and environmental objectives in the planned activity. However, there is still no systematic evidence that this always happens in practice.

Criterion 3: Facilitating an equitable distribution of benefits and costs of development The attainment of this objective is facilitated by taking into account the views and interests of the diverse parties potentially affected by the proposed activities, to increase the likelihood that no group is significantly disadvantaged as a result of the development. Commonly, this is done by incorporating consultation and public participation provisions in appraisal and decision-making systems.

In the SER system, decision making is viewed as a purely technical 'objective' exercise (hence the reliance on standards already discussed above). Therefore SER discourages participation of anyone who does not have technical expertise. The affected public is effectively excluded from SER decision making.

Even public access to information on environmental impacts of proposed activities is significantly limited. Virtually the only mechanism of public participation is the so-called 'public environmental expert review', available, as follows from the title, only to semi-professional environmental non-governmental organizations (NGOs). In principle, the standards and deliberations of experts may account for the interests of affected citizens; in practice the interests of minority groups are often disregarded.

The EA approach gives more opportunities for participation because it provides open access to such information as EISs and incorporates such mechanisms as public hearings. For example, in Slovakia, citizens can participate at the screening, scoping and EIS review stages of the EIA process. The affected public can become a full party to the EIA proceedings by gaining the status of Civic Initiative or Civic Association (George and Kozova 1999 forthcoming). Decision makers in EA systems are typically more accountable than experts of the state expert review boards. However, Slovak NGOs surprisingly refer to public participation in the EA in their country as 'public pacification'. According to their argument, public participation in the EA process is not very valuable if the process rarely affects the decision making. It should be noted that, in CEE as in the EU, the existence of formal provisions for public participation in EA regulations does not guarantee the equitable distribution of development benefits and costs in practice.

7.4 Conclusions: environmental appraisal systems in transitional societies

Most of the countries in transition introduced EA systems at the time of their political and economic reforms during the last decade. CITs seem to have chosen two different approaches to EA. One has been to introduce the SER system of environmental permits; the other to introduce a system of EA modelled along the lines of Western countries. Some of the advantages and disadvantages of these two systems are summarized in Table 7.2.

The SER system seems to have stopped a significant proportion of environmentally dangerous developments. However, it failed to ensure that environmental considerations play a role at early stages of project design (except in so far as it had an indirect influence via the OVOS documentation). It did not result in noticeably better environmental education of the developers and it has also not been encouraging wider participation of the affected parties in the SER process.

On the other hand, the EA system is, in theory at least, a more transparent decision-making procedure and an important learning tool for the developers, authorities and the public. In principle, it can promote significant environmental improvements through encouraging environmental modification of proposed developments early in the planning process and bringing environ-

Table 7.2   Effects of environmental assessment and state environmental expert review

Criteria/ System	Western-style environmental assessment	State environmental expert review
Environmental protection	(+) Environmental modifications are introduced at the design stage of proposed activities (–) There seems to be little influence of EIA on the final decision making	(+) Ensures that environmental rules are observed by rejecting development proposals that violate the standards (–) The standards cannot account for synergistic, cumulative and indirect impacts (–) The system cannot take account of the newest scientific findings and unique local circumstances
Balancing economic and environmental considerations	(+) There is a formal possibility for comparing economic and environmental costs and benefits in a transparent and rational manner (–) There is little systematic evidence that such comparison is done in practice where economic interests seem to prevail over the environmental ones	(–) In practice, socio-economic considerations influence SER resolutions in an implicit and informal manner (–) The system does not encourage early incorporation of environmental objectives in planning the proposed activity (–) Environmental protection is not achieved in the most cost-effective manner
Promoting equitable distribution of costs and benefits of development	(+) There are formal provisions for informing and consulting the affected public (–) Since public participation is often limited in practice, EA proceedings rarely influence the final decision. NGOs often describe public participation as 'token'	(+) Mandatory nature of SER resolutions makes it possible to defend the interests of minorities through bringing them to the attention of SER experts. In some cases the public expert environmental review may exercise a limited influence on the SER (–) In practice, SER is a technocratic decision-making mechanism without any participation procedures of its own and is rarely concerned with the distribution of impacts of the development

mental considerations to the attention of decision makers. In practice, however, there are frequent complaints that developers consider environmental
impacts too late in their planning and design activities and that there is little
documentary evidence of specific environmental improvements due to EA
and, particularly, of dangerous developments being stopped as a result of
EAs. Moreover, NGOs criticize public participation in EA as 'token' because
it has not resulted in changes in decisions to reflect public opinion, and there
is little evidence yet of its favourable distributional effects.

Each of the systems has its own advantages and disadvantages and its 'net'
effect depends on the specific socio-economic circumstances of the transitional country concerned. SER systems are a 'cruder' environmental protection
tool. They work relatively well in societies that have not undergone much
reform in political and economic spheres. Typically, many of these CITs
experience economic stagnation, and most of their existing development
proposals originate domestically and are smaller in scale. The lack of their
own economic resources and relative international isolation makes it very
difficult to strengthen institutional capacity in ways which are necessary for
modern EA systems. Civic society is relatively underdeveloped. Under such
circumstances a standardized system that applies to all developments and is
based on objective standards and existing bureaucratic structures may do the
job more effectively than any viable alternative.

When and if the reforms progress, there is likely to be growing pressure to
introduce more participatory decision-making procedures. Large modern
projects may be proposed which cannot be appraised using the old approaches.
Foreign investors may require the introduction of EA systems which are
'harmonized' with internationally accepted standards. All these factors may
prompt a shift from the SER to the EA system. However, such transformation
needs to be preceded by extensive capacity-building measures to ensure a
higher level of education of government officials and other participants of the
process, to provide sufficient technical and organizational expertise. Also, the
Western-style EA system may only be effective if the country has established
the rule of law, and a strong civic society, and it is not so overwhelmed with
economic problems that its decision makers cannot afford to have other
priorities on the agenda.

There are several examples among CITs (for example, Armenia) where
advanced and ambitious EA laws were enacted in the absence of such necessary preconditions. Their net result has been disappointment in the very concept
of participatory environmental appraisal and deterioration in the traditional
environmental planning system. Equally undesirable, however, is holding back
the reform of SER systems until the resources of the society are sufficient to
establish a state-of-the-art EA system and where the existing procedures cannot
resolve existing social conflicts over contentious new developments.

   More information and insight into the operation and the effects of environmental assessment systems under the unique conditions of transitional societies are needed in order to recommend the right balance of 'old' and 'new' approaches in specific countries or regions. It is more appropriate for developed countries and for international aid agencies to support professionals, officials and representatives of the civil society from the region in finding the right approaches to their EA systems, than to offer them ready-made procedures borrowed from elsewhere.

Notes

1. The term 'environmental assessment' collectively refers to environmental impact assessment (EIA) of individual projects and strategic environmental assessment (SEA) of policies, plans and programmes.
2. The data presented in this study have been collected by the author through a mail survey in 24 countries in transition, interviews in six CITs and research in the archives of the Ministry of the Environment of one country in transition.
3. Armenia, Azerbaijan, Belarus, Georgia, Kazakhstan, Kyrgyzstan, Moldova, Russia, Ukraine, Uzbekistan, Tajikistan and Turkmenistan.
4. Albania, Bulgaria, Bosnia and Herzegovina, Croatia, Czech Republic, Hungary, FYR Macedonia, Poland, Romania, Slovak Republic, Slovenia, and Yugoslavia (Serbia and Montenegro).
5. Estonia, Latvia and Lithuania.
6. In Russian: 'gosudarstvennaya ekologicheskaya ekspertiza', also frequently translated as 'state ecological expertise', 'state environmental examination', or 'state environmental assessment'.
7. The Russian abbreviation for 'assessment of impacts on the environment'.
8. The advantages of comparing Belarus and Slovakia include similar size of the countries, a similar economic situation (moderate economic growth, partially induced by state intervention), and comparable administrative systems. The author conducted extensive surveys in both countries.
9. About one-third of the rejected projects were modified and approved at the second or third resubmission.

References

Bellinger, E., Lee, N., George, C. and Paduret, A. (eds) (1999 forthcoming), *Environmental Assessment in Countries in Transition*, Budapest: CEU Press.
Cherp, O. (1999 forthcoming), 'EIA in the Republic of Belarus', in Bellinger, E. et al. (eds), *Environmental Assessment in Countries in Transition*, Budapest: CEU Press.
Cherp, O. and Lee, N. (1997), 'Evolution of SER and OVOS in Russia (1985–1996)', *EIA Review*, **17**, 177–204.
Council Directive of 27 June 1985 on the assessment of the effects of certain public and private projects on the environment (85/337/EEC), *Official Journal*, L175 05/07/1985: 0040–0048.
Council Directive 97/11/EC of 3 March 1997 amending Directive 85/337/EEC on the assessment of the effects of certain public and private projects on the environment, *Official Journal*, L73, 5–15.
George, C. (1999 forthcoming), 'Testing for sustainable development through environmental assessment: criteria and case studies', *EIA Review*.
George, C. and Kozova, M. (1999 forthcoming), 'EIA in the Slovak Republic', in Bellinger, E. et al. (eds), *Environmental Assessment in Countries in Transition*, Budapest: CEU Press.
Law of the Russian Federation on State Environmental Expert Review (1995), Federal Law No. 174–FZ of 30.11.1995.

Appendix 7A: Main EA legislation in selected countries in transition

Table 7A.1   Main EA legislation in selected countries in transition (as at the end of 1998)

Country	EIA Regulations	Year
Mongolia	Government Resolution No. 121	1994
	Law on Environmental Protection	1995
	Law on EIA	1997
THE BALTIC STATES		
Estonia	Regulation on Conducting EIA in Estonia, No. 314	1992
	Regulation on the Methodological Guidelines for Implementing EIA in Estonia, No. 8	1994
	Law on Environmental Impact Assessment and Environmental Audit	draft
Latvia	Law on State Environmental Review (no longer in force)	1990
	Law on Environmental Protection	1991
	Regulations on Territorial Planning	1994
	Law on Construction	1995
	Law on Territorial Planning Development	1998
	Law on Environmental Impact Assessment	1998
Lithuania	Articles in the Environmental Protection Law	1995
	Law on Environmental Impact Assessment	1996
	Governmental Resolution No. 456 concerning the approval of the list of proposed activities and projects that shall be made subject to the full EIA	1997
	Governmental Resolution No. 1305 on the approval of the order of informing the public about the proposed activity and implementing the proposals	1996
	An amendment to the Law on EIA	draft
CENTRAL EUROPE		
Czech Republic	Czechoslovak Federal Act on the Environment (No. 17/1992)	1992
	Czech National Council Act (No. 244/1992)	1992
	Implementation Decree on Professional Competence in EIA	1992
	EIA Act	draft

Table 7A.1   continued

Country	EIA Regulations	Year
Hungary	Government Decree on the temporary regulations of EIA of certain activities 86/1993 (IV.h)	1993
	Government Decree on the modification of the list of activities requiring EIA 67/1994 (V.h.)	1994
	Environmental Protection Act No. LIII	1995
	Decree No.152 on Activities Requiring the Completion of an EIA	1995
Poland	Environmental Protection and Management Act (with a number of amendments)	1980, 1997
	Landuse Planning Act (LPA) with amendments	1994
	Highways (Toll Motorways) Act	1994
	MoE Executive order on the forecast of the environmental consequences of local land-use plans (connected with LPA)	1995
	MoE Executive order on environmental impact assessment of highways on environment, agricultural and forest lands and cultural heritage (connected with the Highways Act)	1995
	Executive order on hazardous and potentially harmful developments and environmental impact assessment	1995
	Framework EIA Act	draft
Slovakia	Czechoslovak Federal Act No. 17 of 1992 (all articles concerning EIA in this Act were superseded by Act 127/1994)	1992
	The National Council of the Slovak Republic Act No. 127/1994 on EIA	1994
	Regulations No. 52/1995 on the list of authorized experts for EIA	1995

SOUTH-EAST EUROPE

Albania	Law on Environmental Protection	1993
	Regulation and procedure on EIA	draft
Bulgaria	Environmental Protection Act Chapter VI (1991)	1991
	Regulation No. 1 on EIA	1993
	Regulation No. 2 on EIA	1995
	Regulations on licensing EIA experts	1995

Table 7A.1   continued

Country	EIA Regulations	Year
Croatia	Law on Physical Planning and Spatial Arrangement	1980
	Regulations on the Elaboration of EIA Studies (no longer in force)	1984
	Law on Environmental Protection (art. 25–art.32)	1994
	Government Decree on EIA	1997
Macedonia	Law on environment and nature protection and promotion	1996
	Law on physical and urban planning	1996
	Guidelines for issuing approval and decision for the use of facilities	1996
	Law on EIA – draft	draft
Romania	Law 137 on Environmental Protection	1995
	Ministerial Order 125 – The Permitting Procedure for Economic and Social Activities Having an Environmental Impact	1996
	Ministerial Order 278 – Accreditation Rules for EIA and Environmental Audit Performers	1996
Slovenia	Environmental Protection Act	1993
	Regulations on the types of activities for which an EIA is mandatory	1996
	Instruction on the methodology for preparation of a report on EIA	1996
	Decree on Conditions and the Procedure for obtaining Authorization for preparing reports on environmental impacts	1996

NEWLY INDEPENDENT STATES (NIS) OF THE FORMER USSR

Armenia	Principles of Legislation 'On Nature Protection'	1991
	Law on Sanitary-Hygienic Safety of Population	1992
	Law on the Review of Impacts on the Environment	1995
	Law on Environmental Protection	draft
Georgia	Law on Environmental Protection	1996
	Law on Environmental Permits	1996
	Law on State Ecological Expertise	1996
	Law on EIA	draft

Table 7A.1   *continued*

Country	EIA Regulations	Year
Belarus	Law on Environmental Protection	1992
	Law on the State Environmental Review	1993
	Instruction on the Order of Conducting State Environmental Reviews	1995
Moldova	Law 'On the Protection of the Environment'	1993
	Law 'On Ecological Expertise and the Assessment of Environmental Impacts' No. 851–XII	1996
Russia	Law on Environmental Protection	1991, 1993
	Regulations 'On Assessment of Environmental Impacts in the Russian Federation'	1994
	Instruction on Environmental Substantiation of Economic Activities	1995
	Construction Norms and Rules SniP 11.01.95	1995
	Construction Rules SP 11.01.95	1995
	Federal Law on Environmental Review	1995
	State Environmental Review procedures ('*reglament*')	1997
	Regulations on Assessment of Environmental Impacts	draft
Ukraine	Environmental Protection Act	1991
	Law on Ecological Expertise	1995
	Law on Scientific Expertise	1995
	Structure and Content of Documents on Environmental Impact Assessments (OVOS) in Designing and Construction of businesses, houses and buildings. Main designing principles. DBN A.2.2–1–95	1995
Kazakhstan	Law 'On the Protection of the Environment'	1997
	Law on Ecological Expertise	1997
	Tentative Instruction on Procedure of OVOS of Planned Activities	1993
	Instruction on the Procedure of SER for pre-Project and Project Documentation	1997

Table 7A.1 concluded

Country	EIA Regulations	Year
Kyrgyzstan	Law on Environmental Protection	1991
	Law on Environmental Review	draft
	Law on Environmental Protection	draft
	The Instruction on the Order of Conducting OVOS	1997
	The Instruction on the Order of Conducting SER	1997
Tajikistan	Law of the Republic of Tajikistan on the Protection of the Natural Environment	1993
	Regulation on State Ecological Expertise No. 156	1994
	Law on State Ecological Expertise	draft
Turkmenistan	Law on State Ecological Expertise	1995
	Law of Turkmenistan on Nature Protection	1991
Uzbekistan	Law on Nature Protection	1992
	Instruction on the Order of Conducting the State Ecological Expertise	before 1995
	Instruction on the Order of Carrying out OVOS	before 1995
	Law on the State Ecological Expertise	draft

PART II

CASE STUDIES

8 Environmental impact assessment within a multinational enterprise: adaptive EIA in the Camisea project

Murray G. Jones

8.1 Introduction

The Camisea gas project in Peru was a 'green field' development in an area that had previously seen only petroleum exploration. The fact that it would occur in a highly sensitive area required that there be extensive environmental and social planning in concert with project design. At the end of the initial licence period (15 July 1998), commercial agreement was not reached between Shell Prospecting and Development Peru (SPDP) and the Peruvian government. None the less in over two years of preliminary planning and two further years of on-the-ground activity, much was completed and much was learned about the achievement of a high standard of performance. SPDP was the operating company on behalf of partners Shell and Mobil.

This project has involved a progressive decision-making process necessitated by the need to carry out technical studies in advance of a project decision. This would be followed by continuing design of project components (for example, pipelines and fractionation facilities) after the project decision with environmental impact assessments (EIAs) on each project component. The EIA process was adapted to this evolution to ensure that the right levels of studies were carried out in accordance with the engineering design, the probable environmental impacts and the needs, concerns and expectations of the resident native communities.

It was clear from the start that the project would take place in an environment that was highly sensitive. It was sited in Upper Amazonia, in the homeland of indigenous peoples and in an area of high biodiversity. It was recognized that there were many non-governmental organizations (NGOs) and multilaterals who, through direct involvement or through long-standing areas of attention, would have various levels of concern. Thus, in addition to the implementation of a series of EIAs, it was also decided that the process must include longer-term biodiversity studies, extensive community interaction, a wide-ranging consultation and the development of an ongoing social diagnostic connected to community regional planning. This formed an 'adaptive environmental impact assessment' process that allowed not only critical path EIAs to be completed but also a continuous process of learning that could be integrated into project decision making. Improvement within this context does not end with the EIA submission. This process was proving successful in the short term (1996–98) and was viewed as the model by which Camisea would proceed.

This chapter describes the project in terms of the key phases and components providing an insight into the progressive nature of oil and gas decision making. The EIA process was to encompass seven separate but related EIAs each addressing a distinct part of the development and meeting both internal (Shell) and external (government) approval processes. The chapter describes key project aspects of environmental and social management. With the EIA as a core design tool, other processes were developed that would provide the ability to continuously adapt the project to new information and understanding. These included baseline diagnostics, monitoring and consultation processes that would feed into the design and operation of the development. Lessons learned in these processes resulted in a number of fundamental design premises and changes to the intended means of implementation. Some of these key lessons are presented.

8.2 The Camisea project

The Camisea natural gas and liquids reserves are located in the upper Amazonia region of Peru 500 km due east of Lima (see Figure 8.1). The development of these reserves presents a unique opportunity for the country. It entails the largest project of its kind in Peru and enables the country to convert its growing energy deficit into a positive balance. It also offers the country an indigenous source of cleaner energy and the opportunity to attract significant investment in new industries such as petrochemicals.

The project involves the production of natural gas and condensates (natural gas liquids – NGLs) from two reservoirs that lie about 2500 metres deep on either side of the Camisea River. This river feeds Urubamba which in turn flows north to the Ucayali and on to the Amazon. Condensates are small droplets of liquid entrained in the reservoir rock. To maximize the production of these condensates a gas recycling system was planned whereby 'wet' gas would be produced carrying the condensates. The liquids would be extracted from the gas and much of the 'dry' gas would then be reinjected into the reservoir to flush out further liquids. This extraction and recompression would take place in a gas processing plant that was planned to be located on the banks of the Urubamba River. The gas plant would also be the terminus of two pipelines (one for the gas and one for the NGLs) that would extend some 700 km, leading first through some 150 km of rainforest then up to the altiplano and across the Andes arriving at Pisco on the Pacific coast. The pipelines would turn north towards Lima with an intermediate stop at a fractionation plant that would further separate the various liquid and gaseous

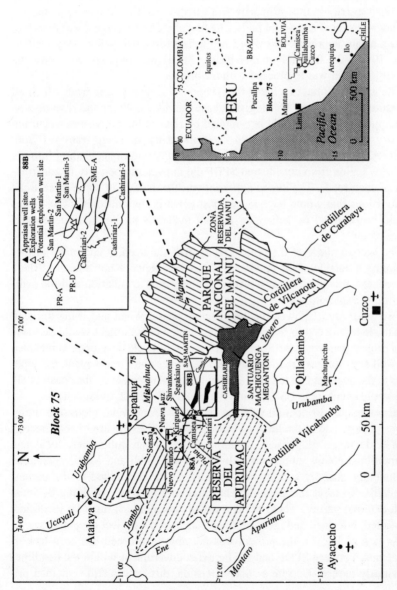

Figure 8.1 Location of the Camisea project

121

streams. The liquids would be exported by boat. The gas pipeline then proceeds to customers in and around Lima.

To make a decision on the gas development project, SPDP first needed a period of study to confirm reservoir conditions, develop models by which the gas and liquids could be economically extracted and most particularly develop the gas markets on the coast. Until Camisea gas reaches the coast, Peruvian energy comes primarily from hydro-electric sources with the remainder from coal and diesel fuels. The first phase of the project was therefore known as an 'appraisal' and was timed to last some two years (May 1996 to May 1998). By the end of this phase, SPDP was required to notify the government if it was to proceed with the project.

The appraisal phase included the creation of a supply base from which all operations would start. This logistics base provided both air and river access. The appraisal project would be supplied by river in the rainy season. During the dry season, operations would be supplied by air cargo transport from Lima. All personnel would arrive by air. There are no roads leading into the Camisea region from outside and SPDP did not want to be party to construction of such roads. The key to appraisal was the drilling of some three wells on locations that would have to be constructed in the rainforest. These sites would be supplied by helicopter and all materials to the well sites would move by air.

The second phase of the project recognized the need to undertake further exploration outside of the previously discovered fields. Known as the 'Block 75 licence', this phase was to involve both seismic acquisition and the drilling of one exploration well.

Two years were allowed for the planning phase. When and if the decision was made to proceed to full field development, a commitment would be made for a project that would last some 40 years. The full field development included the well sites for gas production, infield flowlines and the gas plant, the pipelines to the coast and on to Lima and the fractionation plant on the coast. In all, this would entail some US$3 billion (thousand million) of investment.

Issues related to operating in the rainforest, Amazonia, alongside indigenous persons and in the heart of world-class biodiversity are of core interest to a wide range of parties, including the Peruvian authorities, local and international NGOs, numerous individuals, and Shell and Mobil personnel. Technically, socially and environmentally, SPDP committed to the highest standards. To meet this commitment required a new way of doing business with external parties. These parties, called stakeholders, must be identified, contacted, informed and involved in all stages of the project development.

As is now known, the project was not able to proceed due to a lack of agreement between SPDP and the Peruvian government within the deadlines previously agreed. Despite a short extension, differences still remained primarily around assuring gas markets. However, the project was considered by many, including the native communities and their leaders, as having established a direction and commitment that provided the probability for success in minimizing overall impacts and maximizing benefits. Indigenous leaders have since petitioned the Peruvian authorities, complimenting the work of SPDP and asking that any future development be required to meet the commitments set by SPDP.

8.3   The EIA process
Environmental impact assessments are required by law in Peru for oil and gas activities including seismic operations, drilling and full development programmes. Equally they are a commitment of Shell International. These requirements came together appropriately with the SPDP policy that EIAs would be carried out and the commitment that they would meet the highest standard. From the point of view of external measurement, this implied that a reviewer should be able to compare the resulting EIAs to the requirements of the Shell International *Environmental Assessment Guidelines* (1995a) and *Social Impact Assessment Guidelines* (1995b) – both public documents – or to the World Bank EIA Guidelines (1991). At the same time, the EIAs would meet Peruvian requirements including the important provision that an environmental management plan must be included with any submitted EIA. The latter, which is also a Shell International requirement, provides for an action plan that shows how the EIA will be implemented in reality.

In all, some seven EIAs were considered part of the required process to gain approvals from the earliest (appraisal) phase through exploration and into development. These EIAs covered

1.   appraisal drilling of three wells in the San Martin and Cashiriari fields;
2.   exploration drilling of up to three wells in prospective fields;
3.   seismic exploration over prospective fields;
4.   gas plant, infield flowlines and well clusters;
5.   pre-build access road in Altiplano – Angusmayo to Chiquintirca (to enable pipeline construction);
6.   two parallel pipelines from the gas plant across the Andes to a fractionation plant/export terminal on the coast and on to Lima; and
7.   fractionation plant/export terminal at Pampa de Clarita.

The first three of the EIAs were considered independent studies to 'prove up' the project. The latter four were inter-related, taking into account that impacts of one element of the project could affect another. Thus in scoping documents, briefing materials, and consultation, the components were always described together. For EIA submission it was agreed with the government that each component would become the focus of an EIA due to the complexity of each, the different audiences and the need to obtain approvals for EIAs (4) and (5) ahead of (6) and (7) due to longer construction periods.

SPDP started considering the environmental and social impacts, ahead of the activity-specific EIAs, with an environmental profile in 1994 (ERM for Shell International Exploration and Production 1995c). This document provided a first look at environmental risks associated with the project. It clearly identified for SPDP not only the regional sensitivities but also defined land uses (for example, Manu National Park and the Apurimac Reserve) that would have to be considered. The preparation of the profile included a number of consultation meetings from which a list of key concerns relating to the future as well as to past practices were identified. These 'past practices' were associated with the exploration activities of a different Shell company in the region in the 1980s and represented a clear message of what issues were likely to come on the table from any local consultation.

A scoping report was initiated as the first step in the EIA. The EIA recognized that the project description included a logistics supply base, the logistics transport themselves (air and water), and the construction and drilling of three wells. Field studies were undertaken in the region including visits to a number of communities to inform them of the activities and to gather baseline information. The study design and execution recognized that the EIA was addressing an activity that would last no more than two years and would largely take place outside of areas normally used by communities. Thus it focused on minimizing site-specific impacts and impacts of logistics. The EIA was filed with the Peruvian authorities in July 1996 and approval to proceed was received on 26 August 1996.

Subsequently an agreement was signed for Block 75 providing the opportunity for SPDP to explore for further hydrocarbon prospects outside of the discoveries in Block 88. Exploration was to be carried out in two parts. First an exploration well would be drilled on a prospect known as Pagoreni – a new 'lead' north-west of the Camisea fields. Second, further seismic studies would be undertaken to identify further prospects. Both these activities require an EIA. These were to be undertaken separately. The EIA for the exploration well started in March 1997. Following a public hearing, approval to proceed with the exploration programme was received on 25 September.

The seismic EIA commenced with the design of a scoping report in June 1998. This latter document was just being completed at the time the decision was made not to proceed with the project. Thus the EIA activities on seismic studies ceased at that time.

In all, seven EIAs would make up the submissions required to enable the project to occur as envisaged. Each would have scoping, field studies, consultation, public hearings and environmental management plans. This represents a comprehensive approach to impact identification and management as well as allowing stakeholders numerous opportunities for involvement.

8.4   Consultation

A consultation process was mandated through policy and management commitment as stated in the company's business objectives (Jones 1998). Consultation serves a number of purposes including:

- providing information;
- gaining information;
- developing dialogue such that concerns may be communicated;
- focusing on specific studies such as EIAs;
- providing a participatory route for active involvement in decision making; and
- providing for partnership in joint contribution to a common goal or deliverable.

The consultation process:

- ensures the identification of stakeholders;
- ensures the availability of timely information;
- makes publicly available all environmental and social studies;
- ensures that communication allows for two-way flow of information;
- ensures that SPDP staff listen to the external messages;
- ensures that the information, messages and concerns received are communicated within the system to determine what changes in the project will assist in alleviating or minimizing the concerns; and
- provides feedback to the stakeholders of how their concerns have been addressed.

Early in the process we established a number of key steps to consultation and listed these in 'Briefing Paper 3' distributed in June 1996. (Note: briefing papers are information documents distributed to stakeholders approximately every two to three months.) As originally stated, these steps were:

1. To establish stakeholder identification and prioritization.
2. To hold initial meetings with all key stakeholders (to confirm interests, provide information and seek involvement).
3. To provide information, for example through such means as briefing papers.
4. To repeat meetings with key stakeholders who confirmed their interest in the project (based on mutual understanding with the stakeholders).

5. To recognize stakeholder information, comments and concerns in feedback letters and in environmental and social studies.
6. To integrate consultation results into formal EIA documents.
7. To provide feedback on issues and actions to SPDP management.
8. To establish key external groups for collective discussions (for example, community meetings and topic-specific workshops).
9. To commission specific research or studies to assist in understanding (environmental profile, EIAs).
10. To broaden relations to create partnerships within communities and key stakeholders, to find solutions to problems and to provide delivery of benefits.
11. To establish long-term management relationships for delivery of social capital. (Note: social capital is the inherent ability of a person and/or community to manage their own future through health, education, training opportunity, equality, capacity.)
12. To release EIA documents to the public. The appraisal drilling programme EIA (no. 1) will be used to understand concerns and to help in discussions of the terms of reference for subsequent EIAs.

These steps have provided a good model. Participation means that SPDP must provide information in a timely and efficient manner so that stakeholders can contribute to the process. All reports are considered public. We in turn must indicate how the information received is used and how the project has changed as a result of the input. All information is bilingual and some is translated into Machiguenga. In February 1998, SPDP inaugurated an Internet web site – www.camisea.com – which acted as a repository for this information and is designed to cater for surfers ranging from children to informed NGOs.

Stakeholders
Stakeholders have been identified as those on whom the project will impact (primarily the local native communities which have land tenure and land rights) and those groups or agencies who can impact on the project. The primary stakeholders also include the representative federations.

The indirect (or secondary) stakeholders include those with specific interests in the region or those who have planned programmes that relate to regional improvement or regional study. It is our objective not to interfere with such programmes but to look for synergy with our own activities. Indirect stakeholders also include those who have interests or concerns in the issues at hand – rainforest, indigenous communities, biodiversity and oil and gas operations. Many of the international stakeholders fall into this category. In all some 200 groups or individuals make up the stakeholder list.

Combining direct and indirect stakeholders provides a lengthy list of those with whom we have been, and are, consulting. It has been learned that many groups simply want to be kept informed and aware. Others are more directly involved to the point of weekly and at times daily contact.

Techniques

A variety of techniques are required to deliver and receive information and comments due to the geographic location of the project and its limited infra-structure. In addition, the native communities require a certain formality within which information is received and decisions are reached. Formal notice of visitation is required. Community meetings are held and joint decision making is the social etiquette. Any agreements must be formalized and signed by the full community. This process is repeated for each community visited. We started with visiting about six communities. This has expanded to more than 40, to include all the main communities within our exploration licence block and an additional number outside. This recognizes the wider impacts of the full field development programme as well as the fact that, in remote areas, regional change is of concern to adjacent communities and affects their communications and culture. Thus all affected parties must be considered, not only those directly involved.

To ensure that the communities understand the scope of the project, a number of consultation 'rounds' were devised. Taking place over some nine months, a series of visits were made to the 45 affected communities during which information of increasing depth was provided on the project. At the same time, concerns were identified and fed back to the design team, result-ing in changes to the project in a number of areas. The rounds used a variety of means of presentation to ensure that the cross-section of attendees would understand. These techniques included maps, drawings, pictures, models, copies of guidelines, specifically designed comics, and a puppet show. While some feedback showed concern with repetition of information as progressive layers of data were added, the process did provide a sense that the complexity and extent of the project were being understood. At the same time, the community liaison officers of SPDP were able to introduce the concepts of social capital and sustainability, to provide regional net benefit, and to show corporate commitment to a long-term working relationship with the commu-nities.

Written information is a key to developing and maintaining awareness. This has included a series of briefing papers which provide updates in which we try to indicate both positive progress and also any mistakes or areas requiring particular attention. We were advised that specific papers should be directed at the communities themselves to enhance appreciation of the tech-nology, terminology and general understanding of what is coming in the form of development. This suggestion has been acted upon through 'letters to communities' – four issued in Spanish and Machiguenga. We also provided to communities a special paper on understanding EIA (this paper was drafted for SPDP by the UK Institute of Environmental Assessment) and have drafted a 'community' version of the gas plant EIA to simplify the issues and discussions for presentation to the communities.

Workshops

For other stakeholders, techniques such as one-on-one meetings and workshops are used to generate direct responses. In December 1997 we started on a new phase of involvement termed 'stakeholder workshops'. These workshops took place in Lima, Washington and London and brought together regional stakeholders with an open agenda for dialogue. Three leaders representing the native federations of the Camisea region attended these workshops. The key objectives were to try and understand different positions, to provide information and to identify the major issues. While these issues could not be fully resolved in one day, a few of them did receive detailed debate and all were recorded for continuing consideration within the project study and design.

A second round of workshops took place in late May 1998, which provided project updates based on EIA preparation and an issues discussion. Prior to each workshop an issues report was released summarizing the status of all the issues identified in the earlier workshops. Typical issues that had been identified included: native rights, security presence, sustainable development, need for increased government involvement, need for capacity building amongst NGOs and communities, and integrating NGO and community needs into a business schedule.

In the two-day Lima workshop in May, 46 participants representing 39 organizations attended. In the one-day Washington, DC workshop, 17 participants representing 15 organizations attended. In the one-day London workshop, 15 participants representing 13 organizations attended. Participants included representatives from the governmental, non-governmental, private sector, multilateral and academic sectors.

In addition to Camisea project staff and participants, two Peruvian representatives also attended the Washington, DC and London workshops. These included representatives of the Ombudsman's Office (Defensoría del Pueblo) and the Peruvian Environmental Network (Red Ambiental Peruana – RAP). The Defensoría is the constitutionally mandated, independent state institution responsible for protecting and promoting the rights of the Peruvian people to the Peruvian government. RAP is a consortium of 38 environmental NGOs which is independently monitoring and evaluating project activities.

The difference between the first and second workshops was that the latter resulted in the generation of specific topics for future action, coupled with a statement of interest by participants that they would like to join focus groups on those topics. Workshop reports have been issued to all participants and are available on the Camisea web site.

8.5   Social analysis and community planning

One of the first management events, after the Camisea licence agreement was signed in May 1996, was to hold a workshop in Lima to consider our community programme. It was agreed in the discussions that SPDP wanted to be seen as a 'partner' working with communities and enhancing their abilities for self-sufficiency – sustainability – recognizing that the project would create both short- and long-term impacts and a permanent regional change. The means by which this was to be achieved was by enhancing 'social capital', that is the collective ability of persons and communities to manage their own future. For the communities of the Lower Urubamba, this came to mean enhancement in such areas as health care, education, employment abilities, agricultural practices, women's rights, training programmes and capacity to understand the project and work within the planning process.

As a result of these discussions, a number of baseline studies were commenced. The first was a *health baseline study* which was undertaken in August 1996 prior to the arrival of Shell personnel or contractors. It was led by the Royal Tropical Institute of Amsterdam with participation and support from the Peruvian Ministry of Health, the Proyecto Integral de Salud en la Amazonia Peruana (PISAP) and the Instituto de Medicina Tropical Universidad Peruana 'Cayetano Heredia'. The purpose of the study was:

- to identify the prevalence of disease in the region;
- to identify the state of health care in the region; and
- to make recommendations for improvements.

Workshops were then held with the communities and officials in Lima to set priorities and map a way forward. This resulted in the establishment of an inter regional committee supported by the Minister of Health. After some 18 months, a plan was produced which focused on capacity building, enhancing regional health delivery services and training of local health staff. This plan was being implemented by a team external to SPDP when closure was announced. However, SPDP committed to the completion of the first phase of implementation which will last more than a year.

A second study was a regional *socio-economic review* to provide the regional baseline on which regional planning could take place. SPDP requested that the regional government and NGOs work in the local communities to conduct a socio-economic and ecological review of the region. This covered education and training, women's issues, resource use, business development and other economic issues and will propose initiatives to promote regional sustainable development. It was a partnership between Region Inca, IMA (Instituto Medioambiente) and SPDP. The technical team included representatives of FPCN (Pro Naturaleza), CBC (Centro Bartolome de las Casas), ADARI (Asociation Derecho Ambiental Region Inca), INANDES (Instituto Andino de Ecologia y Desarrollo) and IMA. It relied on both secondary and current information which was revealed at a series of village workshops.

Because sustainable development depends on the situation in the entire region, the review went well beyond the six to eight communities where SPDP had initial operations. It covered the lower Urubamba watershed from the Pongo de Mainique to Sepahua. The field programme for the diagnostic lasted some eight weeks. After completion of the report, workshops were planned to prioritize recommendations and to develop the relevant regional plans. The key was to ensure a basis from which agreements on the future development would be established with the communities and their representatives.

These two baselines were considered key to future planning and the formalization of programmes. These would be facilitated by SPDP but increasingly led by government, NGOs, multilaterals and the communities themselves. This, however, was not the full extent of studies that were either planned or completed at the time that closure was announced. The following additional plans started or were intended:

- *Education baseline study*   This commenced with a workshop between Regional Ministries of Education, community representatives and community teachers and was followed by community visits by the Ministry. The Ministry then began the preparation of a plan to improve education in the region.
- *EIA baseline study*   For every EIA, surveys were carried out of the communities most directly affected. These surveys were undertaken in progressively more detail as the activity changed from the drilling of appraisal wells to the development of full field facilities. EIA studies typically related to the project activity. Given the overall approach to the Camisea development it was decided that a combination of parallel, linked studies would serve the overall project objectives better than using EIAs as the only delivery mechanism. This allowed communities to work at their own pace and for sustainable plans to emerge over a period of one or more years as opposed to the EIA schedules which are typically driven by business schedules. EIA baselines were prepared using direct observation, community visits, interviews and rapid rural appraisal techniques.
- *Federation workshops*   A series of four workshops, called by Federation leaders, and facilitated by SPDP, were implemented by the end of

September 1998. These were typically used to discuss results from the consultation rounds with communities, key issues from the EIAs, proposals to reach a regional agreement on negotiations and compensation, capacity building on EIA monitoring, conceptual issues regarding sustainable development, social capital and net benefit and the programme for social monitoring and social indicators. The workshops were also a means to establish priorities for community programmes. For example, at the May 1998 meeting, the Federation leaders indicated their preferences concerning health, food/nutrition, income, education and housing priorities.

- *Social indicators*   At the start of the project, community representatives expressed concern that their communities could be adversely impacted by the gas development and would not see any benefit from the project. SPDP recognized that some negative impacts would occur and thus an early commitment was made to the concept of 'net benefit'. It was considered that the programmes as discussed above would go a long way to providing that net benefit. The key consideration was how to measure such benefit. A project was formulated to develop a series of performance indicators. This process was elaborated into an 'appraisal and monitoring process' which would not only present the indicators themselves but would also use them to record the changing baseline, inform the communities, and use community resources and capacity in information gathering and identifying appropriate priority measures.

It is clear from the above that an extensive and wide-ranging series of studies were needed, first, to understand the social environment and, second, to jointly plan the future of the region. No single 'one-off' event could provide the necessary baseline, buy-in, prioritization, planning and ultimate delivery given the need to involve such a wide range of players.

In the early days, the communities had a strong interest in receiving compensation. The feeling was that 'Shell is here, get it while we can'. The vision was short term, defensive and entirely understandable. To move to a sustainable approach and succeed in delivering 'net benefit', the communities had to believe that 'up-front' planning would lead to long-term plans and deliveries. To provide assurance on the SPDP intentions, two commitments were made to the communities during the consultation rounds. The first was a commitment from the company in the form of a 'pledge' signed by the general manager. This pledge confirmed that the company would work towards benefits and sustainability in the different geographical and social areas where construction and operations would take place. The programme in the Lower Urubamba, for example, would be quite different from that along the pipeline route or in Lima.

The second approach was to establish a regional 'accord' between the company and the communities at a public signing ceremony. The accord represented the beginning of a joint commitment to a regional development plan. It also represented an understanding by the communities that 'net benefit' was to be seen as regional and shared amongst all communities, not only the few where project activities would actually take place.

An example of a regional benefit can be seen in the initiative to register the 'mothers' clubs'. These clubs are involved in many aspects of community life, including nutrition, shelter, education, and 'all things necessary for the advancement of daily life'. Consultations with communities revealed that while all communities had such organizations, none had been formally registered. Registration was seen as an important step in providing authenticity and the ability to speak on behalf of, or request support for, a mothers' group. As a result, SPDP supported the legal registration of 19 such clubs. By the end of 1998 it also supported an initiative to create an association of mothers' clubs in the lower Urubamba to assist the affiliated organizations. Supporting the activities of these clubs is an important way of ensuring the involvement of women in community development.

8.6   Biodiversity studies

One of the international stakeholders that was identified early in the stakeholder identification process was the Smithsonian Institution. It has a long connection with Peru, particularly concerning the Manu National Park, adjacent to the Camisea region. Initial meetings led to a recognition that the biodiversity of the Camisea region had not been studied and little was known about the changes that might be expected.

The possibility of working together was discussed and led to an agreement resulting in a succession of studies. The first of these, Phase I, was a workshop (October 1996) organized by the Smithsonian with many Peruvian attendees. There were 83 participants representing 38 national and international organizations. The agenda was initially to determine both knowledge and expectations on biodiversity awareness and needs in the Lower Urubamba but the agenda was expanded by the participants to address social links and concerns.

Subsequently the Smithsonian made a proposal to establish biodiversity monitoring plots at the appraisal well sites. A total of six phases were ultimately completed. The Smithsonian also recognized the need for and value of linking the collection and use of biodiversity information to management decisions. In the Phase II Smithsonian report (Dallmeier and Alonso 1997) the adaptive process it developed was explained as follows:

Aspects of the adaptive management process – setting objectives, carrying out an assessment and monitoring plan for forest biodiversity, evaluation and decision-making – have been incorporated into the Lower Urubamba project. This process can be represented as a cycle which is periodically calibrated to ensure that appropriate information from each component feeds the next level. The cyclical nature of the process is maintained through refining the objectives and management decisions based on the ongoing results. Thus, adaptive management gives managers the flexibility to adjust on-the-ground practices.

Adaptive management is well suited to the type of project underway in Urubamba. The process serves as a guide in planning and carrying out a sound forest biodiversity monitoring program. As hydrocarbon exploration continues in Urubamba, pressures to provide adequate development of the identified gas resource in conjunction with conservation of the Urubamba region will likely increase, resulting from greater public and private interest and involvement in use of the local resources. An assessment and monitoring process can aid in evaluating existing management approaches and their impacts on the Urubamba forest ecosystems and define new approaches if needed. (Section B of the report)

The methodology recommended by the Smithsonian was to create a multi-level assessment and monitoring of species of plants and animals in a series of test plots near to the area of proposed operations. These test plots would be thoroughly inventoried by expert scientists who would document six different taxonomic groups: vegetation, mammals, birds, amphibians and reptiles, arthropods, aquatic systems and the integrated ecological system. Established Smithsonian protocols and improved protocols were used. The design, change and improvement of protocols were furthered through two scientific workshops in Washington and Lima, in early 1998, each attracting about 50 participants. A programme of test plot surveys was also planned along 150 km of pipeline route that would pass through a variety of rainforest environments from the gas plant location to the Apurimac River. This unique transect study had started with the choice of ten macro environments that should be surveyed. A team of 32 was helicopter lifted into the first of these locations. The first site investigation was well under way when the decision was made that the project should not proceed. It was agreed, however, that both the first and second site surveys would be completed before withdrawing the team and redirecting them to a final set of follow-up surveys in the Camisea region at the well-site testplots.

While the biodiversity surveys operated to an independent time line from the EIAs, the data acquired supported the much more abbreviated surveys that are normally carried out in the EIA process. Also, the biodiversity team benefited greatly from the EIA information that directed the researchers to specific issues of concern.

The biodiversity surveys were fully designed and executed by Smithsonian personnel and their Peruvian counterpart team representing a number of universities. SPDP exercised no control over the surveys, their locations or methodologies. The agreement provided the team with full access to all areas with an invitation to advise on project decisions. All findings would be in the public domain.

In accordance with this adaptive management approach, opinions were sought from the Smithsonian experts in a number of areas including whether the root zones of trees would create any problems for underground pipelines; the migration patterns of vampire bats which had caused rabies in some communities; the effect of drilling operation noise on the presence of mammals; the effects of a temporary or permanent access route along the infield flowlines in creating ecological fragmentation; and the effects of siltation on downstream biological communities.

8.7 Adaptive EIA
Within the Camisea project, adaptive EIA comprises a series of EIA studies, coupled with long-term social and environmental research and with ongoing consultation programmes at local, national and international levels, to progressively influence design and operations activities to meet the project objectives (see Figure 8.2).

With this as a basis, and as a result of early consultation with the native communities, SPDP made a commitment to 'net benefit' through a programme focused on both meeting legal obligations to the communities and delivering 'social capital' to secure sustainability. This long-term focus then had to be coupled with the shorter-term needs of an EIA process that would gain government approval, help in the design of the activities, and establish the standards and commitments by which the detailed implementation would take place.

It was realized that these could be achieved only if there was increasing buy-in to the programme by stakeholders and that the programme retained flexibility to adjust and change with learning. This could not be accomplished through the EIA process alone. EIAs are, by definition, a planning tool integrating environmental and social information into the decision-making stage of project design. The project, in this case developing the gas of Camisea, develops progressively on the basis of research and learning. Until the appraisal programme was finished it was impossible to predict a full conceptual design. Even after conceptual design was completed it would still be impossible to understand fully the environment and the impacts upon it without continuing studies and consultation.

By the nature of the oil and gas business, further exploration would be needed to better define known reserves and to prove up additional 'leads'. This is done through both seismic and drilling programmes. However, the level of uncertainty that exists within exploration, and the time line of typical activities (no more than a year in a given location), determines the likely scope of the impact assessment.

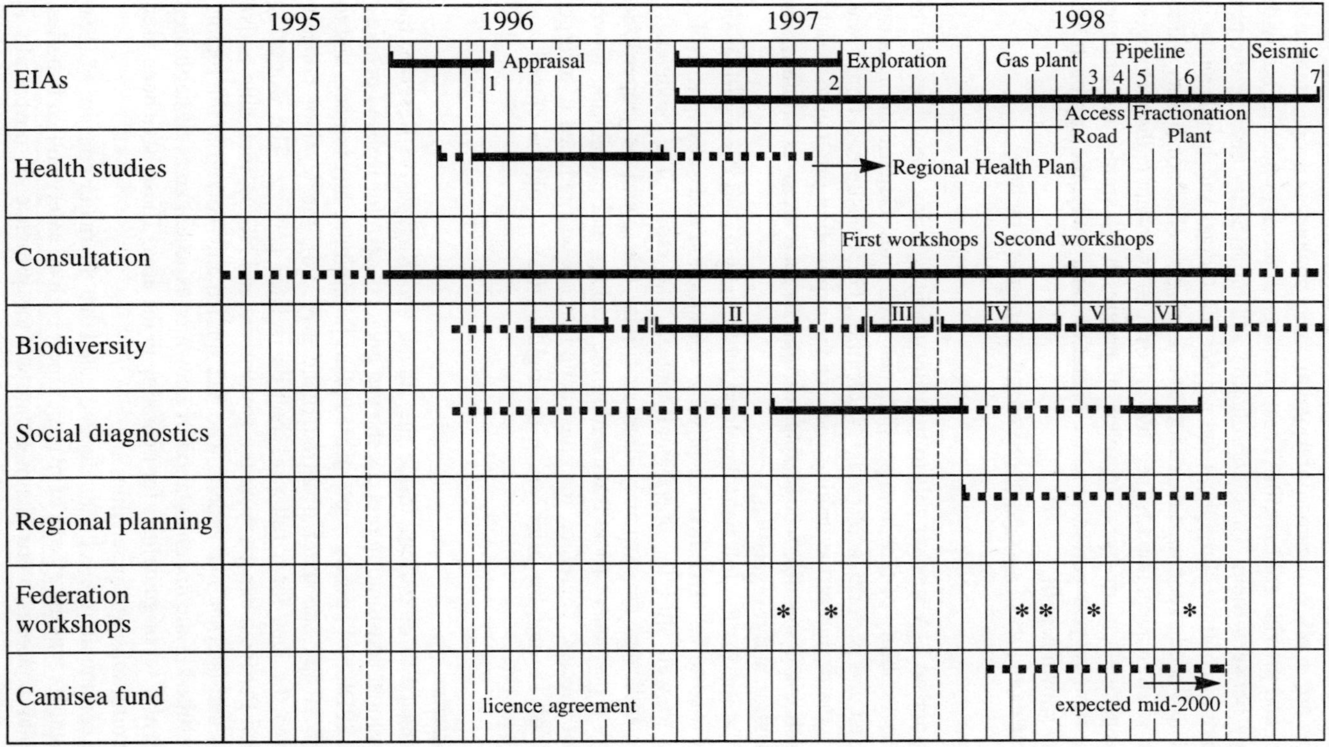

Figure 8.2 Adaptive environmental assessment

The limitations of the EIA process can be overcome by ensuring that other avenues are in place to gather information, make changes in scope, minimize impact and provide for benefits. These avenues all work in parallel but with synergy between them. Thus, consultation and biodiversity became themes that should continue throughout the project life. Social and health analysis would also need to continue to reflect the changing baseline conditions and to recognize subsequent impacts (negative or positive) and adapt to these changes. This represents a life-cycle approach of progressive learning and change. Within the two-year period of active operations and study, the approach has already shown benefit.

Some examples of success of this adaptive approach include:

EIA

The appraisal EIA was not able to fully document baseline conditions due to the inaccessibility of terrain at possible new well sites. Generic information was used and performance standards identified. Once onsite experience was gained, the design of the drilling sites for the exploration programme could be much more specific, recognizing learning in such areas as rainfall, site stabilization and revegetation.

The scope for the full field development initially called for a permanent infield road to be used, first for pipeline construction and subsequently for access to well sites for operational controls and repair. The biodiversity studies indicated an extremely high sensitivity that could be jeopardized through a permanent route fragmenting the ecology and prohibiting movement of species. Therefore, the construction access was reduced to a target period of 18 months, after which the right of way would be closed and revegetated.

Consultation

With regard to operations inside the Nahua and Kugapakori Reserve, the international consultation process showed great concern for isolated peoples. While SPDP had already implemented plans to minimize any impacts and to respond if any encounter occurred (none ever did), the level of concern triggered the idea for a full workshop on isolated peoples. The workshop included Peruvian experts from the government and NGOs, including native leaders and international experts who had studied and worked in the region. This resulted in the documentation of known or expected areas of habitation as well as a set of guidelines for operating in the area. These have been used in planning subsequent activities.

The community consultation demonstrated that the major concern of local communities was the effects of river transport both on safety and on fisheries. Particular concerns were identified around the presence of hovercraft. A series of community meetings, along the riverine route, resulted in a set of operating guidelines developed and supported by the communities and the operating department. A system was put in place to ensure that communities could notify the company of any complaint. With respect to the fisheries issue, SPDP agreed to sponsor an extended fisheries baseline study over many seasons, which included community participation. The results would be provided in regular updates to communities so that changes or effects could be understood jointly.

An early consideration was the possibility of including an electricity generation plant as a part of the project. Siting of the plant both inside and outside the Lower Urubamba were seen as options. Before the EIA was started, consultation was undertaken specifically on the 'power plant option' to determine key concerns and issues. It became clear that there were strong positions that would be taken in relation to a power plant in the rainforest. This information, plus preliminary technical, logistics and environmental studies, led to an early decision that a location in the Lower Urubamba rainforest should not be considered further.

Other examples of the identification of native community concerns and at least part of the response taken are included in Table 8.1.

Biodiversity

The Smithsonian was asked to comment on noise effects on mammal presence and behaviour around rig sites (see Phase II report, Dallmeier and Alonso 1997). This information was needed to determine whether a reduction in mammal presence could result in more difficult hunting for the local communities. After completion of the well-site programmes the observation was made that rig activity did not appear to have a significant offsite effect with all expected species appearing within some 100 metres or less of the rig. An extension and continuation of this programme was planned to include helicopter noise. The intensity of hunting pressure by members of the local communities was the principal factor in determining the distribution and abundance of game species.

Bats

The area is very rich in different species of bats, with 99 per cent of them representing important components of the forest ecology as pollinators and seed dispersers. Several rabies cases were reported over the general area and vampire bats were the probable sources of the disease. Even though the probability of catching rabies from vampire bats is much less than from infected domestic dogs and cats, a programme for their control was in preparation when the project was wound down.

*Table 8.1 Some concerns identified in community consultation and
company response to them*

Concern	Response
Pollution of air, water and land from gas plant operation	Federation leaders visit a 'typical' site in Scotland which would be matched in Camisea
River cargo transportation effects on fisheries and canoes	Long-term fisheries study/River Traffic Safety Booklet produced
Construction noise from pipelines and helicopters on game	Pipelines and helicopters kept away from populated areas and rivers; Smithsonian Institution monitoring noise effects
Pollution of waters from gas plant construction	Gas plant location in previously deforested settlers land/sewage plant to be provided
Increased colonization due to access tracks for pipeline construction	Access tracks to be controlled/reforestation plans in place
Use of flow lines access tracks by loggers and settlers	Flow lines access tracks to be controlled with community participation
Effects on the health of isolated and semi-isolated peoples	Response plan in place/health pass, medical screening for all workers
Effects on community women and daily community life	'Offshore policy': no interaction with communities/community relations guidelines in place
Effects of flaring	Community leaders visit test flares; limited duration; restore surrounding environment and remove flare pit
Pipe leakage	Pipes fully tested/pipes are buried
'Offshore policy' should continue in order to reduce community effects	Commitment that 'offshore policy' will continue
Current operational commitments should be enforced	Agreed; River Traffic Safety Booklet is an example
Employment for community members in construction and production phases	Community members will be employed/outsiders coming to the region will not
Use of access tracks to go hunting and visiting relatives	Community lands should continue under traditional use; access will not be promoted along artificial tracks
Access to medical services in gas plant	Community health services are being enhanced as the preferred alternative
Compensations for land take and nuisance impacts should continue to include more communities	Policy for land negotiation, compensations and net benefits to be recognized in a regional framework agreement

Revegetation

To minimize the possibility of intrusion into the region from outside, a decision had been taken to fully revegetate, with native species, the pipeline right of way from the Apurimac to the gas plant site. There was some concern over whether this could permit the full recurrence of all local tree species due to the possibility of the root systems damaging the pipeline coating. While the pipeline engineers determined the best possible coatings to protect the line for 40–50 years, the Smithsonian carried out literature and field research (at the Pagoreni well site) to predict the types of root penetration by different species. The information gathered provided the assurance that full vegetation could take place.

Education

An important part of the biodiversity programme was to return information to the communities in the form of educational material. In addition, several members of the community were trained by the research staff to carry on with some of the biomonitoring activities.

Social analysis

Communities identified potential concerns over company intrusion into their villages. This intrusion was expected to impact on the economic situation, women, wastes, alcoholism and culture. As a result of these concerns, SPDP established an 'offshore' policy by which all operations would be treated as controlled areas from which workers were not allowed to leave. Communications with communities was strictly limited to community liaison officers or other designated persons. The reasons for the tight controls were explained to the workers and the communities through the SPDP community relations guidelines. Following construction it was anticipated that the offshore approach might move to a partnership based on developed trust and selective initiative implementation.

The health baseline study found that the communities of the Lower Urubamaba could be sensitive to Western diseases, particularly as the Ministry of Health vaccination programmes were not reaching the region. As a result, an extensive vaccination programme was developed for all SPDP employees and contractors to minimize the risk of the transfer of disease. It was also realized that, even with the offshore policy that isolated our workers from communities and with vaccinations, other persons such as traders, loggers, NGOs, tourists, government officials and so forth would still visit the region without similar precautions. Therefore, SPDP agreed to assist the Ministry of Health in its community programme. This consisted primarily of logistics support and establishing a 'cold chain' of strategically placed solar refrigerators to allow for vaccination storage.

8.8   Conclusions

Adaptive EIA recognizes the need for continuing appraisal of environmental and social conditions throughout the project life cycle. In the Camisea project it was determined that this would be done, in part, through preparing a series of impact statements that would provide 'point in time' predictions of impacts and of environmental management plans. The involvement of stakeholders through consultation and participation and leading to partnership is also key to this adaptive process. Societal priorities and perceptions changed through this participatory process, leading to a greater consensus and shared vision and mission by many of the parties. Some key findings are:

- EIA processes must be linked to the business framework and, while this is schedule driven, the relationship can be well handled if started early in the decision-making process.
- Consultation must accompany the EIA activities but must also be a fundamental project commitment extending before and after EIA.
- Consultation must be open and transparent.
- Consultation must use a variety of approaches.
- Stakeholder response will vary, but with an open approach will extend towards those who wish to be kept informed, those who wish to have active involvement and those (a few) who oppose development for fundamental reasons.
- Regional analysis of health and social impacts requires extensive planning, effort and time and must be seen as a supplement to what can be accomplished within the EIA.
- Diagnostic analyses are seen as ongoing tools needing periodic review.
- Measurement of performance and change are required.
- EIA is key to identifying impacts and the means to mitigate these but the ability to address issues and concerns also requires a range of other studies and consultations.
- Meaningful change in the project is possible outside the EIA process.
- Partnerships with communities, NGOs, government and independent agencies provide opportunities for continuing studies which supply inputs to subsequent adaptations of the project.

The project has, in its short life, demonstrated the ability to work within the adaptive approach and to make critical and significant changes to it as a result of the feedback received.

References

Dallmeier, Francisco and Alonso, Alfonso (eds) (1997), *Biodiversity assessment and Long Term Monitoring – Lower Urubamba Region – San Martin-3 and Cashiriari-2 Well Sites Phase II*, Washington, DC: Smithsonian Institution Institute for Conservation and Biology.

Environmental Resources Management (ERM) for Shell International Exploration and Production (1995c), *Camisea Project Environmental Profile*, Environmental Resources Management, Report EP 95–0597, The Hague, February.
Jones, Murray G. (Manager Health, Safety and Environment, Shell Prospecting and Development Peru) (1998), 'Stakeholder Participation – The Road to Successful Oil and Gas Development', Society of Petroleum Engineers' Health Safety and Environment Conference, Caracas, Venezuela, June.
Shell International Exploration and Production (1995a), *Environmental Assessment Guidelines*, Report EP 95–0370, The Hague.
Shell International Exploration and Production (1995b), *Social Impact Assessment Guidelines*, Report EP 95–0371, The Hague.
World Bank (1991), *Environmental Assessment Sourcebook*, vol. III, Guidelines for Environmental Assessment of Energy and Industry Projects, Washington, DC: World Bank.

9 Environmental and social impact assessment in a remote, timber-dependent community in Guyana

Danette Leslie

9.1 Introduction

In 1991 the government of Guyana signed a Timber Sales Agreement with Barama Company Limited (BCL), a jointly owned Malaysian–South Korean plywood company. The agreement gave BCL the rights to extract timber over an area of 1.6 million hectares for 25 years. This area, situated in the North-West District of the country, represents 8 per cent of the country's land area.

BCL's concession, although extensive and rich in tree species diversity, is poor in the hardwood species that are known and readily accepted on the international market. Soils throughout most of the concession are composed of heavy clays with low fertility. As such, commercially valuable timber trees occur with less frequency and are smaller in dimension than in South-East Asia. These circumstances increase costs of extraction per cubic metre and reduce profitability, when compared to South-East Asian forests. Although several hardwood species are harvested by BCL, Baromalli (*Catostemma spp.*) is the main species and comprises 85 per cent of their total harvest (ECTF 1996). Baromalli and other suitable species are processed into plywood at the company's mill, located outside Georgetown.

In an effort to improve the sustainability of their forest operations, BCL contracted the Edinburgh Centre for Tropical Forests (ECTF) to undertake research and to monitor their operations. A full time ECTF staff member was based at BCL's forest operation headquarters. In 1993 ECTF conducted, at BCL's request, an environmental and social impact assessment (ESIA). In the ESIA, potential positive and negative impacts of BCL's operations were identified and recommendations presented on how to promote positive impacts and minimize negative impacts.

The North-West District in which BCL's concession is located comprises 10 per cent of the country's total land area, 90 per cent of which is forested (Forte 1995). The majority of the district's population of less than 20 000 people are clustered around five main population centres. One of these, Port Kaituma, was chosen by BCL as the headquarters for their forest operations (see Figure 9.1). This remote resource-dependent community of 2077 persons (Leslie 1996c) is located in the north of the District. The area around

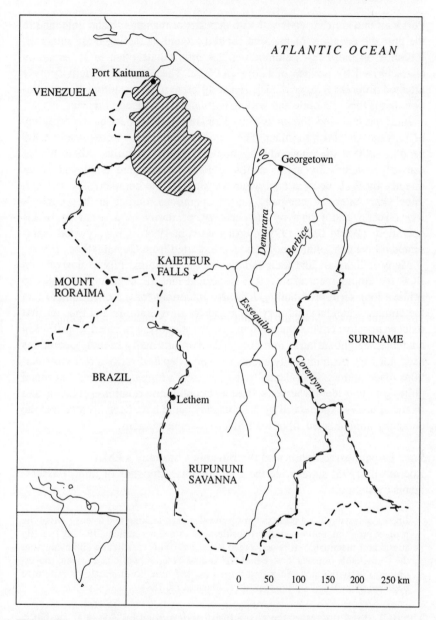

*Figure 9.1   Location of the BCL concession (hatched area) in North-west
Guyana*

Port Kaituma is richly endowed with deposits of manganese and gold, and in the past the economy of the area centred around extracting these minerals. Reliance on these few commodities has unfortunately led to an economy characterized by periods of boom and bust. These cycles of activity have affected different areas of the District at different times, resulting in a population that is highly mobile and willing to migrate to seek employment.

BCL has had, and continues to have, a significant impact on the economy of Guyana and Port Kaituma. The company employs approximately 1300 people, 1000 at the plywood plant and 300 at Port Kaituma. About 47 per cent of economically active adults in Port Kaituma are employed either directly by BCL or by a contractor working for the company. As of 1994, three years after the company started operations, output in the country's forest sector had grown by 70 per cent, primarily as a result of BCL's operations (World Bank 1995). Furthermore, in 1994 BCL's plywood represented 68 per cent of all wood products exported from Guyana (Sizer 1996).

Many individuals and their families in Port Kaituma rely exclusively on BCL for employment and so it is important that the company manages to achieve long-term profitability. It is also important for the environment that the company conducts its harvesting and forest operations in a manner that reduces negative environmental impacts. Profitability, a satisfied workforce, a contented neighbouring community and environmentally friendly operations need not have been mutually exclusive. This chapter discusses recommendations made in the ESIA relating to the company's logging methods and social policy and considers whether subsequent community relations problems and financial losses experienced by the company could have been avoided had the company implemented all of the ESIA's recommendations.

9.2   Impact assessments and the Barama Company's ESIA

Roe et al. (1995) summarize the common characteristics of impact assessments by stating:

> Impact assessment is a process to improve decision-making and to ensure that the project/program options under consideration are environmentally and socially sound and sustainable. It is concerned with identifying, predicting and evaluating the foreseeable impacts, both beneficial and adverse, of public and private (development) activities and mitigating measures, and aims to eliminate or minimize negative impacts and optimize positive impacts. (p. 184)

The BCL ESIA possesses the characteristics described by Roe et al. in that it

> examines the broader environmental and socio-economic context of the BCL forestry operation, discusses the potential negative and positive impacts of this substantial regional development, and produces recommendations for implemen-

tation by BCL and the Government of Guyana for improved planning and forest management in the North-West. (Harrison et al. 1993, p. I).

Although impact assessments share common characteristics, there are no universally accepted guidelines on their methodology. Instead, methods used to conduct assessments reflect the particular country's or agency's agenda and economic situation (Hollick 1986, cited in Wood 1995). Trade-offs often occur between time, cost and quality when conducting an impact assessment, as Figure 9.2 illustrates.

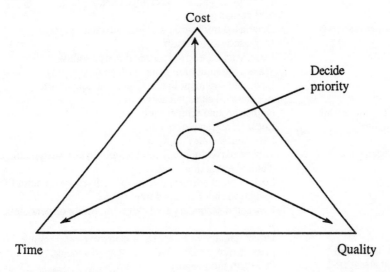

Source: Briner et al. 1997.

Figure 9.2 Trade-offs that may be encountered when conducting an impact assessment

Trade-offs between cost, time and quality were also made by the team that conducted the BCL ESIA. The team comprised a sociologist, a forester[1] and an ecologist and had three weeks in which to compile information for the ESIA and conduct site visits. Although the team met with individuals, Amerindian communities, government officials and non-governmental organizations (NGOs), time severely limited the degree of community participation in meetings and the planning process. Community participation was further hindered by the fact that BCL arranged for the ESIA to be conducted two years after the Timber Sales Agreement was signed and after harvesting had commenced. More community involvement in the planning process may, as will be discussed later, have led to better community–company relations.

Table 9.1 Potential impacts of BCL's activities

Type of impact	Detail of impact
1. *Impacts from selective logging*	
Landform and soil	Slope/bank instability
	Gully/sheet erosion
	Sedimentation
	Channel bed modification
	Loss of nutrients and organic matter
	Decrease in cation – exchange capacity
	Soil compaction
Water resources	Decreased infiltration and groundwater recharge
	Increased storm runoff
	Decreased baseflow, less regular streamflow
	Water contamination from spillage or spraying
	Increased sediment loads, impact on aquatic life
	Accelerated eutrophication
Climate and air quality	Higher ground temperature
	Local or regional desiccation
	Dust, smoke, air pollution
Vegetation	Timber harvesting may not be biologically sustainable at planned extraction levels
	Loss of plant species, threats to biodiversity, genetic loss
	'Isolation shock' to seed trees
	Unwanted secondary forest growth, influx of persistent weeds
	Direct damage to forest from machinery and felling
Wildlife and fisheries	Loss of rare, endangered or protected species, threats to biodiversity
	Loss or damage to breeding and feeding sites, both terrestrial and aquatic
	Population stresses from displaced animals into nearby forest and on agricultural crops
Traditional culture, local and subsistence economy	Reduction or elimination of traditional food, shelter, and other forest resources, loss or changes in fuelwood supply
	Damage to religious, cultural or archaeological sites
Epidemiology	Creation of habitat for disease vectors
	Reduction of diseases by forest clearing
Conservation	Damage to existing, poorly demarcated or legally uncertain conservation areas
	Disruption of conservation potential and loss of amenity
2. *Impacts from roads*	
Direct impacts	Soil erosion and sedimentation
	High runoff or poor regeneration on compacted soils
	Damage to residual trees

Table 9.1 concluded

Type of impact	Detail of impact
Indirect impacts	Water contaminated by hydrocarbons
	Loss of forest through road construction
	Increased hunting pressure, wildlife trade and illegal timber felling
	Increased settlement and shifting cultivation
	Increased mining activities
	Increased transport and communication, change in traditional transport patterns
	Improved access for tourism
	Damage or destruction to wildlife

3. *Impacts from forest activities*

Forestry workforce	Additional pressure on forest resources through hunting and shifting cultivation
	Friction with local residents
Log pond	Generation of polluting wastes
	Interference with navigation, fishermen and local river traffic and fauna by stray logs and barging activities
Chemicals	Contamination of waters by wood preservatives
Other BCL activities	Improvement of living standards through social provisions
	Housing

4. *Impacts from fire*

Forest clearing by fire	Damage to soils, vegetation, fauna and seed banks
Introduction of fire risk	Desiccation and inflammable weed invasion

5. *Impacts from employment, economic development and changing population structure*

Impacts of increased jobs, spending, people	Conflict over job opportunities
	Increased standards of living, trading and market demand
	Disruption to traditional subsistence economy
	Culture shock in remote areas
	Immigration, with increase in settlement and shifting cultivation
	Immigration, with increased hunting and illegal logging
	Introduction of diseases by forestry workers and other incomers

Source: Adapted from Harrison et al. 1993.

Despite the limited time and funds for the study, the ESIA accurately predicted the five main sources of potential impacts, as detailed in Table 9.1, and made pertinent recommendations relating to them (Harrison et al. 1993). Each of the five main sources was further divided into more specific impacts (as shown in the table), which had social as well as environmental consequences.

9.3   ESIA recommendations and their implementation
The remainder of the chapter discusses the major recommendations, made in the ESIA and listed below, which were designed to reduce negative and promote positive impacts:

1.   Choice of road alignment.
2.   Training of felling and skidding teams.
3.   Adoption of a code of practice for chemicals.
4.   Incorporating ECTF's findings into BCL operations.
5.   Hiring a community liaison officer and an Amerindian liaison officer.
6.   Improving markets for foodstuffs.
7.   Providing assistance to improve health care.
8.   Providing assistance to improve the quality of education (Harrison et al. 1993).

The recommendations are discussed in regard to their environmental and social appropriateness and their degree and effectiveness of implementation.

Choice of road alignment
It was recommended that care be taken in road alignment as poorly considered road alignments could unnecessarily damage the forest stand, increase erosion,[2] further fragment the habitat of certain animals and plants and increase access into remote areas for gold miners and animal trappers. It could also impact on migration, traffic and forest loss in particular local settlements. Hence careful planning of road alignments was important not only to avoid the costs of building unnecessary roads, but also to minimize the negative impacts of poorly located roads on the environment and the local community.

Unfortunately, a change in the intensity of the forest survey method used, some time after the ESIA was completed, meant that information on the location of commercial trees was no longer reliable. This change led to two major problems, the building of roads into areas with insufficient commercial trees to cover costs and the inefficient layout of skid trails for extraction of logs from the forest. In addition, valuable trees were left uncut as logging teams no longer had information on their location. Road building costs constitute a major proportion of the costs of a logging operation and have a large impact on the physical and social environment. Had the company followed the recommendations concerning roads in the ESIA and their own Forest Management Plan, the environmentally damaging and costly exercise of building inappropriate or unnecessary roads could have been avoided.

Road construction had the following social impacts: (i) increased transport between communities within the concession; (ii) increased access of previously inaccessible areas by gold miners; and (iii) increased settlement along roadways. Of households surveyed during the 1996 Household Survey (HHS), 76.5 per cent stated that transport was easier then than pre-BCL (Leslie 1996a). Although walking was the most common form of primary transport, free transport in BCL vehicles was the next most common form.

The ESIA recommended that a road usage policy be adopted as unregulated use of heavy vehicles on the wet clay roads caused considerable damage to the roads, resulting in increased maintenance, particularly grading, at BCL's expense. In 1996, several years after the request was first lodged, the government accepted BCL's request to allow the company to control usage of its roads by non-BCL vehicles. In March 1997, private commercial vehicles were required to pay a toll when they used the company's roads and were prevented, like BCL's own vehicles, from using the roads when they were wet. Although the levying of tolls was a legitimate attempt by BCL to recoup some of the additional road maintenance costs they had incurred, after five years of free use the tolls were not well received by all members of the community. Had the government and BCL agreed on and implemented a road usage policy before access was allowed, any damage to community relations which resulted from restricted road use could have been avoided. Further, BCL's rehabilitation of several overgrown and disused public roads in the area, in an attempt to keep private vehicles off their own roads, was overshadowed by the late introduction of the road usage policy.

Training of felling and skidding teams
The ESIA recommended that felling and skidding teams receive training in the felling of trees and their removal from the forest. According to the ESIA, training felling and skidding teams[3] would minimize 'needless waste, damage and risk to the regeneration of residual forest stand' (Harrison et al. 1993, p. viii). As BCL intend to harvest their concession on a continuous and cyclical basis, reducing damage to saplings and seedlings was imperative to their long-term operational success. In addition to reducing damage to the forest, training the operators of the machinery would have ensured better use of machines, some of which cost hundreds of thousands of pounds, thereby reducing costs through fewer breakdowns and repairs and by increasing their working life.

Initially, when BCL started operations, felling and skidding teams were trained by two Canadian loggers. However, the periodic and thorough pro-gramme of professional training recommended in the ESIA was never implemented. Because of high labour turnover, one year after the start of operations there were members of felling and skidding teams whose only training had been from their fellow team members.

This situation led to costly and damaging harvesting practices. Environ-mental impacts were greater than necessary due to a lack of planning in the layout of skid trails and lack of understanding by logging teams of the environmental and efficiency benefits of directional felling and winching. This resulted in increased costs to the company and greater damage to the forest. Machinery also suffered from a lack of trained operators; at one time, 40 per cent of the company's heavy machinery was inoperable and awaiting repairs (Chan 1996). Had the training programme been implemented, as identified in the ESIA, timber harvesting and extraction would have been better planned and executed resulting in more timber being harvested,[4] less damage to the residual forest and reduced machine downtime. Striking a better balance between costs of training and costs from poor practice could have increased company profits.

Adoption of a code of practice for chemicals
Various fuels and chemicals are used during the course of BCL's operations. The ESIA recommended BCL produce and implement a code of practice for chemicals, notably insecticides. This code was to cover storage and use, thereby reducing pollution of the environment and increasing the safety of employees. Pollution of the area in which BCL sprayed their logs,[5] before the logs were loaded on to barges and transported to their plywood mill on the coast, was of particular concern since the area drained into the main water source from which the community obtained their water for drinking and household use.

In 1995 BCL requested that ECTF produce a chemical code of practice. The introduction of the code of practice has led to major improvements in BCL's use of chemicals. Further improvements still need to be made, but chemicals are now stored in specific areas where smoking is not permitted and staff are provided with appropriate safety equipment (ECTF 1996).

Unfortunately, during the two years that elapsed between the initial recom-mendation for a chemical code of practice being made and BCL applying tighter control of chemicals, stolen Basiment[6] was widely used as a house-hold and farm insecticide by the community. As of 1997, the chemical could still be obtained through company employees despite the chemical being stored in a locked shed. Not only is Basiment unsuitable for household and farm use, but once it has left the company's compound there is no monitoring of its use or disposal and it is doubtful whether those applying it used the appropriate safety gear. Had the company implemented a chemical code of practice, preferably before they started operations and at the latest when it was recommended in the ESIA, there may not have been a supply of Basiment, or a demand for it, within the community.

Incorporating ECTF's findings into BCL operations

ECTF was contracted to monitor BCL's operations and provide it with advice on ways in which it could improve the sustainability of its forest operations as well as 'monitor the wider aspects of BCL's forest management planning, including long term impacts on Amerindian communities' (Harrison et al. 1993, p. i). An adviser, employed by ECTF, was stationed full-time at BCL's forest operations. The ESIA noted that the data collected by the adviser and BCL's research team would be vital to identify areas of BCL's operations that were operating successfully as well as those that needed improvement.

ECTF has been undertaking operational research and making appropriate recommendations, some of which BCL have adopted. In other cases, BCL has retained the familiar logging practices of South-East Asia.

Hiring a community liaison officer and an Amerindian liaison officer

The community liaison officer (CLO) was to be responsible for improving communication and investigating complaints, of both an environmental and social nature, between BCL and the community. The CLO was also to monitor the prices of common goods at local markets and shops to determine the effect of BCL's operations on market structure. A CLO was never hired.

The appointment of a CLO to improve company–community communication would have been particularly helpful as forest operations, based at Port Kaituma, have experienced a very high turnover of senior management, which has resulted in a lack of continuity in both activities and policy. Meetings between the community and senior management to explain policy occur very infrequently, and as such there is no formalized channel for residents to present their complaints and concerns. Community relations have not been ideal, as the following experience relating to the company's water and electricity policy illustrates.

The government of Guyana does not provide basic infrastructure services to the community. When BCL arrived in Port Kaituma the then general manager indicated to the community that BCL would rehabilitate the community's piped water and electricity supply[7] and would maintain and provide both services free of charge. Within three years the community had grown in size and become more affluent. The demand for electricity increased, with the number of appliances growing from a few shop freezers to 66 chest freezers, 21 refrigerators, 65 TVs, 79 fans and numerous other small electrical items[8] (Leslie 1996a). In total, 217 of the 411 households in the community had electricity in their homes. The generators, being old and overloaded, became less reliable. Similarly the demand for water increased and the pump for the water system also began to break down more regularly. Although BCL still provides free electricity and water, subsequent managers have been less committed, with the result that repairs take longer and the services are less reliable. As both utilities are provided free of charge, residents do not repair broken pipes or conserve electricity as there is no incentive to do so. The situation has led to poor community relations because BCL feels that the community does not appreciate the provision of the services and the community feels that BCL is not meeting their promise to provide the services. The community now views free water and electricity as a right, rather than as an offer of goodwill. As no effective channel of communication exists, the problem continues to fester. If a CLO had been appointed, the community–company relations problem could have been reduced, even if not fully resolved.

The Amerindian liaison officer (ALO) was to deal specifically with Amerindians and had a similar remit to the CLO. In addition, the ALO was: (i) to establish a committee 'to advise and cooperate with BCL and Amerindian groups in the concession' (Harrison et al. 1993, p. 50); (ii) to conduct a population survey of the area to determine the location of Amerindian settlements and mining activity, so that harvesting operations could avoid such areas; and (iii) to mark the boundaries of designated Amerindian areas within the concession, thereby avoiding operating in Amerindian areas.

An appointment was made by the company, but the ALO, who was based in Georgetown,[9] flew into the area only sporadically and then for just a few days at a time. Some population surveys of Amerindian communities were carried out, but the committee proposed in the ESIA was never created. The appointment of the ALO was terminated in 1997 and there has been no replacement.

Improving markets for foodstuffs
Port Kaituma is very remote and accessible only by light aircraft and boat. Before BCL's arrival, the availability of goods and foodstuffs was limited and prices were much higher than those on the coast. As the government was not involved in the development of local agriculture or market infrastructure, the ESIA recommended that BCL should offer assistance.

BCL decided to allow shop owners and community residents to transport their goods on company barges from Georgetown to Port Kaituma,[10] charging only for the cost of employing the security guards who accompany the goods. This had a positive outcome and prices of goods in Port Kaituma decreased by 15 per cent between 1995 and 1996 (Leslie 1996b). The heavy subsidization of goods transport led to more people, without substantial capital, opening small shops.

BCL also established a ration store which sold basic foodstuffs and goods to employees on credit. The store, which applied only a 10 per cent markup on basic food stuffs, further increased competition between shop owners, which also helped to decrease prices and increase the diversity of goods available. Pre-BCL, 53.1 per cent of households stated that they could buy all the goods they required; as of 1996, this figure rose to 75.3 per cent (Leslie 1996a).

Employment in BCL has also had a positive impact on most residents' standard of living, as 65.4 per cent of households stated that their income was greater in 1996 than pre-BCL while only 24.7 per cent indicated that their income was less (Leslie 1996a). This increase in income has generated a further demand for goods and services. Fifty-eight per cent of households stated that they consumed more food in 1996 than pre-BCL, while 34.6 per cent said that consumption had remained unchanged (ibid.).

These positive changes are reflected in community attitudes as 75.3 per cent of households stated that they were more positive about their future in 1996 than they were pre-BCL, although 19.8 per cent remained unchanged in their view (ibid.).

One of the concerns expressed in the ESIA was that BCL's scale of operations would disrupt the traditional subsistence economy. The area's traditional economy, since the late 1800s, has revolved around small-scale gold mining, agriculture and the activities of whichever large company or companies were operating in the area at the time. As such, residents of the North-West District are used to moving to 'boom' areas. In fact, 88 per cent of heads of households in Port Kaituma in 1996 were not originally from Port Kaituma, 56 per cent of them arriving during the period 1990–96, yet 60 per cent of these immigrants were born within the North-West District (Leslie 1996c).

Households that have employment with BCL have a more stable existence than they had previously. However, problems do arise when a household member becomes unemployed. Within households, particularly Amerindian households, clearing and preparation of farm land was undertaken by men while the planting and harvesting were the responsibility of women. When the men were employed by BCL they had less time to undertake their farming responsibilities, and some returned to their communities and homes only once a fortnight. As a result, 62.9 per cent of households stated that they farmed less land in 1996 than they did pre-BCL (Leslie 1996a). Food production also decreased in 51.4 per cent of households, with less time available for farming work being cited as the primary reason. Once households started buying produce and stopped producing it themselves they became extremely vulnerable if the employed member of the household lost his/her job; it took months before crops could be harvested and during this time the family had neither income nor home-grown food.

As a result of the increase in population and disposable income,[11] and decreased agricultural production by many households, the market for the agricultural produce of local farmers has increased. In fact, 37.1 per cent of households that farm were cultivating more land in 1996 than they were pre-BCL (ibid.). However, BCL's own purchasing practices did not contribute to this increase, as the company bought most of its produce in Georgetown and airfreighted it to Port Kaituma. If local farmers could have organized the production of their produce to meet BCL's requirements, then their market would have increased further.

Although BCL did not have a formal policy to help in the development of the area's markets, it would seem, almost by default, that their barging policy and provision of a ration store, combined with income they injected into the area's economy from the employment of workers, has fulfilled in part the relevant ESIA recommendation.

Providing assistance to improve health care
Before BCL started operations the average person, within the area of the company's concession, caught malaria one and a half times per year (Salvador 1996). There was only one poorly staffed and equipped hospital within the concession's boundary. Port Kaituma had only one unqualified health worker, and access to medical facilities and care in the more remote areas of the concession was even worse. It was not unusual for residents to have to paddle in dugout canoes for days to reach medical care. The ESIA envisaged that by recommending that the quality and availability of medical care be improved by BCL (in particular screening and treatment facilities for malaria) then BCL would be providing a needed community service and reducing the number of days its employees were absent from work because of illness.

BCL has implemented this recommendation quite successfully by rehabilitating and staffing the previously disused hospital[12] in Port Kaituma. All maintenance costs, most of the staff costs and the costs of all drugs are met by BCL. The hospital treats anyone, free of charge, regardless of whether they are a company employee or community resident. Hospital staff are also engaged in disseminating health information. Increased access to quality medical care has meant that 59.5 per cent of households view their health as being better in 1996 than pre-BCL, while 37 per cent stated that their health remained unchanged (Leslie 1996a). Although the health service it provides costs BCL a substantial amount of money, their workers are healthier and work approximately 2730 more man days per year, since the rate of malaria has decreased (ibid.).

Providing assistance to improve the quality of education
The majority of the residents within the concession area have only a basic education, if any. Many are based some distance from a school and the schools themselves provide education of a limited standard as the government provides only limited support for hinterland schools. The government school at Port Kaituma, for example, had its teaching staff paid by the government, but had no budget to buy books or materials, or to maintain the school building.

The lack of a well-educated populace meant that BCL was unable to recruit highly qualified staff from neighbouring communities. As of 1997, all of the company's administrative managers had been recruited from the coast. However, employing qualified staff from the coastal areas to work in Port Kaituma was not entirely successful as coastlanders were reluctant to forgo the facilities of a city for a basic existence in the forest. Coastlanders tended to view their employment as a way of gaining experience and saving a substantial amount of money before returning to their families on the coast. As a result they did not remain in their posts long. If BCL were to have supported and improved the level of education within the concession, a resource of qualified people could have been developed who considered the area their home and who may have been more likely to retain their jobs on a long-term basis.

To this effect the company has sponsored two voluntary services overseas (VSO) teachers to teach at the Port Kaituma Secondary School. It has also donated lumber to a Canadian youth challenge group to rehabilitate the school buildings. Also, some training seminars have been held for the Port Kaituma administrative staff. However, these measures are effective only to a point, as the majority of the workforce still has only basic reading and writing skills. For these workers, seemingly simple tasks such as completing a machine time sheet, reading an instruction book or drawing a map are too complicated to be conducted successfully.

Nevertheless, 55.6 per cent of heads of households felt that their skill levels had increased since pre-BCL, while 43.2 per cent felt that they had remained unchanged (Leslie 1996a). Of those who stated that their level of skills had increased, 34.6 per cent attributed this to learning new skills while being employed by BCL.

9.4 Conclusions
An impact assessment can help to ensure that the project/programme being undertaken is environmentally and socially sound and sustainable, as well as improve decision making relating to project implementation. Ideally the impact appraisal should be undertaken willingly by a project's promoter, rather than simply to meet government regulations. Recommendations arising from

the impact assessment must be adequately supported by project management if maximum benefits are to be gained from the assessment.

BCL was not required by the Guyana government to conduct an ESIA. Rather, management saw the potential benefit of an ESIA and commissioned ECTF to undertake it. Additional resources may have enabled the identification of other important factors that affect the operation, such as the degree of racial discrimination[13] that exists between the different ethnic groups of Guyana. However, most of the important impacts and issues were correctly identified in the ESIA.

The problems described in this chapter highlight the importance not only of conducting an ESIA but also of developing a structure that enables the recommendations to be implemented. Work plans should be part of the output of an ESIA, to guide management in implementing the recommendations. Responsibilities of different groups, in this case the government, BCL and the community, should be clearly defined and should be developed through a participatory approach.

As the forests of North-west Guyana are relatively poorly stocked with commercial trees, a high level of planning is required if harvesting is to be profitable. Planning should provide for: (i) the construction of roads only where they are necessary; (ii) the harvesting of all commercial trees; and (iii) the efficient operation of logging teams. The recommendations in the ESIA addressed these activities and if BCL had implemented them there could have been a marked reduction in their harvesting costs. BCL's executive director stated in February 1998 that BCL has lost US$20 million since starting operations in 1991 (Stabroek News 1998). If the ESIA's recommendations had been fully implemented, it is believed that this financial situation could have been significantly improved.

BCL is operating in a community which receives only limited government financial support. As a result, the population has come to expect BCL to provide basic services normally provided elsewhere by the government. The BCL experience shows the dangers of generating unrealistic expectations in a local community as a result of not having a clear policy. If the ESIA had been conducted sufficiently early, prior to operations, and had used a consultative approach, BCL could have better predicted the growth in demand for services, analysed the implications of that growth and devised its community support policy accordingly.

The BCL case study demonstrates the importance of fulfilling the following requirements of an effective impact assessment:

- It should be conducted prior to the commencement of operations.
- It should be supported with sufficient resources to enable all relevant

information to be collected, up to the point where the cost of collection exceeds the benefits from that additional information.

● It should use participatory methods to develop a sense of ownership in all stakeholders.
● Mechanisms should be developed to ensure that recommendations, once accepted, are implemented.
● The assessment's recommendations and predicted outcomes should be monitored against actual impacts, so that recommendations can be updated and revised where necessary.

Notes

1. The forester was permanently based at Port Kaituma before, during and after the ESIA was conducted.
2. A Food and Agriculture Organization (FAO) report, cited in Dykstra and Heinrich (1992), stated that 90 per cent of all erosion occurring was a result of roadbuilding.
3. Skidding teams are responsible for extracting logs from the forest using either bulldozers or machines (known as skidders) specially built for the purpose.
4. ECTF surveys suggest that a larger volume of commercial timber is left in the blocks than is actually harvested (ECTF 1997).
5. Logs are sprayed to prevent insect infestation and the resulting damage to the logs.
6. Basiment is sprayed on debarked logs to prevent pin-hole borers from attacking the logs.
7. The water and electricity supply was originally installed by a company mining manganese which operated in the area from 1961–68.
8. Numbers are most likely underestimates as people were reluctant to report electricity usage.
9. In the ESIA it was envisaged that the ALO would be based in Port Kaituma.
10. Barges transport logs from Port Kaituma to the plywood mill on the coast and return empty.
11. At month's end now, 60.5 per cent of households have more money left over than pre-BCL (Leslie 1996a).
12. The hospital was erected and staffed originally by the manganese corporation.
13. Nepotism, discrimination and corruption have plagued BCL's forest operations.

References

Briner, W., Hastings, C. and Geddes, M. (1997), *Project Leadership*, USA: Gower Publishing Ltd.

Chan, S.K. (1996), Personal communication.

Dykstra, D.P. and Heinrich, R. (1992), *Sustaining Tropical Forests Through Environmentally Sound Harvesting Practices*, in *Restoration Forestry: An International Guide to Sustainable Forestry Practices*, Kivaki Press.

ECTF (1996), *3rd Annual Report by Edinburgh Centre for Tropical Forests on its Programme of Monitoring and Research for the Barama Company Ltd. North West Guyana Sustainable Timber Production Programme*, Edinburgh: LTS International Ltd.

ECTF (1997), *4th Annual Report by Edinburgh Centre for Tropical Forests on its Programme of Monitoring and Research for the Barama Company Ltd. North West Guyana Sustainable Timber Production Programme*, Edinburgh: LTS International Ltd.

Forte, Janette (1995), *Situation Analysis: Indigenous Use of the Forest with Emphasis on Region One*, Georgetown: Overseas Development Agency.

Harrison, M.J.S., Allen, E. and Sutton, G. (1993), *Barama Company Limited Environmental and Social Impact Assessment*, Edinburgh: LTS International.

Hollick, M. (1986), 'Environmental impact assessment: an international evaluation', cited in Wood, C. (1995), *Environmental Impact Assessment, A Comparative Review*, Harlow: Longman.
Leslie, Danette (1996a), 'Results of 1996 Port Kaituma Household Survey' (unpublished).
Leslie, Danette (1996b), 'Price basket comparison 1995–96, Port Kaituma' (unpublished).
Leslie, Danette (1996c), 'Census of Port Kaituma 1996' (unpublished).
Roe, D., Dalal-Clayton, B. and Hughes, R. (1995), *A Directory of Impact Assessment Guidelines*, London: International Institute for Environment and Development.
Salvador, Raul, Dr (1996), Personal communication.
Sizer, N. (1996), *Profit Without Plunder*, Washington, DC: World Resources Institute.
Stabroek News (1998), 'Low plywood price forces BCL austerity', *Stabroek News*, 2 February.
World Bank (1995), 'Guyana recent economic trends', http://www.iadb.org/ipes/enghtm/guy.htm.

10 Evaluating trade-offs between uses of marine protected areas in the Caribbean

W. Neil Adger, Katrina Brown, Emma Tompkins, Peter Bacon, David Shim and Kathy Young*

10.1 Introduction

This chapter describes a method to enhance decision making being developed and applied to marine and coastal resources. The approach combines stakeholder analysis and environmental valuation within a framework of multiple criteria analysis. It uses stakeholder participation in an iterative process to derive weights for economic, social and ecological criteria and aims to develop a decision-making tool which enables different stakeholders' perspectives and values to be explicitly included in the analysis.

This approach is developed within the context of a multiple-use marine protected area, the Buccoo Reef Marine Park in Tobago, West Indies. Such resources are crucial both in terms of the close environmental interactions in coastal zones and in terms of their economic and recreational use linkages, particularly within small-island developing countries. The multi-criteria analysis model uses eight criteria which cover social, ecological and economic aspects. Preliminary results demonstrate that there are evident trade-offs between the identified criteria, and that individual stakeholders rank or weight these criteria differently. However, involvement by stakeholders in the process of developing the model, and in discussing the recommendations derived from different weightings, provides an opportunity to explore and construct alternative development outcomes. This makes explicit the different perceptions and values of the different actors, which creates an opportunity for decision making and management based on consensus rather than conflict. This chapter argues that such an approach where stakeholders are involved in deliberative and participatory management is likely to enhance the feasibility of sustainable development in a variety of resource management contexts.

10.2 The basis of trade-off analysis for marine protected areas

The need for an adaptive approach to support decision making in natural resource management
Economic valuation of environmental resources for decision making is limited in its application. Although economic approaches have been a rapidly

evolving aspect of resource management, there remains a need to incorporate interdisciplinary analysis both in understanding how resource users decide on their priorities, but also on who participates in decision making. Economic valuation studies of resource management issues have focused on ecological functions and environmental services and linkages to the economic system. Importantly, however, most valuation studies do not explicitly identify the extent of conflicts between different values or uses of the environment, or the possibility of trade-offs inherent in different policy options or management strategies.

Critiques of economic valuation point to the limits of such techniques in capturing motivation for decision making and in representing the nature of human relations with the physical environment (for example, Sagoff 1998; Gregory and Slovic 1997; Norton et al. 1998). In addition, the exclusion both of non-economic values and of important stakeholders from the decisions themselves through the process of valuation is argued to lead to poor implementation of policies and reduced legitimacy in attempting to realize sustainability goals (for example, O'Riordan 1997). Indeed, the trade-off between valuation and consensus decision making has been argued to be starkly that between 'best' policies (derived by expert-based rational analysis) and 'correct' policies (that can draw the maximum stakeholder support) (Davos 1998).

The participation of stakeholders in making decisions about natural resources which directly or indirectly affect them represents a major challenge to researchers, policy makers, and those involved in resource management. Many of the approaches which have been advocated for enhanced participation rely on consensus-building techniques or on feeding direct information on preferences upwards to decision makers within a hierarchical structure (for example, Cohen 1997; O'Riordan and Ward 1997). Alternative frameworks have been developed by economists such that information from stakeholders can be translated into monetary terms (Emerton 1996) or to validate economic valuation studies (Brouwer et al. 1999).

Although these approaches engage stakeholders in order to derive information, they rarely address the need to incorporate stakeholders at the outset in order to frame the resource management issue or thereby 'construct' their values. Gregory and Slovic (1997) argue that a comprehensive approach involves processes whereby stakeholders and researchers construct preferences and information. This position is argued on the basis of the constraints and limitations of economic valuation of preferences mentioned above, particularly on the information provision in any contingent valuation exercise and the dependence of such techniques on familiarity with market choices for the resources in question. But Gregory and Slovic also recognize the need for decision making to be based on such preferences, and recommend an approach which involves various steps: setting out objectives of decision making; allowing participating stakeholders to make trade-offs across these objectives; and the construction and comparison of alternatives. The multi-faceted nature of many environmental problems can be appraised within such a framework using the tools of decision analysis and multi-criteria decision making.

The purpose of the study reported in this chapter is therefore to develop an approach which can assist decision makers in the development of appropriate management strategies for marine protected areas (MPAs). This objective is based on a recognition of the need to incorporate participation into decision making and to diversify and construct indicators of value familiar to stakeholders own perceptions and the management issues. In the context of the management of protected areas, this objective involves translating economic criteria, social aspects of development, and complex ecological data to understandable information. The approach proposed brings users and regulators together to discuss issues and resolve conflicts at all levels. Enhanced participation increases the likelihood that the key stakeholders are heard and their concerns are incorporated into protected area design and implementation.

This chapter provides an overview of the objectives and the methods to be used in the present study of trade-offs in MPAs. The rationale for studying conflicts in resource use is that these conflicts are the key determinants of both the ecological sustainability of the protected areas, and sustainability in the sense of being socially equitable and desirable. The approach seeks to identify and explicitly highlight conflicts in resource use between different groups affected by management of a resource (primary and secondary stakeholders), and to present this information in a systematic fashion to groups who are either dependent on the resource or managing the resource on behalf of society. Thus the evaluation process itself feeds directly into promoting acceptability and sustainability.

The approach adopted is termed 'trade-off analysis' in this study to highlight the objective of enabling decision makers to consider trade-offs between various types of criteria upon which they evaluate alternative management options. Thus the economic, social and ecological implications of management options of MPAs are presented to different stakeholder groups, and their appraisal of relative priorities are relayed to the decision-making bodies. Trade-off analysis, in the working definition used here, utilizes a number of methodological tools. The framework by which the information is organized for discussions with stakeholder groups is that of multi-criteria analysis (MCA). The relevant actors with whom the dialogue is opened are identified through formal and informal analysis of stakeholder interests. The conflicts are quantified, where relevant, with reference to the techniques of environmental economics, to social analysis, and to ecological modelling.

The methods used (environmental economic valuation, stakeholder analysis and MCA) are themselves relatively new, having been developed during the past decades: only during the 1990s has MCA been applied systematically to natural resource projects (reviewed in Powell 1996). This project focuses on the Buccoo Reef Marine Park in Tobago but it is anticipated that the approach can be applied to support natural resource decision making in the context both of small-island developing states and of coastal zone management in general.

Environmental impacts of tourism development
Small-island developing states face particular constraints on both environmental management and more widely on social and economic development. In the economic and social domain these constraints are associated with the burden of governance and lack of human resources, the impact of globalization and the dependence on trade and lack of opportunities for self-reliance in agriculture and other sectors (see Streeten 1993). Despite these constraints, some small-island economies have produced spectacular economic success, sometimes based on international tourism. However, the impacts of tourism both on the local environment and on social change in certain circumstances can be negative, particularly where there is major dependence on this sector of the economy (Brown et al. 1997). For small-island nations in particular there is a close interaction between water resources, land use and the coastal environment, and degradation of these is likely to impact on the sustainability of livelihoods of the local populations and the long-term viability of any development strategy which includes tourism. Tisdell (1993) has highlighted the need for taking account of environmental sustainability constraints when considering the options for development in such small islands, where the social and natural capital can be undermined by tourism and other large-scale infrastructure. One traditional route by which important coastal and marine resources are managed and conserved in the face of such pressures is through their designation as protected areas.

Marine protected areas exist in most of the island states of the Caribbean region, being typically established over the years by a central regulatory body following recognition of declining resource quality by users and beneficiaries. They have been established with the expectation that enhanced management improves resource quality and assures sustainability. However, deterioration of the marine and coastal environments in many of the designated MPAs in the Caribbean, and more widely, has not been arrested simply by protected area designation and management (for example, Dixon et al. 1993; Cesar et al. 1997). In some cases this is due to ineffective management of the MPAs resulting from inappropriate environmental legislation, or failure of the governments to effectively intervene and manage the resources. In other cases the causes of resource depletion can be traced to the marginalization of important stakeholders who feel excluded and withhold support for the MPA concept (for example, Mak and Moncur 1998; Hoagland et al. 1995). The failure of MPAs to achieve their objectives are often due to the utilization of ineffective decision-making approaches, during the conceptualization, planning and implementation of the MPAs, resulting in overexploitation of resources. Consequently, the MPAs, initially established to assist users and beneficiaries alike, remain either undermanaged or have not achieved their stated objectives (Dixon et al. 1993).

Degradation of marine and coastal areas designated for conservation is one manifestation of the numerous competing demands on the coastal resources of the developing nations. These are especially acute in small-island states where coastal zones are the focus of economic activity and are also relied upon for waste assimilation, storm protection and numerous other ecological and environmental functions. For the Caribbean, the pressures on these resources stem from diverse human impacts on these systems including increases in economic activity in agriculture and other primary economic activities; indirect impacts from pollution from industry and households; and the impact of tourism development (for example, Ceballos-Lascurain 1996).

Tourism is a significant generator of revenue in Tobago, but the rapid expansion of tourism is causing a number of problems, many related to degradation of the natural resources which form part of the attraction for tourists. Experience in the Caribbean and elsewhere shows that coral reefs are especially vulnerable to unregulated use by tourists for activities such as reef-walking, diving, boating and snorkelling (for example, Dixon et al. 1993; Mak and Moncur 1998). There are also believed to be trade-offs between recreational uses of reef systems and other economic uses. In addition there are trade-offs between recreational users and ecological values such as biodiversity conservation and ecological functions. These trade-offs become acute when the environmental impacts are uncertain or when the assimilative capacity of the environment is under stress.

Strategies for managing conflicts between tourism and other land uses have focused primarily on visitor management, and notions of sustainable tourism have come to prominence (for example, Driml (1997) on the Great Barrier Reef, Australia; Ceballos-Lascurain (1996) more generally on protected areas). Ecotourism or environmentally-sensitive tourism has become the watchword for tourism development and is increasingly cited as a means to generate revenue from protected areas and make conservation more 'integrated' with development objectives (Goodwin 1996). However, critical analysis of a range of issues, including careful assessment of the extent and magnitude of trade-offs and conflicts, is clearly required to make such rhetoric reality. These approaches need to take account of the biophysical, economic and psychological dimensions of tourism and allied developments.

10.3   An integrated approach to trade-off analysis

A framework for the research
The research framework uses stakeholder analysis initially to inform the design of the economic, social and ecological evaluation of options and in framing who should be involved in the deliberative processes for enhanced management. The process then involves evaluating these issues using multi-criteria analysis. The social, economic and ecological evaluation of the impacts of options is generated by the use of primary and secondary data on these aspects. The scenarios and information derived from this exercise is used to deliberate with the stakeholder groups. The subsequent stakeholder participatory process defines and refines the objectives of management of the marine protected area in an iterative manner.

A schematic representation of the research process is given in Figure 10.1, showing that the major analytical input by researchers to enhance the participation in decision making is in three stages:

- defining the scenarios and scope of the MCA on the basis of stakeholder interests;
- quantifying the economic, social and ecological impacts of the chosen scenarios; and
- enabling the participation process to inform the models and the ultimate management of the park.

However, a prior stage in this approach is to identify and appraise who the stakeholders are and what their interests and impact on successful management may be.

Stakeholder analysis
As discussed above, an economic framework in which the trade-offs inherent in ecological and tourism objectives of Buccoo Reef Marine Park (BRMP) are brought into a monetary numeraire would not necessarily provide insight into where and to whom the values and impacts accrue. This latter dimension is critical when there is a need to consider the conflicts and trade-offs between different development options, so that the different actors involved can be considered. Stakeholder analysis, first developed by management scientists, is becoming more widely used in project appraisal and natural resource management. Grimble and Chan (1995, p. 114) define stakeholder analysis as 'an approach and procedure for gaining an understanding of a system by means of identifying the key actors or stakeholders in the system, and assessing their respective interests in that system' (see also Grimble and Wellard 1997). The term 'stakeholder' includes all those who affect and are affected

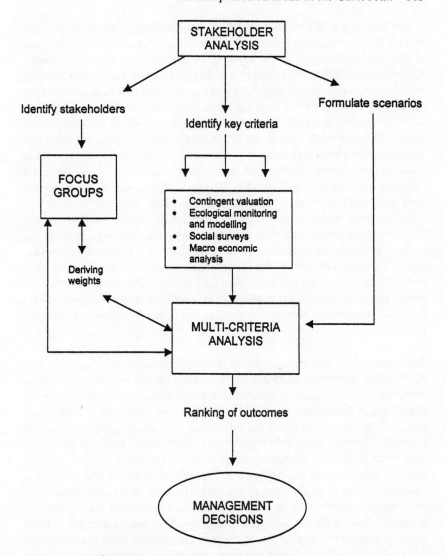

Figure 10.1   Stakeholder analysis and the research and management process

by the policies, decisions and actions of the systems. They can be individuals, communities, social groups or institutions of any size, aggregation or level in society. Thus, in the context of MPAs, policy makers, planners, administrators in government and non-governmental organizations (NGOs), as well as local commercial and subsistence users are stakeholders.

The first step in stakeholder analysis is to identify the stakeholders in any project. Stakeholders are 'groups of people with common objectives and sets of interests with regard to the resource in question and the environment' (Grimble et al. 1994, p. 4). Within a natural resource management context, stakeholders are identified as those groups who can have a material outcome on developments designed to bring about a particular transformation. Thus the identification of stakeholders and the impacts of resource management on these stakeholders are seen as important for meeting the objectives of management. Identifying stakeholders at the outset is particularly appropriate in cases of collectively managed or open access resources where there are different levels of stakeholders with different interests, and where trade-offs need to be made at the policy level over the use of the resources.

In this study, stakeholder analysis is used initially to identify and classify the groups and individuals who are impacted by the state regulation of the marine resources. To ensure that stakeholder analysis is effective, it is necessary to be comprehensive in the identification of stakeholders in the project and all their objectives and conceptions of value of the good or service in question; and to analyse the conflicts of interest (and areas of commonality) that exist between the various stakeholders and determine what trade-offs are feasible.

Economic, social and ecological data in multi-criteria analysis
MCA offers opportunities to present the trade-offs and ranking of different priorities and criteria in a systematic manner which does not specify an overall single value framework. Rather, it allows the sensitivity of both social and physical data to be tested for robustness, and which makes explicit the trade-offs between competing impacts and stakeholders. Decision processes have been defined in management texts as having three separate stages: problem identification, developing possible courses of action, and selecting a course of action from the choices available (Janssen 1994). The actual process can be characterized as flows of inputs of information into a decision procedure leading to the output of a decision. This means that MCA must effectively generate information on the decision problem from available data and ideas, effectively generate solutions (alternatives) to a decision problem and provide a good understanding of the structure and content of a decision problem.

Cost–benefit analysis can be effective when used as the sole decision-making tool, if the objective is to maximize economic efficiency. When other issues, such as social implications, ecological and environmental conservation or biophysical impacts of decisions are also important to decision makers, MCA can be a more appropriate analysis tool. Proponents of MCA believe it to be superior to cost–benefit analysis as it allows 'soft criteria' that cannot be expressed in monetary terms to be included in the analysis (van Huylenbroeck and Coppens 1995). MCA is particularly useful as an analysis tool in projects where there are conflicting objectives or priorities of different stakeholders. Another benefit of MCA is that it provides decision makers with a set of feasible solutions, rather than one economically efficient outcome.

MCA has been widely applied to land-use planning (Makowski et al. 1996; Macmillan et al. 1998; Joubert et al. 1997; Malczewski et al. 1997). The lessons from research on applying MCA, where the aim is to achieve outcomes which are broadly acceptable to the relevant user groups, can be summarized thus: while MCA is a valuable tool for achieving resolution of environmental conflicts there are several constraints to this in practice. Critical elements which must be clearly identified to enable participation in decision making include the relevant interest groups, the interactions between the interest groups and the socio-economic activities undertaken by the interest groups. Following from these lessons, a participatory approach to decision making using MCA as the organizing framework is adopted for application in the case of marine resources management in South-west Tobago. However, as illustrated in Figure 10.1, the overall objective is to utilize this information so that the participation of stakeholders in and around this conservation area can be ensured.

The first step in undertaking MCA is to define as far as is possible the actual problem, such as overuse of resources and degradation of the resources, ideally in discrete measures of the environmental impact, such as the size of area involved or the scope of the natural resources involved. A set of possible suitable alternatives (henceforth referred to as *scenarios*) for improving site quality are identified and compiled. These scenarios are generally derived using expert judgement, and should cover all extremes of possible policy and management action. Scenarios have been developed in this case giving greatest emphasis to one stakeholder group, the park regulators, as that group is the key to the management process. An assessment of the possible scenarios might include increasing the size of the MPA, limiting access rights, or prohibiting any activity within the park area.

The potential effects of each scenario on each criterion are estimated. Due to differences in the methods and scales of measure of the different effects, there are likely to be variations in the accuracy of measurement. One means of standardizing these generated measures of effect is to apply a *value function*, which converts the values into scores that range between 1 and 100 (Janssen 1994). Some MCA software packages perform this task automatically for the user. Alternative scenarios can be evaluated in terms of their efficiency (ratio of achievement of objectives to the costs and other means of achieving those objectives) and their effectiveness (the level of achievement of a set of objectives).

To determine effectiveness and efficiency, the relevant importance of the criteria must be distinguished. This can be achieved by weighting at the level of the major criteria (for example, economic impacts versus biological impacts) and at the level of subcriteria (for example, different types of economic impacts, net costs versus employment impact). In many applications of MCA these weights are set by the analyst to reflect their judgement of the relative importance of the criteria, or are derived through the opinion of elite groups or experts, sometimes through a Delphi method. But the major objective of this study is to bring stakeholders into the process of decision making. As outlined below, this is initiated through allowing each stakeholder group to appraise the criteria and set their own weights.

Ultimately, the application of MCA should produce a single most acceptable alternative given weights determined by the decision makers. The trade-off analysis proposed in the present study utilizes MCA, where trade-offs between different criteria can be analysed. This type of analysis is particularly useful where the criteria can be subgrouped into two or three major criteria which offer conflicting solutions. The trade-offs that exist between alternative development paths are presented to the different stakeholder groups in consultative meetings, thereby building consensus on which scenarios should be implemented.

10.4   Participation in management options for Buccoo Reef Marine Park, Tobago

The case study and the stakeholders
Buccoo Reef and Bon Accord Lagoon Complex which make up the Buccoo Reef Marine Park (BRMP) are located in South-west Tobago (11°10′N and 60°50′W). This park is a large reef system which protects an extensive shallow reef lagoon bordered by a fringing mangrove wetland and covers an area of 150 ha with a terrestrial area of 300 ha (described in John 1996; DRDE 1996) (see Figure 10.2). The economy of Tobago is less diverse than that of Trinidad and more dependent on tourism and agriculture. Being a smaller island (300 km^2) the management of the coastal margins are intertwined with all its coastal and marine resources. The heavy use of its marine and coastal resources for both the tourism industry and for commercial and subsistence use ensures that the major resource conflicts in Tobago are played out in this land–water interface.

Understanding the institutional arrangements surrounding the utilization of coastal resources by these various stakeholders is the key to designing better management of regulated common property resources. This has long been recognized in the analysis of marine as well as terrestrial common resources (Berkes and Folke 1998), where the necessary conditions for the institutions

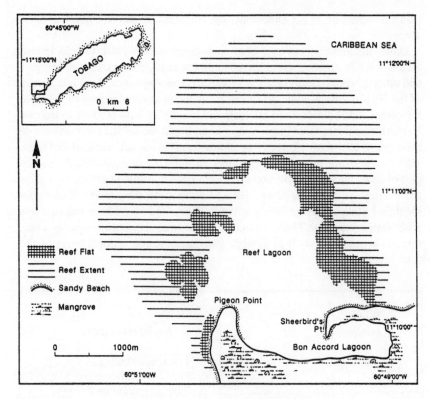

Figure 10.2   Location of Buccoo Reef Marine Park, Tobago

to produce a sustainable utilization outcome have been analysed, but where 'success stories' are more difficult to identify and observe. In the case of protected areas, state intervention, regulation and ownership of these resources often increase the conflicts between stakeholder groups (Brandon and Wells 1992) and, by demarcating areas, locks resource use into patterns which may not be appropriate for local residents, or even for long-term ecological management.

As part of the development of BRMP, a management plan drawn up in 1995 by the Institute of Marine Affairs (IMA 1995) identified the main stakeholders who could influence the management of, or were important beneficiaries of, the BRMP. The IMA noted that in order of importance these groups included: park management, reef tour operators, hoteliers (managers and owners), formal and informal businesses involved in the tourism trade, dive tour operators, ground handlers, jet ski operators, fishers and fish processors, and taxi drivers. However, these stakeholders with a direct interest in the park management do not encompass the complete human and political land-scape.

Other institutions, not explicitly mentioned in the IMA (1995) report, include NGOs, regional agencies, government organizations, land developers and other interested individuals who also have an impact on the management of the BRMP area. Additional research has led to a reassessment of the most important stakeholders, their interests and objectives with relation to Buccoo Reef Marine Park, their impacts on the park and the relative importance of their group to it (either directly or indirectly). This is summarized in Figure 10.3 for the major primary stakeholders, recognizing that individuals may be part of more than one institution and hence have multiple interests, as well as the overlap between the categories and institutions themselves. The major identified stakeholder groups are the primary and secondary stakeholders with vested interests. These include the reef tour operators and other commercial interests, as well as foreign and domestic recreational users of the resource.

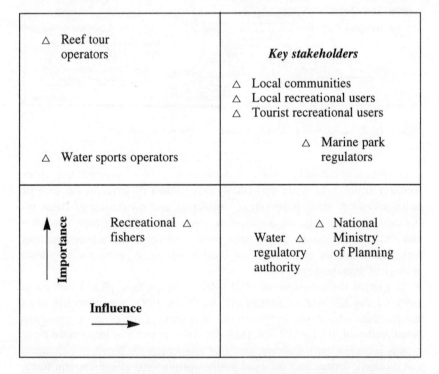

Figure 10.3   Classification of primary and secondary stakeholders in Buccoo Reef Marine Park, Tobago

Scenarios and criteria estimation for multi-criteria analysis

Development of the scenarios recognizes the key management issues which become the scenario descriptors, for which alternatives are identified and numerical values generated. For BRMP two descriptors are used: tourism development and environmental management. They have been chosen primarily because of their relevance to park management; because they encompass broad development priorities in South-west Tobago; and because they take into account the scale and type of tourism development and environmental management plans which affect Buccoo Reef Marine Park.

Combinations of the scenario descriptors are used to create specific scenarios based on permutations of tourism development plans which may be expansive or limited; and of environmental management efforts in BRMP and more widely in South-west Tobago which may be complementary to enhanced status of the park. These four scenarios outlined in Table 10.1 encapsulate very different development paths. To ensure that there is clear and consistent understanding of the scenarios, they have been more explicitly described in terms of factors that affected them. A review of the developments in South-west Tobago, for example in strategic planning documents for the island (DRDE 1996) highlights driving forces of change. These are the number of new tourism developments in South-west Tobago; subregional population growth; and waste treatment. The specific scenario drivers used and highlighted in Table 10.1 (number of new tourism beds, population growth, and percentage of waste treated to tertiary level) are selected on the basis of measurability and likely impact on the criteria. Numerical measures of these 'drivers' are used to describe each scenario in detail (see Table 10.1).

Within MCA, the criteria are an embodiment of potential multiple impacts of the development issue, and they tend to reflect the differing perspectives of the various stakeholders. In the case of BRMP, these can be summarized as predominantly related to national and local economic growth, community, social and cultural development, and environmental conservation (referred to here as economic, social and ecological criteria). As with the scenarios, these concepts are broad to enable discussion of their importance, but are complemented by more specific subcriteria. The subcriteria do not describe the entire system under consideration, they are an indicator of important aspects of the overall picture.

For BRMP, selection of the subcriteria has been undertaken by a multidisciplinary group of specialists which includes representatives of one stakeholder group, the regulating agency of the park. Subcriteria are considered for inclusion in the MCA only if they were measurable and if they varied under the different scenarios. 'Relevance' is determined in the process through ongoing stakeholder analysis as the project progressed, which served to highlight the important, but often implicit, preferences of the key stakeholders.

Table 10.1   Scenarios for Buccoo Reef Marine Park and the driving forces
              of change

Scenario	New tourist beds in BRMP area*	Population in BRMP area*	Percentage waste treated
A: Limited tourism development without complementary environmental management	240	6900	9
B: Limited tourism development with complementary environmental management	240	6900	49
C: Expansive tourism development without complementary environmental management	1580	7400	18
D: Expansive tourism development with complementary environmental management	1580	7400	69

Note: *   'BRMP area' refers to the watershed draining into Buccoo Reef Marine Park.

Table 10.2 describes the criteria and the selected subcriteria with a brief explanation of the means of calculating those data. Operationalizing the MCA involves estimating the effects of the scenarios on each subcriterion in quantitative or semi-quantitative form. The strategy for data collection involves wide-ranging modelling techniques across the ecological, social and economic criteria.

For example, the economic criteria focus on macro-economic benefits and recreational user benefits. The first of these is the domain of economic planners who may want to maximize this criterion. However, the recreational value of the tourist visitors is an important non-market benefit which captures aspects of the benefit to that stakeholder group and the sustainability of tourism based in part on the quality of the marine and coastal environment. The first economic subcriterion, 'Macro-economic benefits that accrue from tourism developments in South-west Tobago', has been calculated by first estimating total annual visitor expenditure in that area. This number is multiplied by the marginal propensity to import for Tobago, to estimate the proportion of visitor expenditure which remains in Tobago. This figure is then multiplied by the 'tourism multiplier' to reflect the benefits that accrue across the economy from the initial round of tourist expenditure, thereby showing the macro-economic benefits that accrue to South-west Tobago. The

Table 10.2   Criteria for assessing management options for Buccoo Reef Marine Park and method of estimation

Criteria	Subcriteria	Measure/basis of calculation	Sources of data
Economic criteria	1. Macro-economic benefits of tourism to Trinidad and Tobago	Tourism revenue × economic multiplier × (1 – marginal propensity to import)	Secondary data from government statistical sources
	2. Tourist benefits	Consumer surplus of recreational users of BRMP	Contingent valuation survey of visitors and residents
Social criteria	3. Local employment in tourism	Additional full-time 'quality' jobs × proportion of jobs to Tobagonians	Continuous Sample of Population (Trinidad and Tobago); UN Economic Commission for Latin America and the Caribbean; Tobago House of Assembly management report on BRMP
	4. Informal sector benefits	No. of additional persons with 50% of livelihoods coming from informal sector	Primary data collection – informal business survey
	5. Costs of local access to BRMP	Change in costs of accessing BRMP for recreation and subsistence extractive purposes	Private access costs, public access costs, expert judgement of BRMP manager
Ecosystem health criteria	6. Water quality	Nutrient concentration – nitrate loading and concentration	Secondary existing data and modelling using scenarios of tourist sector development
	7. Mangrove habitat	Change in area of mangrove (ha) % change in area	Historical aerial photographs and projected tourist development
	8. Productivity – nursery function of sea grass	Unit productivity; nos of small fish, diversity of species per area	Surveys using rapid assessment techniques and modelling
	9. Coral reef health	% live coral cover	Surveys using rapid assessment techniques and modelling

results are estimates of net present value ranging from US$9.1 million to US$18.7 million over a ten-year period across the scenarios, as shown in Table 10.3. The second economic subcriterion, 'Recreational user benefits', reflects visitor enjoyment of BRMP. It has been estimated as the total willingness to pay of visitors through BRMP using a contingent valuation survey, based on a randomized survey of 1000 visitors and residents. The resulting estimates show a consumer surplus of between US$0.6 million and US$2.5 million in net present value terms, depending on the resulting environmental quality implied by the scenarios (Table 10.3).

The social criteria are distinct from the economic criteria in that they reflect the distribution and impact of some of the economic criteria. The social criteria describe only costs and benefits affecting the local community in terms of human development impacts, or social change. The social criteria

Table 10.3   Estimated impact of four development scenarios for Buccoo Reef Marine Park area on the economic, social and ecological criteria

	Scenario			
Criteria	A	B	C	D
Economic				
Economic revenues to Tobago (US$ m)	9	11	17	19
Visitor enjoyment of BRMP (US$ m)	1.2	2.5	0.6	1.2
Social				
Local employment (no. jobs)	2500	2600	6400	6500
Informal sector benefits (score)	5	4	3	2
Local access (score)	6	5	6	7
Ecological				
Mangrove health (ha)	65	73	41	65
Sea grass health (g dry weight/m^2)	18	19	12	15
Coral reef viability (% live stony coral)	19	20	17	18
Water quality (μg N/l)	1.5	1.4	2.2	1.9

Notes:
Scenarios (as explained in Table 10.1):
A: Limited tourism development without complementary environmental management.
B: Limited tourism development with complementary environmental management.
C: Expansive tourism development without complementary environmental management.
D: Expansive tourism development with complementary environmental management.

are local employment, contribution of the informal sector to local livelihoods, and local access to the resource, and have been estimated using the methods outlined in Table 10.2.

Not all criteria are best represented in quantitative terms. A qualitative survey of a sample of informal business vendors was undertaken to ascertain the employment impacts of development as a social factor important to many stakeholder groups. The informal sector vendors were asked their attitudes to: the level of environmental control and informal sector control introduced by the government agencies; the size and nature of the hotels to be developed in South-west Tobago; and the type of tourists who are likely to visit Tobago. Their qualitative responses are scored and transformed into ordinal data for the MCA through use of scales with single indicators. Similarly, access by Tobagonian residents to the BRMP for recreational activities is an important factor identified by local residents and is included in the MCA using a simple scaling device, which are scaled and converted to ordinal data (see for example, Bernard 1994).

The results of the modelling are shown in Table 10.3, demonstrating the diversity of units in the assessment across the economic, social and ecological data. Evaluation of the scenarios through their impacts on the criteria as shown in the table is the first step in the MCA and generates an ordered ranking of the development scenarios; the highest scoring scenario can be considered the most desirable one. This set of systematically ordered information is then used to engage with stakeholder groups in achieving increased knowledge of preferences and desired outcomes (see Figure 10.1). This is brought about through deriving weights and focused discussions of the implications of the scenarios and options for management of BRMP and development more generally in South-west Tobago.

Participation in resource management decision making
The most important facet of this research framework is the participation of the stakeholder groups in enhancing the decision-making process. The first major interaction with the stakeholders in terms of the multi-criteria assessment is in generating weights to reflect the importance of the criteria and subcriteria to each group. For each of the criteria, the relative importance of the subcriteria can be determined by stakeholders through informal interviews; through discussions with key informants; or through focus groups. The third step of the MCA and trade-off analysis process is to begin the iterative process of stakeholder interaction to generate weights for the main criteria.

A series of meetings with each stakeholder group is used to elicit stakeholder weights. The first round of meetings is a general introduction to the project, the method used, and the analysis undertaken. Second-round meetings require the stakeholders to order the main criteria, according to their specific preferences. The culmination of the two rounds of meetings is a set of weights for the major economic, social and ecological criteria from each stakeholder group. In some cases, particularly that of tourists, the stakeholder group is diffuse. In developing the weights of the visitors to the major criteria for managing BRMP, questions have been incorporated into the survey allowing derivation of weights from the responses.

The various stakeholders' preference ordering of the criteria, quantified as the weights they attach to the criteria, are likely to alter the ranking of the development scenarios and lead to a different 'best' scenario. These involve presenting the sets of weights of the diverse stakeholder groups and the resulting rank ordering of development options to regulators of BRMP and the other relevant decision-making bodies, as well as to the groups themselves. The iterative focus group meetings and dialogues make explicit the objectives of apparently conflicting groups where such information is not easily available or articulated in such a fashion.

The final iteration is to return to the stakeholders in a joint discussion group involving representatives from each stakeholder group, and identify where consensus can be found, where conflicts exist and where trade-offs are possible. Using participatory methods, or consensus-building techniques, a narrower set of weights can be generated that can again be taken to the decision makers for their consideration. Repeating this process and incorporating the decision makers into the focus groups should lead to a more satisfactory development outcome for all parties. The process of participatory action research is more dynamic and fluid than the organization and modelling of quantitative and qualitative data within the multi-criteria analysis. The key issue in this context is to determine the impact of the participatory process itself. There is often uncritical acceptance of participation as a means of promoting sustainable resource management through harnessing and empowering local stakeholders. In the context of Buccoo Reef Marine Park, this research is facing the ongoing challenge of appraising the usefulness of the process itself.

10.5   Conclusions

There is a cogent case that participation in decision making is an essential element in sustainable management and use of natural resources. Evidence from many countries and different contexts of resource use support this argument. Participation is particularly relevant for complex multiple-use resources, such as in the conflicts surrounding conservation and development for example, where different stakeholders with different needs may lead to conflicts in use and management. Such participation leads to greater flexibility and more robust institutional processes. It has been argued (for example,

Sanderson 1995) that such institutions are a critical means by which developing states, and small-island developing states in particular, can develop strategies which enhance self-reliance while maintaining resource integrity. The research reported in this chapter is providing further evidence in this context, but ultimately aims to critically appraise the role of participation of stakeholders in management processes.

Current approaches to decision analysis fail to include key stakeholders at critical points and are unable to resolve the kinds of conflicts in resource use which arise in many instances of natural resource management. We argue that a constructive approach to decision making is required which allows different stakeholders to express their priorities and preferences and to feel ownership of decisions and their outcomes. We have developed a methodology to analyse the trade-offs between different uses and users and are applying this to a marine protected area in Tobago. But we believe that the approach is widely applicable, not only to other marine protected areas, but to other natural resource management situations.

Our approach attempts to overcome the problems identified in other approaches to decision making in natural resource management. We use a multi-criteria framework and combine other techniques, most importantly stakeholder analysis and environmental economic analysis, within this general framework. By engaging with stakeholders we are able to derive and set weights applied to different criteria within the multi-criteria framework. However, stakeholder participation is not limited to this stage of analysis, and we use MCA as a tool by which we can explore different scenarios with stakeholders in an iterative process. MCA is therefore simply a tool which we use as part of a constructive participatory process.

The development of this approach is not simply an academic exercise in combining sophisticated techniques. There is an urgent need to find ways of resolving conflicts and making decisions which stakeholders can support and comply with. In the Caribbean, many MPAs suffer severe degradation that threatens ecological integrity as well as having economic and social impacts which potentially undermine livelihoods and the resilience of the communities reliant on those coastal resources. Including stakeholders in decisions about these ecosystems is an important first step to ensuring more sustainable management. A challenge remains to facilitate the more widespread adoption of such approaches, and to refine methods of incorporating stakeholders in active management to ensure resource integrity for multiple users.

Note

* The authors thank Jane Powell for comments, while retaining full responsibility for the final version. This chapter is an output from a project funded by the Land Water Interface Programme of the UK Department for International Development (DFID) for the benefit of developing countries. The views expressed are not necessarily those of DFID.

References

Berkes, F. and Folke, C. (eds) (1998), *Linking Social and Ecological Systems: Management Practices and Social Mechanisms for Building Resilience*, Cambridge: Cambridge University Press.

Bernard, H.R. (1994), *Research Methods in Anthropology: Qualitative and Quantitative Approaches*, 2nd edn, Thousand Oaks, CA: Sage.

Brandon, K.E. and Wells, M.P. (1992), 'Planning for people and parks: design dilemmas', *World Development*, **20**, 557–70.

Brouwer, R., Powe, N., Turner, R.K., Bateman, I.J. and Langford, I.H. (1999), 'Public attitudes to contingent valuation and public consultation', *Environmental Values*, **8**, 325–47.

Brown, K., Turner, R.K., Hameed, H. and Bateman, I. (1997), 'Environmental carrying capacity and tourism development in the Maldives and Nepal', *Environmental Conservation*, **24**, 316–25.

Ceballos-Lascurain, H. (1996), *Tourism, Ecotourism and Protected Areas*, IUCN (World Conservation Union) Protected Areas Programme, Gland, Switzerland.

Cesar, H., Lundin, C.G., Bettencourt, S. and Dixon, J. (1997), 'Indonesian coral reefs: an economic analysis of a precious but threatened resource', *Ambio*, **26**, 345–50.

Cohen, S.J. (1997), 'Scientist–stakeholder collaboration in integrated assessment of climate change: lessons from a case study in Northwest Canada', *Environmental Modelling and Assessment*, **2**, 281–93.

Davos, C.A. (1998), 'Sustaining co-operation for coastal sustainability', *Journal of Environmental Management*, **52**, 379–87.

Department of Regional Development and Environment and Town and Country Planning Division (DRDE) (1996), *Planning for Sustainable Development: South West Tobago*, Government of Trinidad and Tobago and Organization of American States, Port of Spain.

Dixon, J.A., Fallon Scura, L. and Van't Hof, T. (1993), 'Meeting ecological and economic goals: marine parks in the Caribbean', *Ambio*, **22**, 117–25.

Driml, S.M. (1997), 'Bringing ecological economics out of the wilderness', *Ecological Economics*, **23**, 145–53.

Emerton, L. (1996), *Participatory Environmental Valuation: Subsistence Forest Use around the Aberdares, Kenya*, Applied Conservation Economics Discussion Paper No. 1, African Wildlife Foundation, Nairobi.

Goodwin, H. (1996), 'In pursuit of ecotourism', *Biodiversity and Conservation*, **5**, 277–91.

Gregory, R. and Slovic, P. (1997), 'A constructive approach to environmental valuation', *Ecological Economics*, **21**, 175–81.

Grimble, R.J., Aglionby, J. and Quan, J. (1994), *Tree Resources and Environmental Policy: A Stakeholder Approach*, Natural Resources Institute Socio-economic Series 7, Natural Resources Institute, Chatham.

Grimble, R. and Chan, M.K. (1995), 'Stakeholder analysis for natural resources management in developing countries', *Natural Resources Forum*, **19**, 113–24.

Grimble, R. and Wellard, K. (1997), 'Stakeholder methodologies in natural resource management: a review of principles, contexts experiences and opportunities', *Agricultural Systems*, **55**, 173–93.

Hoagland, P., Kaoru, Y. and Broadus, J.M. (1995), *A Methodological Review of Net Benefit Evaluation for Marine Reserves*, Environmental Economics Series No. 27, Environmental Department, World Bank, Washington, DC.

Institute for Marine Affairs (IMA) (1995), *The Formulation of a Management Plan for the Buccoo Reef Marine Park. Volume 1 – Executive Summary*, Carenage, Trinidad and Tobago: Institute of Marine Affairs.

Janssen, R. (1994), *Multiobjective Decision Support for Environmental Management*, Dordrecht: Kluwer.

John, G.M. (1996), 'Quantitative characterisation of land-based sources of marine pollution in the vicinity of the Buccoo Reef Marine Park, Tobago', Unpublished MSc Thesis, Department of Biology, University of the West Indies, Cave Hill, Barbados.

Joubert, A.R., Leiman, A., de Klerk, H.M., Katau, S. and Aggenbach, J.C. (1997), 'Fynbos vegetation and the supply of water: a comparison of multi-criteria decision analysis and cost benefit analysis', *Ecological Economics*, **22**, 123–40.

Macmillan, D.C., Harley, D. and Morrison, R. (1998), 'Cost-effectiveness analysis of woodland and ecosystem restoration', *Ecological Economics*, **27**, 313–24.

Mak, J. and Moncur, J.E.T. (1998), 'Political economy of protecting unique recreational resources: Hanauma Bay, Hawaii', *Ambio*, **27**, 217–23.

Makowski, M., Somlyody, L. and Watkins, D. (1996), 'Multiple criteria analysis for water quality management in the Nitra Basin', *Water Resources Bulletin*, **32**, 937–51.

Malczewski, J., Moreno-Sanchez, R., Bojorquez, L.A. and Ongay-Delhumeau, E. (1997), 'Multi-criteria group decision-making model for environmental conflict analysis in the Cape Region, Mexico', *Journal of Environmental Planning and Management*, **40**, 349–74.

Norton, B., Costanza, R. and Bishop, R.C. (1998), 'The evolution of preferences: why sovereign preferences may not lead to sustainable policies and what to do about it', *Ecological Economics*, **24**, 193–211.

O'Riordan, T. (1997), 'Valuation as revelation and reconciliation', *Environmental Values*, **6**, 169–83.

O'Riordan, T. and Ward, R. (1997), 'Building trust in shoreline management: creating participatory consultation in shoreline management plans', *Land Use Policy*, **14**, 257–76.

Powell, J.C. (1996), 'The evaluation of waste management options', *Waste Management and Research*, **14**, 515–26.

Sagoff, M. (1998), 'Aggregation and deliberation in valuing environment public goods: a look beyond contingent pricing', *Ecological Economics*, **24**, 213–30.

Sanderson, S.E. (1995), 'Ten theses on the promise and problems of creative ecosystem management in developing countries', in Gunderson, L.H., Holling, C.S. and Light, S.S. (eds), *Barriers and Bridges to the Renewal of Ecosystems and Institutions*, New York: Columbia University Press, pp. 375–90.

Streeten, P. (1993), 'The special problems of small countries', *World Development*, **21**, 197–202.

Tisdell, C. (1993), 'Project appraisal, the environment and sustainability for small islands', *World Development*, **21**, 211–19.

van Huylenbroeck, G. and Coppens, A. (1995), 'Multi-criteria analysis of the conflicts between rural development scenarios in the Gordon District, Scotland', *Journal of Environmental Planning and Management*, **38**, 393–407.

11 Social acceptability in project EIA in the Philippines

Lourdes Cooper and Jennifer Elliott

11.1 Introduction

Demonstrating social acceptability is a requirement for project developments involving environmental impact assessments (EIAs) in the Philippines. Because of this policy, the implementation of EIA has taken on an added dimension due to its potential to address issues other than the environment. EIA is now considered the main institutional mechanism for participation in decision making on projects of national significance (Smith and van der Wansem 1995).

Since 1996, detailed provisions for project documentation include reports on public consultation meetings and public hearings and endorsements of local community representatives to certify public acceptance at this level (Department of Environment and Natural Resources (DENR) Administrative Order No. 37, 1996). Furthermore, the 1987 Constitution, the Local Government Code of 1991 and the Philippine Agenda 21 (1996) require public consultation with local government units, non-governmental organizations, people's organizations and other concerned sectors of the community to be affected by projects and programmes.

This chapter identifies briefly the origins of these legislative developments in the Philippines and considers recommended government procedures for identifying and securing social acceptability in project EIA. The substantive content of the chapter focuses on an analysis of how project proponents across key sectors are seeking to demonstrate social acceptability. The problems in securing proof of social acceptability are considered briefly and the chapter concludes by considering the effects of the social acceptability criteria on EIA practice and how the procedures might be improved.

11.2 Background: the Philippine environmental impact statement (EIS) system

The Philippines adopted the EIA process in 1977 through the Philippine Environmental Policy (Presidential Decree 1151). In 1978 the EIA system, called the Philippine EIS system, was established with the signing of Presidential Decree No. 1586 which defined the scope, coverage, organization and sanctions for non-compliance. Philippine policy first sought to limit the application of EIA to environmentally critical projects (such as those in heavy industry, resource extraction and large-scale infrastructure) and projects located in environmentally critical areas. However, the EIA system became operational only in 1982, after the rules and regulations for implementing PD 1586 were issued.

The EIA process was initially a decentralized one with approval of EISs being issued by government lead agencies. The process was centralized in 1979, with approval of EISs issued from the National Environmental Protection Council (NEPC). All projects covered by the EIA system have to obtain an Environmental Compliance Certificate (ECC) before a project can be implemented.

The overthrow of the authoritarian regime in 1986 and the establishment of a democratic government was to usher in changes in natural resources and environmental administration. In 1987 the implementation of EIA was transferred to the Environmental Management Bureau (EMB) under the Department of Environment and Natural Resources (DENR). In 1992, the system was partially decentralized, through the DENR regional offices. Currently, the EIA division of the EMB and the regional offices of the DENR are the primary implementing agencies for EIA. The procedural review of EISs is conducted by staff from these agencies while the substantive review is conducted by an EIA review committee consisting of experts and academics.

In operation, the EIA process in the early 1980s was limited by the fact that environmental issues were not considered a priority by government and the private sector and there was a lack of environmental awareness by the public (Balagot and Briones 1994). In addition, the martial law conditions at that time prevented people from participating in decision making. There was little evidence of public involvement and only five public hearings have been conducted under the EIA system since 1981 (Abracosa 1987).

Having evolved from a planning instrument to the regulatory mechanism it is today, the EIA system has become the main tool for environmental management in the country (RCG/Hagler, Bailly, Inc. 1993). With the establishment of a democratic system in 1986, two policies adopted by government were to have a significant effect on the EIA system. First, the government decided to strictly enforce environmental regulations (Balagot and Briones 1994). As a result, all sectors of the economy have regarded the pursuit of environmental protection more seriously and the implementation of the EIA system has been enforced vigorously. Second, it became government policy to require all national agencies and offices to conduct consultations with local government units, people's organizations and affected communities before any project was implemented in their area (Local Government Code 1991). This policy has a major importance for EIA since it is essential for the public to have access to the decision-making process to express their concerns.

During 1986–92, stricter enforcement necessitated certain changes and the adoption of innovative implementation approaches. These included the social acceptability criteria, requiring the establishment of an environmental guarantee fund for certain highly polluting projects (such as mining) and multisectoral monitoring. A major change in EIA policy was the introduction of the social acceptability criteria in 1992, resulting in changes in procedures and requirements for project EIAs. Because EIA requires public acceptance of a project before it can be implemented, it has the potential to consider social issues in the process. Thus, for some disadvantaged groups such as indigenous peoples, EIA is one of the most important means of protecting their rights (Smith and van der Wansem 1995).

In spite of nearly two decades of implementation constrained by inadequacy of resources and lack of political support, EIA in the Philippines is now regarded as a major policy instrument for attaining environmental objectives while pursuing economic growth (Balagot and Briones 1994).

11.3   Legislative developments and emerging concerns regarding social acceptability in the EIA process

Increased public participation in the EIA process in the Philippines can be seen as the product of two main factors, the legislation that required public participation in development activities and the recognition that many problems regarding projects were due to the lack of consideration of social issues (Guerrero et al. 1993). Under the 1987 Constitution, the newly established democratic government recognized the effective and reasonable participation of people's organization at all levels of social, political and economic decision making as a constitutional right. The Constitution likewise mandates the establishment of adequate consultation mechanisms within development activities.

Public participation in environmental management was also reinforced in the 1989 Philippine Strategy for Sustainable Development, the 1991 Local Government Code and within the Philippine Agenda 21. All recognize the important role of the people in nation building, as non-governmental organizations (NGOs) and as members of people's organizations (POs), and strongly endorse people's participation in environmental management. Furthermore, a key strategy under the current national plan is the improvement of the quality of life through the empowerment of POs and one of its guiding principles is democratic consultation (Philippine Medium-term Development Plan, 1993–98).

It is now appreciated that a lack of communication with local people and public involvement in the EIA process led to many problems in the first decade of implementation, including protracted conflicts between proponents and affected communities. Conflicts also arose between key sectors in the

EIA system, between project proponent, the NGOs and the affected community or between the regulatory agency, the proponent and the affected public. Two brief examples below illustrate some of the limitations of the EIA process when there is insufficient consideration of the social, cultural and political dynamics of projects.

Benguet Antamok gold operations (BAGO)
An EIS for an open pit mining project in Itogon, Benguet, was submitted by Benguet Corporation in 1989 (Benguet Corporation 1989), and an Environmental Compliance certificate was issued by the DENR on 27 June 1990 with 22 conditions. After more than 80 years of underground mining, Benguet Corporation (BC) decided to expand its operation at the surface of the Antamok gold vein deposits. The communities adjacent to the open pit mining areas were opposed to the project as it would deprive them of their main source of livelihood, small-scale gold mining.

The people were not consulted over the project and quickly protested by filing petitions with the DENR and the DENR Cordillera Autonomous Region (CAR) offices. The municipal government, the church and media groups supported the community. Furthermore, a report was published questioning the technical soundness of the EIS (Alcantara and Gimenes 1991). Prolonged legal battles, barricades and rallies followed, during which the DENR–CAR mediated between BC and the community.

Eventually, a Memorandum of Agreement (MOA) was signed between BC and some groups that decided to cooperate. The MOA addresses the issues raised by the local community and required BC to submit an environmental rehabilitation plan, identify relocation sites, pay compensation for damages caused by their blasting operations and fund improvements in community facilities. A multisectoral team, called 'a multi-partite monitoring team', composed of representatives from DENR, other concerned agencies, NGOs and representatives of the affected community, was formed to assess compliance with the MOA and ECC conditions. The locations of the BAGO project and other cases cited in this chapter are shown in Figure 11.1.

The Mount Apo geothermal project (MAGP)
Mount Apo is considered by several tribal groups as their ancestral domain and a sacred burial place. It is the country's highest mountain, with a diversity of flora and fauna and was declared a national park in 1936. It is the source of 28 rivers and the watershed of several provinces in the island of Mindanao. It is also the abode of the Philippine eagle, an endangered species.

The Philippine National Oil Corporation (PNOC) started exploratory activities on Mount Apo in 1985 without first securing an ECC (Sales 1994). Although an ECC was issued in April 1987 to cover the exploration, no adequate environ-

184   *Case studies*

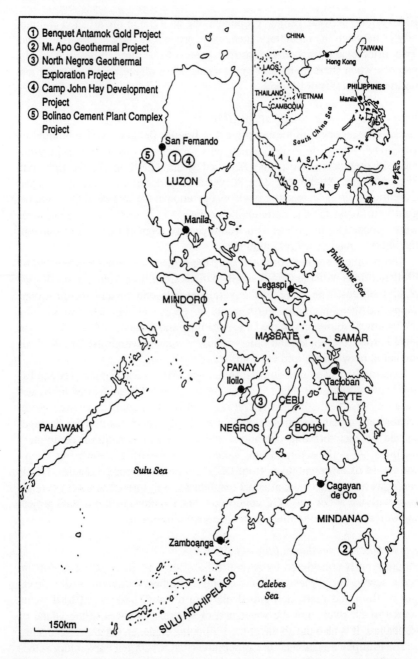

Figure 11.1   Map of the Philippines showing the locations of case studies

mental and social studies had been made (Guerrero et al. 1993). *Datus* (chiefs) of tribes filed petitions with the office of the Philippine president and the protest against PNOC intensified in the late 1980s. Those opposing the project included the tribal communities, church and religious groups, NGOs, and other organizations in the affected provinces. Opponents of the project identified two main issues: the first was that the government was pursuing economic development at the expense of ecological damage to the environment and the second was the right of the indigenous peoples to their ancestral land (ibid.).

In spite of the DENR suspending the ECC in September 1987, however, the PNOC continued with their drilling operations until December 1988 (Sales 1994). On 22 December 1988, PNOC submitted an EIA of the Mount Apo geothermal project. After negotiations and granting of concessions to those affected by the development, eventually, the project was endorsed by the tribal peoples and the local government units of the affected communities. MAGP was issued an ECC on 14 January 1992 after three years of consultations, a public hearing and militant action. The acute power shortage in the country and the need to generate power for industrialization were the main factors in the DENR's decision to allow the PNOC to proceed with the geothermal project on Mount Apo.

Because the project stirred so much controversy, it was the first major energy facility required to pass DENR's social acceptability rule (Arquiza and Mercado-Carreon 1997). The ECC contained nine conditions, one of which was the establishment of an environmental and tribal trust fund to be funded annually by PNOC. Like the social acceptability criteria, this is the first time that an energy project has been required to establish such a fund.

The two case studies mentioned above illustrate that consultation between the project proponent and the public took place only as result of protests by the affected public. However, it was the experience from the Batangas coal-fired thermal project (Calaca II) that led to a change in EIA policy requiring proof of social acceptability for all project EIAs before granting ECCs (Mendoza 1998). The Calaca project consisted of two units. The first one was exempted from EIA requirements and completed in 1984. However, the plant operations resulted in serious pollution and respiratory problems in the community. When the National Power Corporation applied for an ECC for Unit II, there were organized protests from the community. As a result, the funding agency (Overseas Economic Cooperation Fund of Japan) agreed to approve the loan only under certain conditions, including 100 per cent social acceptability. Before signing the MOA that showed acceptance of the project, however, the community requested assistance amounting to several million pesos (Guerrero et al. 1993). An ECC was granted on 14 July 1992, with 13 conditions.

As these case studies show, reconciling differences after a project has been designed and publicly opposed is a tedious and costly process (ibid.). Guerrero et al. further observe that assessing its social acceptability early on as part of project planning is more sensible, practical and cost-effective. As a result of the experiences from these projects, EIA procedures were improved and public participation in the process has been strengthened.

11.4   Public participation and social acceptability in the Philippine EIA process

Social acceptability is fundamentally about acceptance of a project by the community. The criteria of acceptability of a project to the community was introduced in 1992, when the rules and regulations of the EIA system were revised under Department Administrative Order (DAO) No. 21. In order to demonstrate public acceptance, comments and recommendations received during the consulting stage of the EIS (and replies to these comments) were required in the EIS documentation. Endorsements from the local government unit (LGU) or the regional development council were also required (EMB 1992). However, in operation there were misgivings as to the representativeness of the LGU or the council and the adequacy of the endorsements to support a project's acceptability. It was evident that specific guidelines for determining social acceptability and strengthening public participation in the EIA process needed to be developed.

In 1996, DAO 96–37 was issued, revising the rules and regulations for EIA implementation. Public participation in the EIA process was conceived as the essential means for achieving social acceptability, which is defined by the DENR as 'the result of a process that is mutually agreed upon by the DENR, stakeholders, the proponent to ensure that the concerns of stakeholders, including affected communities, are fully considered and/or resolved in the decision-making process for granting or denying the issuance of an ECC' (DENR 1997, pp. 6–16). The DAO 96–37 procedural manual further states that social acceptability can be achieved only if the decision is informed; the process of decision making is agreed through a democratic process; the stakeholders have been empowered to decide for themselves; and those involved in the project understand the risks and related responsibilities and accept them (ibid.).

One of the major changes introduced in DAO 96–37 is mandatory scoping for all EISs. Scoping reports now have to be prepared by the proponent and endorsed by stakeholders and submitted as part of the EIS documentation. One outcome of the scoping sessions is that it gives the proponent an indication of whether the project will be acceptable to the local community. The project proponent can then decide whether to proceed with the project or avoid having to prepare a costly EIS that would eventually be rejected. The EIS is prepared based on the parameters identified in the scoping report.

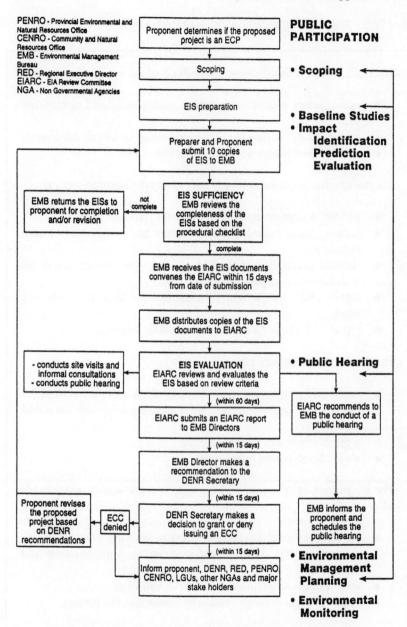

Source: Adapted from Department of Environment and Natural Resources (1997).

Figure 11.2 Opportunities for public participation in the Philippine EIA process

Box 11.1 Indicators of social acceptability, DAO 96–37

For *ecological and environmental soundness* of the proposed project:

- management plan, environmental management and monitoring plan;
- municipal and *barangay* (village) resolution endorsing the project;
- endorsement letters from local NGOs and POs.

For the *effective implementation of the public participation process*:

- process documentation reports signed by stakeholders;
- scoping report signed by all key parties and stakeholders' representatives;
- detailed description of the EIA process with concurrence of all stakeholders who participated;
- signed MOA for the establishment of a multipartite monitoring team;
- report of the hearing officer during public hearing.

For the *resolution of conflicts*:

- negotiated agreements on conflicts should be included in an MOA between the proponent, the DENR, local government units and stakeholders;
- a resettlement and relocation plan;
- social development programme.

For the promotion of *social and intergenerational equity and poverty alleviation*:

- an environmental management and monitoring plan which includes a social development programme, compensation and resettlement plan;
- endorsement letters from local NGOs and POs;
- municipal and *barangay* resolution endorsing the project.

Source: DENR (1997).

DAO 96–37 also identifies the stages in the EIA process when public participation should be elicited as shown in Figure 11.2. Effective implementation of the public participation process is then identified as one part of the required demonstration of social acceptability. According to DAO 96–37, social acceptability also involves consideration of the following: ecological/environmental soundness of the proposed project; effective implementation of the public participation process; resolution of conflicts; and promotion of social and intergenerational equity and poverty alleviation. Guidance is then given in terms of indicators for identifying social acceptability in practice as shown in Box 11.1.

11.5 Demonstrating social acceptability: an analysis of experiences of project proponents from key sectors

Securing acceptance of the project by the community involves negotiations and an adequate amount of resources and time on the part of the regulatory authority and the project proponent. It also means employing approaches that facilitate the active participation of the affected community in the process. The examples below illustrate how project proponents seek to demonstrate social acceptability.

Northern Negros geothermal exploration project (NNGEP)

The Northern Negros geothermal exploration project is located in the municipality of Murcia and Bago in Negros Occidental. The purpose of the project is to develop three exploratory wells as a possible source of steam for geothermal power development to augment the energy requirement in the Visayas (central area in the Philippines) grid.

Drawing lessons from its past experiences with energy projects such as the Mount Apo geothermal project, the Philippine National Oil Corporation appointed a consulting firm to undertake the EIS for the NNGEP in early 1993. The consulting firm's participatory EIA scheme sought to involve the affected community in the entire EIA process to ensure an open, transparent and credible process and to incorporate local knowledge and perspectives into the process as stated in their aims (PNOC 1993).

In order to make the EIA process participatory, a two-day training on EIA was conducted for the local officials, representatives of NGOs and POs and concerned citizens of the affected *barangays*. Various participatory approaches were used including:

- assistance from the local community in baseline data gathering;
- discussion of initial findings and recommendations with consultants and the DENR;
- walk-through project sites involving the proponent and other

stakeholders, which resulted in a decision to relocate the road to be constructed to minimize possible losses to the community (Factoran and Metin, in Sales 1994);
- participation in public hearings by various stakeholders;
- training of some local community members on the socio-economic survey and assistance as enumerators and to pre-test, finalize and translate into the local dialect the survey instrument prepared by the consultants for the development phase of the NNGEP; and
- community representatives as members of the multi-partite monitoring team.

Various sectors of the community (the local communities, NGOs, the church and religious sectors, the LGUs and academia) participated in the process. By involving the community in the EIA process, there were opportunities for concerns to be raised and discussed. Objections by a coalition of NGOs included the heavy denudation of the Negros forest ecosystem, vague assurances of PNOC's proposed mitigation measures and inadequate information on the projects costs and benefits (Sales 1994). After community validation meetings and public hearings, the ECC for the NNGEP was granted on 1 December 1993. The ECC conditions reflected the process of negotiation with and participation of the local communities. The conditions included the following:

- a mutually agreed compensation scheme in cases of damage to properties;
- formation of a multi-partite monitoring team composed of representatives from government agencies and local communities; and
- implementation of the alternative livelihood plan and employment opportunity policy for local residents.

Camp John Hay development project (CJHDP)
The development of the Camp John Hay special economic zone is intended to be a private sector undertaking to assist the government develop and manage one of the US military facilities that reverted back to the Philippine government in 1992. Camp John Hay is located within the John Hay Military Reservation in Baguio City, Benguet. Located in the Mountain Province, Baguio City is referred to as the summer capital of the Philippines, because of its cool climate. The CJHDP is to be developed as an integrated eco-tourism development complex. The proposed project is essentially a tourism development scheme which includes a golf course, hotels, cottages, conference centre, camping areas and a managed forest area. The overall framework for the development of the leased area is the approved Master Plan by the Bases Conversion Development Authority and the Baguio City Council.

The Camp John Hay Development Corporation (CJHDevCo) acquired the lease to develop the facility. Considering the eco-tourism thrust of the proposed development, the existing facilities and infrastructure, its fragile location and the ecological role of the John Hay watershed, the general methodology and process employed for the EIA included:

- application of carrying capacity assessment for land-use intensity, population, water supply (domestic and golf course), sewage and waste generation;
- visual impact assessment as they related to view corridors and overall landscape configuration; and
- a participatory approach which used a modified participatory resource system appraisal (PRSA) methodology including a report on how the EIA process was conducted. A formal scoping process was undertaken including public consultations to generate perceptions and acceptance of the project (ENR Consultants 1997).

Specific participatory methods used during the EIA process involved a social preparation programme, site visits and informal meetings including the following:

- a scoping session on 21 January 1997, with selected stakeholders' representatives, to determine potential/perceived environmental issues and concerns and agree on the major focus of the EIA. The scoping exercise served to clarify certain issues (ancestral claims) and initiate and agree on pending activities such as the tree inventory. The issues/concerns raised were used as a basis for the EIA. The main environmental concerns on water supply, solid wastes and tree cutting were raised;
- an awareness and perception survey was undertaken through discussions with the different stakeholders and concerned individuals;
- public consultation meetings to present the results of the EIA in order to generate comments for clarification and further consideration and articulation of specific agreements/commitments on the EIA and the project; and
- other consultations and information dissemination were undertaken and copies of the EIS were provided to stakeholders.

Evidence of social acceptability included endorsements from the local city council, endorsement by *barangay* captains around the site of the EIA and its environmental management plan and an understanding between CJHDevCo and the city government to pursue jointly additional water sources and a solid waste disposal facility for CJHDP and Baguio City.

A portion of the managed forest of the proposed project is currently part of an ancestral land claim. The proponent and stakeholders agreed that the claims will be considered as pending until the final ancestral land law is passed. Once the claims are decided, any claims within the leased area will be turned over to the government to award to claimants and the proponent will be reimbursed of costs incurred in the development of the area. An ECC was issued for the CJHDP on 26 January 1998 with 38 conditions, including 19 set by the city government.

Bolinao cement plant complex
The proposed Pangasinan cement plant complex (3.2 million metric tons) to be located in Bolinao was seen by the government as a means of developing an area where there are no major industries. The majority of the rural population live close to the poverty line and depend on small-scale fishing and farming. The development involves quarrying, a cement plant and port facilities. It was estimated that the proposed project would provide employment for 700 workers when fully operational and it was largely for reasons of local wealth generation that the project was expected to be acceptable at this level (see Gaia South, Inc. 1994).

However, the proposed project was expected to be controversial because of its proximity to the town and to the University of the Philippines Marine Science Institute (UPMSI) Bolinao Marine Laboratory, the large quarry area involved (6280 hectares), the freshwater requirements and the potential effects on the marine resources and the local community.

Economic losses from the proposed development included 274 hectares of ricelands, 225 hectares of fruit trees and 500 hectares of ipil plantation. Furthermore, the project would result in the economic displacement of 2600 families of farmers and fishermen living along the nearby Lingayen Gulf. The prospect of losing control over their land moved the community to stand up for its right to a sound environment (Ramos 1997). Opposition came from various sectors of the community:

- *Movement of Bolinao Concerned Citizens* This group is composed of farmers and fishermen in the area. The limestone quarrying operation of the proposed development would cover five *barangays* creating social impacts that would be difficult to mitigate.
- *Academics* represented by UPMSI. The Institute has a marine laboratory 500 metres away from the proposed site. The institute argues that siltation and port activities will result in irreplaceable damages to the Bolinao reef system which is a reservoir in invertebrates for the whole of the Lingayen Gulf (UPMSI 1995).
- *Lingayen Gulf Coastal Management Commission* The Commission,

created under Executive Order 171 in April 1994, identifies eco-tourism as an appropriate strategy for Bolinao in the Commission's Ten-year Development Plan for the Bolinao–Anda area. The proposed project is also inconsistent with the regional and provincial development plans, the Regional Physical Framework Plan for 1990–2020 and the National Integrated Protected Areas Act of 1992.

• *Other research and scientific groups, church groups and women's groups* The issue of the displacement of women has been raised since more than 10 000 women are directly dependent on the Lingayen Gulf for their livelihood (Ramos 1997).

Position papers by those opposed to the project were submitted to the Environmental Management Bureau and to the Philippine President, voicing their concern over the ecological and social impacts of the proposed development. Public hearings were held in February and March 1995.

The EIA review committee recommended the rejection of the proposed project, for reasons including the evident policy conflict between industrialization for the Bolinao area and environmental conservation in the light of its designation as an environmentally critical area under both the Presidential Proclamation 156 and the Lingayen Gulf Coastal Area Management Plan. There was also a lack of presentation of alternatives. However, the main reason for the denial of an ECC was the failure to demonstrate social acceptability. This was the first time that a project had been rejected for this reason and as a result the public's perception of the EIA process and that of public participation changed as they realized that their opinion would be taken into account. Previously, very few projects were denied ECCs and these were mainly for other reasons, such as land disputes.

11.6 The effect of the social acceptability criteria on the EIA process

By requiring social acceptability for projects, the EIA process in the Philippines has adopted a 'consensus-building/management' strategy. In this approach, EIA is used as a tool for identifying and exploring issues as well as resolving them, and public participation plays a central role in this process (Smith and van der Wansem 1995). Early consideration of alternatives and of mitigation measures is a fundamental element in the search for broad-based support for proposed activities.

Recent practice, however, has revealed a number of constraints on public participation in the EIA process. Evidently, fulfilling the social acceptability criteria has meant increased costs in preparing EISs and additional demands on the project proponents. For example, demonstrating social acceptability has meant that EISs should be able to withstand public scrutiny in terms of their scientific soundness and still be clearly written for a layperson to understand. In a country where there are 70 dialects spoken, the EIS (originally written in English, one of the official languages) often has to be translated into the local dialect of the project area. Some technical terms may be difficult to translate and meanings may change. A further difficulty is that the staff in the EMB and the consultants come from Manila and may not understand the local dialect during public consultations and hearings. Although translators are used there is still a communication barrier.

Affected communities may also experience difficulty in assimilating highly technical information which further limits their participation in the EIA process. These difficulties include the inability to read the EIS, to comprehend the concept of EIA or to express concerns regarding the project. In some cases, the local residents may not have the expertise to argue their case. Using the proposed cement project in Bolinao as an example, the academics from UPMSI have the expertise to question the technical and scientific soundness of the EIS. However, in the case of the proposed Agno cement plant and quarry project (Ecosys Corporation 1998), which is 20 km from the Bolinao project on the other side of the island, the fishermen and farmers who will be affected by the Agno project have no such expertise. At the time this chapter was written (September 1998), no final decision had been made by the DENR Secretary although the EIA review committee have recommended approval of the project. The Agno fishermen continue to protest, supported by environmental NGOs and POs.

In many areas of the country, NGOs support communities and may even lead the advocacy. In the case studies mentioned, the NGOs played an important role in bringing attention to the many issues of the project. In the NNGEP, for example, 20 NGOs as well as people's and students' organizations formed a coalition to strengthen their advocacy efforts (Sales 1994). Other problems that arise when securing social acceptability for a project are that it may result in conflicts within the community and between some members of the community or the public may take the opportunity to pursue minority interests.

In order to secure social acceptability, there is evidence that project proponents in the Philippines are now working to ensure that in all phases of the EIA, local government units, NGOs, POs and other concerned agencies and members of the affected community are informed and given opportunities to participate. This allows the discussion of issues before the public hearing and provides avenues for conflict resolution between the proponent and other stakeholders. In the case of the North Negros geothermal exploration project, for example, an alternative route for a road was identified during the reconnaissance with community representatives around the site. In the Camp John Hay development project, issues raised by the public in the scoping sessions were widely discussed and mitigation measures identified.

The social acceptability requirement also brings further benefits to the EIA process. There is some evidence, for example, that the quality of EISs has improved as a result of mandatory scoping and that project proponents are preparing better-quality EISs since the EISs will be scrutinized not only by government assessors but also by the public (Cooper 1998). In addition, the adoption of consensual methods of decision making moderates the previous emphasis on technical and economic considerations in project studies. Lastly, through harnessing the participation of a range of stakeholders in the EIA process, the social acceptability requirement enhances the credibility, transparency and openness of the process.

11.7 Conclusions

To make EIA effective, it is necessary to include social and economic assessments. Experience in the Philippines has shown that problems encountered in previous development projects were due mainly to the lack of consideration of social factors. As a result, securing social acceptability of projects has been required since 1992. In order to secure social acceptability, project proponents are involving the public at different stages of the process. Consequently, the level of misinformation and distrust is reduced and this improves decision making.

In determining social acceptability in the Philippines, more attention is now being given to the social costs and benefits of a project. However, the EIA system is still focused on gaining acceptance rather than on the assessment of the social impacts and changes that may occur because of the project. Community consultations should lead not only to public acceptance but also towards the assessment of social changes and the review of policies and practices.

References

Abracosa, R. (1987), 'The Philippine Environmental Impact Statement (EIS) System: An Institutional Analysis of Implementation', PhD Dissertation, Stanford University, USA.

Alcantara, R. and Gimenes, L. (1991), *Special Report on the Antamok Gold Project*, Baguio City: Cordillera Resource Center for Indigenous People.

Arquiza, Y. and Mercado-Carreon, L. (1997), 'People or Power?', in Gamalinda, E. and Coronel, S. (eds), *Saving the Earth: The Philippine Experience*, 4th edn, Manila: Philippine Center for Investigative Journalism, pp. 211–19.

Balagot, B. and Briones, N. (1994), *Strengthening Environmental Impact Assessment Capacity in Asia: A Case Study on the Philippine EIA System*, Environment and Resource Management Project Report No. 13, Dalhousie University, Halifax, and University of the Phillipines, Los Banos.

Benguet Corporation (1989), *Environmental Impact Statement for the Grand Antamok Project*, Baguio City.

Cooper, L. (1998), 'An analysis of quality in the Philippine EIA process', MSc thesis, University of Brighton.

Department of Environment and Natural Resources (DENR) (1997), *Procedural Manual for Department Administrative Order No. 96–37*, Quezon City.

Ecosys Corporation (1998), *Environmental Impact Statement for the Agno Cement Plant and Quarry Project*, Manila.

Environmental Management Bureau (EMB) (1992), *Amending the Revised Rules and Regulations Implementing Presidential Decree No. 1586 (Environmental Impact Statement System), Administrative Order No. 21, Series of 1992*, Department of Environment and Natural Resources, Quezon City.

ENR Consultants, Inc. (1997), *Environmental Impact Statement for the Camp John Hay Development Project*, Manila.

Gaia South, Inc. (1994), *Environmental Impact Statement for the Pangasinan Cement Plant Complex Project*, Manila.

Guerrero, S., Flor, A., Kroske, H. and Cardenas, M. (1993), *Public Participation in EIA: A Manual on Communication*, Manila: Environmental Management Bureau and the Asian Development Bank.

Mendoza, C. (1998), 'The role of public participation in the EIA process: the case of the Batangas coal-fired power project', Master's thesis in Environmental Studies, University of Melbourne, Australia.

Philippine National Oil Corporation (PNOC) (1993), *Northern Negros Geothermal Exploration Project: Environmental Impact Assessment Report*, Vol. 1, Manila.

Ramos, V. (1997), *The Governance of Ecology: Struggles and Insights in Environmental Statemanship*, Quezon City: Environmental Centre for the Philippines.

RCG/Hagler, Bailly Inc. (1993), *Environmental Risk Assessment and Pollution Reduction Planning in the Philippine Environmental Impact Statement (EIS) System*, Policy Study No. 8, Industrial Environmental Management Project, DENR, Manila.

Sales, R. (1994), 'Public participation in environmental impact assessment: lessons and perspectives from the experiences of two energy projects in the Philippines', MSc dissertation, Wye College, University of London.

Smith, D. and van der Wansem, M. (1995), *Strengthening EIA Capacity in Asia: Environmental Impact Assessment in the Philippines, Indonesia and Sri Lanka*, Washington, DC: World Resources Institute.

University of the Philippines Marine Science Institute (UPMSI) (1995), *A Proposed Cement Plant Complex in Balinao, Pangasinan: Potential Conflicts in the Coastal Zone*, Position Paper, Quezon City.

12 Public valuation and decentralized decision making: environmental health risks assessment and valuation of water supply and sanitation facilities in rural Nepal[*]

Dirgha Tiwari

12.1 Introduction

The provision of clean water and hygienic means of sanitation are basic to human health, yet about 20 per cent of the world's population lack access to a safe water supply, while 50 per cent lack access to adequate sanitation. The World Health Organization (WHO) estimates that a total of more than five million people die each year just from diseases caused by unsafe drinking water and a lack of sanitation and water for hygiene (CSD 1997).

Despite the urgency of the need to address environmental health concerns associated with inadequate and contaminated drinking water, there is a lack of integration of these concerns into the development decision-making process in the developing countries. While the government health policy and programmes rarely show an adequate concern for the environmental causes of health risks, environmental policy decision-making process often disguises the health risks associated with the increasing level of pollution. Managing the environmental health risks associated with water pollution and lack of safe drinking water requires integration of both the health risk concerns and public perception into the decision-making process.

A sizable environmental management and economics literature has attempted to identify human health risks associated with water pollution using both the conventional health risk assessment and contingent valuation methods. Most of these studies however, have been limited to the developed countries. For example, Harrington et al. (1987) provide a model for the evaluation of morbidity risks due to waterborne diseases outbreak taking into account worker productivity loss and the medical expenses. Kask and Shogren (1994) developed benefit transfer protocol for long-term health risk valuation associated with surface-water contamination. With few exceptions, such as USAID (1991), empirical studies attempting health risk evaluation due to water contamination in the developing countries are very rare. Briscoe et al. (1990), Whittington et al. (1990) and Bohm et al. (1993), use the contingent valuation method (CVM) for measuring the value of improved

197

water supply benefits in Brazil, the Philippines and Haiti, respectively. Although these studies have attempted to measure users' willingness to pay (WTP) for improved water supply facilities, they do not directly address the question of health risks. In response to this lacuna, this chapter presents an analytical framework for decentralized decision making using public valuation techniques and incorporating public perception and values into the decision-making process for sustainable management of water supply and sanitation (WSS) facilities by presenting a case study of rural and suburban areas of Nepal.

The organization of the chapter is as follows. Section 12.2 presents a brief review of inconsistency problems in the application of public valuation techniques and the implications for applications in rural Nepal. An analytical framework for decentralized decision making is presented in Section 12.3. Section 12.4 presents preliminary estimates of health costs associated with water-related diseases and the supply costs of WSS facilities in the case study areas. The results of the case study and the determination of user charges and cost-sharing mechanisms are presented in Sections 12.5 and 12.6. Finally, some conclusions are drawn for further applications of the decentralized decision-making framework in the context of the developing countries.

12.2 Environmental health risks and impact assessment: theoretical insights and practical problems

Environmental health risks and impact assessment
In principle, quantitative assessment of environmental health risks due to water pollution or other environmental hazards is straightforward and involves four main steps – hazard identification, dose-response, exposure assessment and assessment of risks. Hazard identification involves identification of the pollutant and level of concentration; exposure is assessed in terms of the dose of the contaminant per kg body weight per day; and the population at risk is the total number of people affected by the contaminant water. The health risk is then computed by multiplying the dose, potency factor and population exposed, which gives the total number of cases of health risks. The application of a dose-response function for environmental health risks analysis in the case of developing countries, however, is limited due to data and information limitations. Hershaft et al. (1974) point out that the dose-response function represents a complex and dynamic relationship, and is beset by a number of major difficulties relating to accuracy and reliability. Depending upon the nature of the commodity, or the pollutants, estimates of the health risks depend largely on the reference doses. The difficulty of meeting these conditions in the context of developing countries limits the accuracy of the estimation method (USAID 1991).

In the case of morbidity, unlike quantitative health risk assessment based on the dose-response or the probability density function, the analysis can be based on the estimation of restricted activity days, bed disability days, symptom days, and the reported cases of diseases related to the specific pollutants (Cropper and Freeman 1991). Harrington et al. (1987) developed a relationship for the valuation of health risks of waterborne diseases, incorporating leisure and expenditure variables as the determining factors into the individual's utility function. They showed that changes in the value of health risks associated with individual response to increased water contamination are related to direct disutility of illness, lost work productivity, value of lost leisure, and medical expenses. The application of costs of illness approach also, however, has two major problems when applied in the developing countries. The first is concerned with the value of time lost due to illness, and the second is attached to the ethical issue of excluding an individual's perception of his/her suffering. The high level of disguised unemployment, especially in the rural sector in the developing countries, raises the problem of accurate valuation of the time or productivity loss due to illness. While this may be corrected to some extent by using a shadow wage rate, the second issue, however, requires the application of public valuation techniques to identify individuals' stated preferences.

Public valuation techniques such as the contingent valuation method contain several of the elements required to elicit theoretically valid measures of peoples' willingness to pay (Mitchell and Carson 1989). Valuation of environmental health risks using the CVM approach has received wide attention in recent years and the application of this method helps directly measure the economic value of reductions in the health risks, rather than expressing it in physical units. The underlying concept is that an individual's preferences provide a valid basis for making judgements concerning changes in the environmental health risks which should be valued according to what an individual is willing to pay to achieve them (Cropper and Freeman 1991).

Public valuation: inconsistency problems
Various studies carried out in the past, such as Cropper and Freeman (1991), Haneman (1994), Johansson (1995) and Lindberg et al. (1997), have outlined several inconsistency problems in the application of CVM. These problems are usually known as starting-point bias and information bias. While starting-point bias is related to how respondents perceive the hypothetical experiment, information bias is related to the lack of required information, the procedural steps in asking questions including starting of the bids, and commodity specification bias.

Although most of these inconsistency problems are also common to the application of CVM in the developed countries, several additional difficulties arise in its application in the case of the developing countries. The first is the disparity in income and subsistence nature of the economy, which may lead to difficulties in measuring the true income of households. Second, because of lower income and lower ability to pay, WTP for public services is also expected to be lower (Vincent et al. 1991).

To what extent do these issues limit the application of CVM for evaluation of health risks in the developing countries? Hanemann (1994) pointed out that inconsistency in the household's response applies to all kinds of household surveys and not only for CVM studies. Past studies, for example, Whittington et al. (1990), Briscoe et al. (1990), Whittington et al. (1993), Bohm et al. (1993) and Tiwari (1998), have shown that CVM studies can be successfully carried out at localities having poor and illiterate populations. Whitehead and Houtven (1997) emphasized that the CV approach is more useful in valuing safe drinking water as it allows the researcher to have better control over the valuation scenario even under uncertain health outcomes. There are also ways for verifying the outcome of survey responses, for example, comparing the WTP value with the estimated price of water obtained using indirect valuation methods (Tiwari 1998).

While these various studies have shown that a CVM exercise can be meaningful for decision-making purposes in the developing countries, none of them have directly addressed the environmental health risks associated with water pollution or the lack of safe drinking water in the rural areas. Thus, environmental health risk evaluation related to lack of water supply and unsafe drinking water still appears to be a field for further research in the context of developing countries.

The context of rural Nepal

In rural Nepal the majority of the population (more than 60 per cent) still lack WSS facilities; such facilities are highly subsidized and drinking water is still regarded as a public good. So far, no clearly defined property rights exist. In this context, the application of public valuation techniques as a basis for decentralized decision making may not be straightforward. When property rights are not well defined and users are less aware of the price to be paid for water, there can be problems in fixing the maximum or minimum ceiling to be asked using closed-ended questions for identifying users' WTP. Likewise, as people are not used to expressing their WTP, they might think that they could influence investment or policy decisions by not answering the questions or by expressing a low level of WTP. Further, people may overstate their WTP if they know that some donor agencies or the government have already decided to provide them with water services free of charge. Both the design and administration of questionnaires need to avoid such strategic bias. Various measures can be taken in the study design and survey to overcome some of these possible biases:

- evaluation of preliminary health risks, to provide a basis for designing closed-ended questions and communicating information on existing and potential health risks to the respondents;
- use of shadow wage rate for computation of the costs and benefits due to reduction in health problems from the improved water supply facilities in the project area;
- estimation of the supply cost, average incremental cost (AIC), cost recovery including operation and maintenance cost of the existing schemes and so on, which help provide a basis for determining upper and lower limits for designing dichotomous choice questions; and
- description of the scenario and design of questions, which lead successively to both the dichotomous choice and open-ended questions for measuring users' WTP, and pretesting of questionnaires, and redesign if necessary, in order to avoid the hypothetical bias.

12.3 Analytical framework for public valuation and decentralized decision making

Conceptual framework

Failure to account for public values and opinions in environmental decision making has often frustrated the policy implementation process (Davos and Nienberg 1980). While most of the decision support systems (DSS) are often computer based, a decentralized decision-making structure involves a set of processes including measurement of public perception, valuation, analysis of financial sustainability and equity concerns and investment decision making at the lowest level of the decision hierarchy. A simplified decentralized decision-making process (DDMP) for public valuation and investment decision making in the WSS sector involves: (i) water quality and preliminary health risk analysis associated with water pollution, (ii) estimation of supply costs, (iii) measurement of public perception and WTP, (iv) evaluation and analysis involving public perception, financial sustainability and equity aspects, and (v) analysis of the decision situation. Figure 12.1 shows a conceptual framework for a public valuation and decentralized decision-making process combining these various components and sub-components.

The *preliminary health risk or impact analysis* involves compilation of available reported cases of water-related diseases in the project and non-project areas, estimation of shadow wage rate in the rural areas and estimation of the impacts and cost estimates using a costs of illness approach. Although this approach as mentioned in Section 12.1 does not help directly in decentralized decision making, it provides a sound basis for avoiding starting-point bias in the application of public valuation techniques.

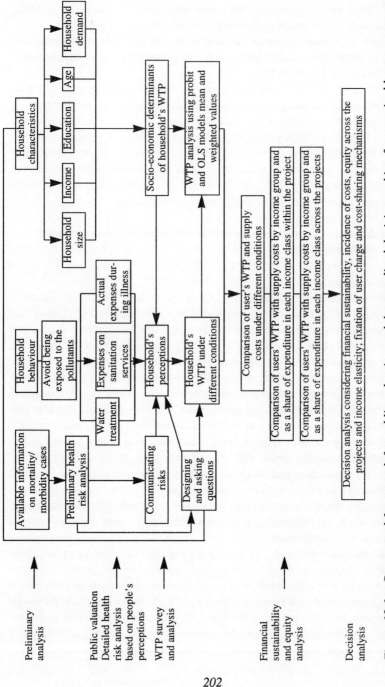

Figure 12.1 *Conceptual framework for public valuation and decentralized decision making for sustainable management of WSS facilities*

The *supply costs* of most of the development projects are readily available or can be estimated in terms of operation and maintenance costs, cost recovery amount and average incremental costs on a per household per month basis, during the project life period. The estimation of supply costs provides a basis for the design of dichotomous choice questions and for financial sustainability analysis.

Measurement of *public perception and willingness to pay* provide the basis for decentralized decision making by incorporating users' perceptions on the improved health conditions and their willingness to pay for it. The rest of this section provides a methodological framework for a public valuation and decentralized decision-making process.

Public valuation

Theoretical framework   The standard approach in the economic valuation technique is to incorporate the environmental quality into the conventional utility function and derive the willingness to pay of the individual or the household for a change in the environmental quality, in this case, changes in health benefits due to improved water supply conditions. The utility function in this case can be written as:

$$U = U(X, Q) \tag{12.1}$$

where, X denotes a vector of goods consumed, and Q denotes the improved water supply services. In some cases, however, especially in the rural areas, as no water treatment facilities are usually provided, provision of public water supply facilities does not guarantee improved water quality. To differentiate supply from quality, we denote water supply by q and quality by q'. In both the cases, a household maximizes welfare across a vector of consumer goods X, and water availability q and quality q'. Where water quality of the sources provided does not change, the utility function is given by $U = U(X, Q)$ and $Q = q$ in this case. But when both the level of quantity available and the quality change, the utility function is given by: $U = U(X, Q)$ where $Q = q + q'$. We have differentiated the utility function to fit into our model of evaluation of health risks as perceived by the users separately from water availability. An individual's willingness to pay for improved water availability and quality for an increase from Q_0 to Q_1 is given by:

$$WTP = e(p, Q_1, U_1) - e(p, Q_0, U_1) \tag{12.2}$$

where, U_1 refers to the post-change level of welfare, p is a price vector for household goods X, $e(.)$ is an expenditure function. The individual will be willing to give some level of consumption of good *X*, in order to receive an improved water supply, and better quality of water. User's WTP in this case is the amount of income or expenditure which must be taken from a household after improved water is provided in order to return to the wellbeing at the previous level (Bohm et al. 1993).

Determinants of the household's WTP   Existing health conditions as perceived by the households can also be one of the determining factors for the demand for good quality water. In the WTP survey, it is assumed that the demand for water by a household is a function of these variables other than the price of water itself, and in functional form it can be expressed as:

$$WTP = f\,(INCOM, EDCN, FASIZE, AGE, FLABOR,$$
$$WRANK, WDIST, WSUFF, HCONDN) \qquad (12.3)$$

where,

WTP	= willingness to pay of household in Rs/month
INCOM	= household income in Rs/month
EDCN	= household's level of education
FASIZE	= family size in nos
AGE	= age of the household head in years
FLABOR	= family labour force in nos with age between 15 and 60 years
WRANK	= water quality ranking in qualitative scale of 1–4.
WDIST	= existing distance for water source in miles or km
WSUFF	= household's perception on water sufficiency (yes/no)
HCONDN	= number of cases of water-borne diseases.

This functional form provides a basis for the questionnaire design and analysis of the WTP survey outcomes.

The survey structure, site selection and field survey   The household questionnaire covered: (i) general characteristics of the households, (ii) local people's perceptions on water supply, sanitation and environmental health conditions, (iii) WTP for improved water supply and sanitation conditions, (iv) WTP for existing water supply services, (v) WTP for averting health risks due to unsafe water, and (vi) WTP for the improved sanitation services. The dichotomous choice questions were designed for high to low and low to high bids in each of these cases. For administering the questions, questionnaire sets were translated into Nepali and also a different set of questionnaires was designed for the existing and new schemes. The issue of hypothetical bias was addressed by pre-testing and re-designing of the questionnaires in some selected locations. The survey was conducted over a two-month period in five project areas and three water-scarce areas. In total, 501 households were surveyed from these eight locations. The research team consisted of well-trained university graduates, resource economists and social scientists.

Methods of data analysis   The functional form (12.3) can be used for regression analysis with cross-sample data on WTP and determinants of the WTP, and can be expressed as:

$$WTP = \beta_0 + \beta_1 INCOM + \beta_2 EDCN + \beta_3 FASIZE + \beta_4 AGE +$$
$$\beta_5 FLABOR + \beta_6 WRANK + \beta_7 WDIST + \beta_8 WSUFF +$$
$$\beta_9 HCONDN) \qquad (12.4)$$

where, β_0 is constant and $\beta_1 \dots \beta_8$ are the regression coefficients. All other variables are as defined in (12.3). Generally, a positive relationship is expected with income, education, water distance and water sufficiency, and a negative one with age and family size.

In the case of dichotomous choice questions, mean *WTP* is given by the expected value $E(WTP)$ of the cumulative probability distribution curve linking the probability of obtaining a 'yes' response to the level of bid, and is usually analysed using limited dependent variables techniques. Such variables are introduced as a dummy variable (yes/no) and the estimation is carried out using a probit (normal) or logit (exponential) model to analyse the relationship between users' WTP and other socio-economic and physical variables. In this case, the ordered probit model was used to explain the variations in *WTP*. Whittington et al. (1990) show that the probability P of a 'yes' response in the case of an ordered probit model is given by:

$$P(y_h = i) = F(u_i - C_h B) - F(u_i - 1 - C_i B)$$

where, C_h is the vector of household characteristics, B is the estimation parameters and $F(.)$ is the cumulative standard normal density function. In the case of dichotomous choice questions, the ordered probit model was used for analysing users' WTP in all of the areas studied.

Public perception, values and decision analysis   Any rational decision-making process involves consideration of the costs and benefits of policy action (OECD 1989). Unlike conventional decision-making processes, such as estimation of net present value or internal rate of return, the decentralized decision-making process aims to incorporate local people's perceptions as a major decision variable. These provide a sound basis for measuring financial sustainability of the projects, determining the level of user charges, and analysing equity issues both at the household and regional levels. The decision rule in these various cases can be set as:

- *Rule 1*   The project is sustainable if users' WTP ≥ supply cost (operation and maintenance cost).
- *Rule 2*   Financial sustainability of the project is met if users' WTP ≥ supply cost (cost recovery amount).
- *Rule 3*   Long-term financial sustainability, or inter-generational equity is met if users' WTP ≥ supply cost (average incremental costs).
- *Rule 4*   Adopt user fees only if (i) the majority of the users know the mechanism and support such fees, and (ii) the distributional impact at the household level is minimum.
- *Rule 5*   Part of the revenue recycling is possible and sufficient for compensating the poorest of the poor if there is a high incidence of costs for such groups.

12.4   Preliminary health risk analysis and water supply costs

Water quality conditions in the case study areas
Available data from water quality tests of the existing and improved water supply schemes carried out by the project provided a rough indication of the water quality in the project area. These bacteriological tests indicated that more than 50 per cent of the existing sources of water in the *terai* (plain areas) (such as hand pumps and wells) were polluted in both the dry and rainy seasons, existing sources of water supplied under gravity schemes before the project situation were found to be highly polluted, especially during the dry season, and the drinking water in 48 per cent of the project areas was highly polluted.

Health conditions and preliminary health risk evaluation
Data available from a health survey study in the project area (New Era 1997) provided a basis for the evaluation of health risks in the study area. The health impact assessment is based on the 'with and without' project conditions using information as reported in the field survey carried out by New Era. The comparison of the health cases obtained from the project and control areas estimated that on a per household basis, the days lost due to waterborne diseases were 1.15 days during the two-week period before the interview. The lost days per household on a monthly basis were then estimated to be 2.29 days. Using a shadow wage estimated at Rs 25.0 per month (US$1 = Rs 59.0 at 1997 price), the benefit of health improvements due to the provision of water supply provisions in the project area was estimated to be Rs 57.50 per household per month.

Communication of health risks or the cost to the public is an important task while asking people for users' WTP for reducing health costs. While carrying out a WTP study for averting health risks, the respondents were informed of the estimated benefits of the improved water supplies due to reduction in health risks, and WTP questions were asked under both the informed and prior to the informed conditions.

Supply costs of WSS facilities

Cost recovery and operation and maintenance costs   The World Bank Report (World Bank 1996) provided estimates of the cost recovery amount for both the gravity and shallow tubewell schemes, assuming a life span of 20 years and at an interest rate of 10 per cent. For the gravity schemes the cost per person per year is estimated at Rs 221.7, which gives each household Rs 110.85 per month, assuming an average family size of six people. For the shallow tubewells, cost recovery on a per household basis was estimated to be Rs 33.60.

Average incremental costs   Ideally, decision regarding water pricing is based on marginal cost. The marginal cost is calculated by adding the marginal construction costs, the marginal user cost and the marginal environmental costs. However, in practice it is not so easy to calculate marginal cost as water supply investments are often lumpy and information on the marginal user cost as well as marginal environmental costs is not available. In such cases, marginal construction cost, or average incremental cost (AIC) can be estimated by dividing the total incremental costs by the total incremental quantity of water supply. Using a stepwise marginal construction cost method, the average incremental cost of water supply in Nepal at 1996 prices was estimated to be Rs 50 per cubic metre, or US$0.9 per cubic metre.

12.5   Public perception, users' WTP and consistency of results

Introduction to the case study areas
The case study was carried out for the Finnida-supported Rural Water Supply and Sanitation Project (RWSSP), Lumbini zone. Five project areas (Deuchuli, Deurali, Kharjyang, Mukundapur and Gorusinge), and three water-scarce areas outside the project (Agyoli, Wamgha and Sandi) with no WSS facilities were selected for the case study. These projects and control areas, located in the four districts of western Nepal, represented both the gravity and shallow tubewell schemes, hilly and *terai* ecological belts, rural and semi-urban areas, various ethnic composition and income groups, relatively successful and unsuccessful projects, and water-scarce and water-abundant areas.

Revised health risk estimates and users' WTP
Environmental health risks associated with unsafe water quality and lack of
drinking water were estimated based on the users' perception in both the
project and control areas. The health risk estimates were based on the cost of
illness approach including both the loss of income incurred for baby care
during illness, and costs of medical treatment per hospital visit for each child
on each occasion. The results indicated a higher incidence of costs in the
water-scarce areas and considerable costs in the other project areas. Figure
12.2 shows existing health costs in the five project areas.

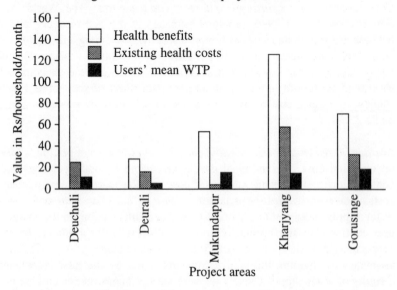

*Figure 12.2   Health benefits, existing health costs and users' mean WTP in
the five project areas*

Users' WTP for averting health risks provides another basis for measuring
the health benefits (Cropper and Freeman 1991) of WSS facilities. Although
the quality of water was improved, and health risk was reduced considerably,
the morbidity cases associated with water-related diseases were still found to
be higher. For this reason, users were asked for their WTP for averting health
risks by improving the quality of water they received. The WTP bids included
both the open- and closed-ended WTP questions (from low to high and high
to low bids). Questions were put to the respondents, after asking their WTP
for the existing or improved water supply availability, about an additional
amount they would be willing to pay for reducing health costs. In the case of
users' mean maximum WTP for reducing health costs, the amount varied
from Rs 7 to Rs 20 in the project areas, and from Rs 9 to Rs 17 per household

per month in the control areas. In the case of dichotomous choice questions, in most of the areas, a higher percentage of respondents said 'yes' at Rs 10.0 per household per month. As shown in Figure 12.2, in most of the cases, except for suburban areas, users' WTP is quite low compared to the health benefits from the project and existing health costs.

Users' WTP for drinking water availability
The analysis of the users' WTP obtained in both the open and dichotomous choice questions indicated that: (i) users responded to the slightly higher bids in the case of high to low bids compared to the low to high bids; (ii) users' mean maximum WTP was estimated to be in the range Rs 27 to Rs 40.0 per household per month, for the existing and improved water supply facilities; (iii) the majority of users in the project areas were willing to pay the full costs of system operation and maintenance; (iv) more than 60 per cent of the households both in the project and control areas were interested in private tap connections with mean WTP at Rs 4000 per tap per household; (v) users were willing to share the initial investment costs of WSS projects up to 40 per cent of the total costs, that is about Rs 3000 per household in the water-scarce areas (vi) compared to the initial cash contribution asked by the project officials, users' WTP for initial cost sharing was many times higher in the project areas. As reported by the users, the amount paid varied from Rs 50 to Rs 100 per household. Likewise, users' mean maximum WTP for toilet construction was found to be in the range Rs 934 to Rs 2584 per household in different project and control areas.

Consistency of users' WTP survey results

Users' WTP for averting for health costs   The statistical analysis of the users' WTP was carried out using both the probit and OLS models relating to various physical, environmental and socio-economic factors. These included: qualitative ranking of existing water quality, number of cases of people suffering from water-related diseases, sex, age, education, occupation, income, family labour size, number of children in the family and so on. The analysis indicated that:

- in the case of dichotomous choice questions, households responded more positively in the case of high to low bids at or below Rs 10 per household per month compared to the low to high bids;
- savings in health costs due to improved water supply in the project areas are significantly higher compared to the users' WTP;
- in most of the cases, households' WTP was positively and significantly related to the number of those suffering from ill health, and education and household income;

- the lower WTP in the non-project areas is justified, because they have yet to realize the benefits of water quality improvements;
- users' WTP was also largely influenced by the level of education and income; and
- in the case of open-ended questions, the same results were found with significance at or below the 10 per cent level and positive relationships with education, income and ill health. The adjusted R-square varied from 0.29 to 0.32.

Users' WTP for existing and improved water availability   In most cases, the probit and OLS estimates of users' WTP for existing and improved water supply showed both positive and significant relationships with some of the included socio-economic variables such as education and income. Positive and negative relationships were obtained with other variables such as child numbers, family labour size, and water collection time, with varying levels of significance and association in different project and control areas. The model validity varied in different cases with the R-square value ranging from 0.17 to 0.78. The results obtained were found to be similar to those of studies carried out on measuring users' WTP for WSS facilities in other developing countries. The regression results in the case of open bids for both the project and control areas are shown in Tables 12.1 and 12.2.

12.6   Decentralized decision making: public perceptions, financial sustainability and local and regional equity analysis

Public perceptions and financial sustainability
The issue of financial sustainability of the WSS projects has been a major concern in developing countries, and is usually examined by comparing the users' WTP with the AIC, cost-recovery amount and operation and maintenance costs of the facilities provided (David Pearce, March 1996, personal communication; Tiwari 1998). The comparative analysis carried out in the case of the five projects showed that users' average WTP lies seven to nine times below the average incremental cost estimated for the whole of Nepal. Likewise, compared with the project cost-recovery amount, users' average maximum WTP covers only about 46 per cent in Kharjyang, 77 per cent in Deuchuli, 26 per cent in Deurali, 54 per cent in Mukundapur and 100 per cent in the case of Gorusinge. Comparison of the users' mean maximum WTP with the project operation and maintenance costs indicated that users were at least willing to pay to cover these costs. Thus, if viewed on a project-by-project basis, shallow tubewell projects in the *terai* appeared to be financially sustainable, while some projects, such as those at Deuchuli and Kharjyang, showed 'win–win' situations of higher WTP, proper maintenance of facilities

Table 12.1   Regression analysis of users' maximum bid for existing water supply facilities in the project areas

S. no.	Independent variables	Deuchuli Coeff./ t-value	Deurali Coeff./ t-value	Mukundapur Coeff./ t-value	Kharjyang Coeff./ t-value	Gorusinge Coeff./ t-value
1	Constant	−14.23 (−0.58)	65.32 (−1.69)***	31.27 (−1.41)	48.38 (1.03)	65.28 (3.99)*
2	Cast	2.83 (1.75)***	−10.18 (−1.12)	0.56 (0.37)	−3.76 (−0.84)	−0.64 (−0.25)
3	Sex	−1.65 (−0.18)	−6.34 (−0.56)	2.14 (0.30)	−50.03 (−1.59)	−16.75 (−2.00)**
4	Age	0.18 (0.86)	−0.18 (−0.90)	0.007 (0.03)	0.88 (1.41)	−0.14 (−0.66)
5	Education	18.47 (2.53)*	8.16 (1.78)***	3.12 (0.46)	22.68 (1.30)	3.57 (0.61)
6	Non-agriculture occupation	3.13 (1.77)***	3.33 (1.06)	2.37 (1.55)	−2.10 (−0.61)	3.59 (1.27)
7	Family child	−3.76 (−2.31)**	−1.42 (−1.19)	−1.79 (−1.03)	0.19 (0.06)	0.22 (1.14)
8	Family labour	0.85 (0.64)	4.37 (3.06)*	2.70 (2.00)**	0.22 (0.06)	−1.35 (−0.91)
9	Total monthly income	0.002 (1.84)***	−0.002 (−1.15)	0.0005 (1.07)	0.0002 (0.10)	0.001 (1.36)
10	Water collection time	−0.27 (−0.81)	−0.54 (−1.00)	−0.45 (−1.13)	−2.17 (−1.95)***	0.24 (0.66)
11	Water sufficiency	1.67 (0.30)	6.52 (1.14)	−2.41 (−0.49)	−2.84 (−0.21)	−12.57 (−1.95)**
12	Water quality	3.21 (0.77)	1.24 (0.43)	−2.90 (−1.20)	3.83 (0.61)	0.11 (0.04)
13	Water consumption per day	−0.07 (−0.42)	−0.03 (−0.12)	1.10 (0.77)	−0.36 (−0.72)	−0.10 (−0.89)
14	Health cases	1.73 (0.78)	0.29 (0.41)	0.34 (0.14)	9.25 (4.15)*	−0.29 (−0.38)
	R^2	0.45	0.36	0.26	0.78	0.37

Notes:
* Significance level ≤ 1%.
** Significance level ≤ 5%.
*** Significance level ≤ 10%.

and a more reliable water supply. But some projects, like the one at Deurali, showed low WTP, lack of maintenance of facilities, and low reliability of water supply.

When the cost-recovery amount of the adjoining project areas was considered, users' average WTP in all the control areas was found to be lower than the cost-recovery amount. However, users' willingness to pay an initial cash

Table 12.2   Regression analysis of users' maximum bid for improved water supply facilities in the control areas

S. no.	Independent variable	Agyoli Coeff./*t*-value	Wamgha Coeff./*t*-value	Sandi Coeff./*t*-value
1	Constant	40.16	−1.15	28.69
		(1.64)***	(0.04)	(1.18)
2	Cast	−1.7	0.41	−2.44
		(−0.79)	(0.15)	(−0.76)
3	Sex	−1.59	−12.97	−3.52
		(−0.14)	(−1.47)	(−0.24)
4	Age	0.40	0.10	0.01
		(1.34)	(0.42)	(0.11)
5	Education	8.24	14.98	8.48
		(0.92)	(1.67)***	(2.28)**
6	Non-agriculture occupation	1.59	0.35	−1.53
		(0.57)	(0.12)	(−1.02)
7	Family child	−2.89	−2.27	0.12
		(−1.70)***	(−1.37)	(0.15)
8	Family labour	−1.52	2.14	−0.67
		(−0.76)	(1.05)	(−0.85)
9	Total monthly income	0.001	0.0008	0.0007
		(1.63)***	(0.64)	(2.67)*
10	Water collection time	−0.03	0.33	−0.22
		(−0.17)	(1.94)***	(−0.72)
11	Water sufficiency	−8.79	−6.67	2.21
		(−0.90)	(−0.67)	(−0.45)
12	Water quality	−2.98	5.07	−2.42
		(−0.69)	(1.68)***	(−1.24)
13	Water consumption per day	−0.15	−0.15	0.05
		(−1.11)	(−0.74)	(0.67)
14	Health cases	0.18	0.26	0.28
		(0.19)	(0.37)	(0.30)
	R^2	0.26	0.17	0.28

Notes:
*   Significance level ≤ 1%.
**   Significance level ≤ 5%.
***   Significance level ≤ 10%.

contribution as well as for system management provided a more optimistic scenario for cost recovery in these areas so long as water supply facilities are provided at a reasonable cost. Likewise, more than 50 per cent of the households indicated their willingness to bear almost the full cost of private tap connection. Thus, the analysis indicated that although application of the user pays principle based on the full cost pricing is not possible in the context of rural and semi-urban areas in Nepal, partial cost recovery may be possible by arranging initial cost-sharing mechanisms in the new areas, extending facilities in the existing systems, and by charging user fees with necessary institutional arrangements.

Public perception on the implementation of user fees
Public support is the basic criterion for implementing user fees. The size of the revenue stream generated with public support provides a basis for political support. Political support is also considered as a necessary condition, because powerful vested interests of political groups may slow, divert or even stop a desirable reform (Dinar et al. 1998) and thus is useful in the passage of financial laws and regulations for implementing water user fees in the rural and semi-urban areas. Users' perceptions about water sufficiency and their response towards rationing of water and introducing fees, and their willingness to pay, provide an indication of public support. In all of the project areas except one, more than 50 per cent of the respondents said that project-supplied drinking water was sufficient for them, and supported the installation of water measuring devices if the project, or the water user committee, would be willing to introduce pricing mechanism based on the volumetric pricing for the efficient use of available drinking water. More than 60 per cent of the users also expressed the view that system operation and management would improve if they were given full responsibility for it.

Incidence of costs and benefits at the household level
The incidence of costs and benefits at the household level can be analysed by comparing the suggested user charge (for example, based on the operation and maintenance costs and cost recovery amount per household per month), with the users' demand for water (for example, users' WTP). The analysis carried out both in the project and control areas indicated that:

- as the users' WTP is higher than the per unit operation and maintenance costs (with the exception of Deurali), household surplus is positive;
- if the user charge is to be based on the maximum mean WTP household surplus may not be negative, but still full cost recovery is not possible;
- when the user charge is fixed equal to the cost recovery amount and the benefit is valued in terms of maximum mean WTP, the household surplus will be negative; and

- household surplus may be positive in some cases such as in Kharjyang, Gorusinge and Sandi when the user charge is set equal to that of the weighted average WTP (weighted by income).

Likely distributional impacts at the household level
How would the incidence of costs and benefits be distributed among different household groups? Such distributive implications are of growing concern when setting the user charge. The distribution of costs and benefits of the pricing structure can be measured in terms of how the programme (in this case user fee-based water supply improvement programme) alters the physical environment of different groups (Cropper and Oates 1992). As suggested by Dorfman (1977), distributional concerns such as excess burden to the households can be addressed by comparing the users' WTP with the average cost share per family under different income categories. Gianessi and Peskin (1980) addressed distributional concerns by comparing the costs of water pollution control measures across the households by income categories. The comparison of a uniform user charge based on the cost recovery with average WTP of the users under different income categories in each project and control area indicated that:

- the percentage share of family expenditure for the lowest-income group is almost four times higher than that of higher-income groups;
- even in relatively successful projects such as that in Deuchuli, the incidence of costs borne by the lower-income groups was found to be almost double that of the higher-income groups. This indicates that charging user fees based on the average maximum WTP would result in welfare loss for the lower-income groups.

For these reasons, either the user charge should be set lower than the average maximum WTP, or some compensation mechanism needs to be developed to compensate the lower-income groups by recycling part of the revenue generated. Dorfman (1977) has shown the high burden of the pollution control programme costs to the lower-income groups in the case of a water pollution control programme in the United States. However, usually it is the lower-income group who have to travel a long distance for the collection of drinking water, and who bear a high incidence of health costs in terms of suffering and loss of earnings due to the use of unsafe water.

In other cases, such as the mean maximum WTP for private tap connections, the WTP bid was usually found to be higher with the higher-income group. In this case, mean maximum WTP could be charged to the households of any income group as they already have an alternative source of drinking water to the public taps if they cannot afford to pay for private taps. The implementation strategy for the user fee-based model should be towards charging the private users for an additional amount depending upon the location and the cost of facility expansion, with the user charge at a level equal to the highest level of users' WTP for operation and maintenance. As users are willing to pay a large amount in each locality, this will help generate more revenue and maintain users' welfare as well.

Regional equity concerns

Comparative analysis on a project-by-project basis showed that the incidence of cost was likely to be much higher in some projects such as those in Deurali and Kharjyang located in the hills and lower foothills, compared to the other areas. This indicates that the present implementation strategy based on the fixed rule of sharing the initial investment at a ratio of 30:70 between users and the government as well as uniform water charges based on location-specific cost recovery or maintenance costs may not be justified. The regional equity concern is also linked to the rural–urban disparity, and how much users in the urban areas are paying for drinking water. The water charge for drinking water supplies even in the urban areas in Nepal is not based on a proper pricing mechanism. For example, in the capital city, the water charge on volumetric basis is only 40 per cent of the average incremental cost of water supply. Compared to the increasing demand for water, and escalating costs of water supplies, the present water-pricing system in urban areas which cover only 40 per cent of AIC, is neither financially sustainable, nor justifiable from a regional equity perspective. It is evident, therefore, that there exist regional disparities both in the provision and sharing of the costs of the water supply and sanitation facilities in Nepal. These aspects need to be considered when making investment decisions and fixing water charges.

Decision analysis

The Nepalese government is presently facing the twin challenges of providing water supply facilities in new areas as well as maintaining existing water supply schemes. The rising demand for water in other sectors such as for irrigation, construction work and industry causes increased conflict over sharing water resources. On the other hand, available water sources, which could be diverted at relatively lower per unit cost, are shrinking due to increased environmental degradation. This situation indicates the growing demand for water on the one hand, and physical limits in terms of escalating costs of water supply on the other. Lack of financial resources and proper institutional arrangements are threatening sustainability of the existing water supply schemes. Unlike the conventional method of decision making such as benefit–cost analysis, the decentralized decision-making framework analysed in this chapter provides several guidelines for investment decision making in new areas and sustainable management of the facilities provided. The analysis indicated that:

- application of decision rules 1 and 2 (see Section 12.3) indicates that financial sustainability of the projects except for shallow tubewells in the plain areas was not met;
- long-term financial sustainability, or inter-generational equity appears to be a distant objective in all cases of gravity schemes both in the rural and semi-urban areas;
- adoption of user fees is possible as the majority of the users are familiar with the mechanism and would support such fees;
- the distributional impacts at the household level for the poorest group are likely to be adverse because of their low WTP and higher percentage of income and expenditure to be allocated for water charges;
- user charges cannot be fixed equal to cost recovery or AIC except for shallow tubewell projects; and
- estimation of the likely revenue under the suggested schemes indicates that part of the revenue recycling could be possible to compensate the poorest of the poor if the necessary institutional arrangements are established.

Tables 12.3 and 12.4 illustrate the basic issues analysed, and suggest different levels of user fees as an instrument for capital-revenue-generating mechanism in some of the projects and control areas.

12.7   Conclusions

As in many other developing countries, Nepal is presently facing high environmental health risks associated with increased water pollution and lack of safe drinking water in rural and semi-urban areas. There is an urgent need for the integration of environmental health concerns into the decision-making process with incorporation of local people's perceptions to address these risks. This chapter has analysed inconsistency problems in the evaluation of environmental health risks, developed an analytical framework for a decentralized decision-making process, and presented the results obtained from a case study carried out using public valuation techniques in different ecological belts of Nepal. Likewise, the chapter provided an analytical framework for incorporating public perception and values and extended the results obtained for financial sustainability, equity and decision analysis of the WSS projects. This demonstrates public valuation techniques for the evaluation of environmental health risks associated with the lack of safe drinking water. The chapter also shows that use of public valuation techniques can be very helpful in adopting a decentralized decision-making process in developing countries.

Table 12.3   Summary of users' WTP, supply costs and incidence of costs and benefits and suggested user charges in some of the project and control areas

Study areas	Users' WTP (mean)	Users' WTP (WTD)	User charge (O&M)	User charge (CR)	Incidence of costs and benefits*	Nature of income distribution and income elasticity	Distribution of costs and benefits at the household level	Recommendations /suggested user charges
Deuchuli (rural; gravity system)	34	35	17	44	Compared to the user charge based on O&M costs, households generate surplus, but will be in loss if user charge is based on cost recovery	Majority in middle-income bracket. Relatively higher income elasticity	Higher for middle-income group as their WTP is lower than lower- and upper-income groups	Charge scheme should cover full O&M and partial cost recovery (Rs 30–40/month/HH)
Mukundapur (suburban; gravity)	37	42	30	69	Incidence of costs will be positive if charged for full cost recovery	Majority in middle-income class, very low income elasticity	Negative impact on lower-middle-income groups	User charge should cover full O&M and partial CR with compensation to the lower groups (Rs 45/month/HH)
Gorusinge (rural; tubewells)	37	41	5	12	Households will generate surplus in both cases	Almost even distribution and lower-income elasticity	Positive impact on all groups of households	User charge should be at least be based on the full cost recovery (Rs 15/month/HH)
Agyoli (semi-urban; gravity; control area)	40	46	30	69	While households will generate surplus in the case of user charge equal to O&M costs, incidence of cost will be positive if charged for full cost recovery	Majority of the population fall in middle- and upper-income category Very low income elasticity	Negative impact on all income groups when charge is considered equal to full cost recovery amount	User charge should cover full O&M costs and partial cost recovery (Rs 40–45/month/HH)
Wamgha (rural; gravity; control area)	30	35	35	86	Households will generate surplus in the case of user charge based on O&M costs but incidence of cost will be positive, if charged based on cost recovery	Majority in the middle- and upper-income group Relatively lower elasticity of income	Although on average user surplus is positive, distributional impact analysis shows negative impacts on lower-income groups	User charge should cover full O&M costs and partial cost recovery (Rs 35–40/month/HH)

Notes:
* WTD = Weighted mean; O&M = Operation and maintenance costs; CR = Cost recovery amount; HH = Household.

217

Table 12.4 Users' WTP for sharing initial costs, distributional issues and suggested charge for sharing initial costs in the water scarce (control) areas

Study Areas	Users' WTP for sharing costs (%)	Users' mean WTP (Rs)	Users' WTP for private taps (Rs)	Users' WTP and relation with household's income	Distributional issues at the household level	Recommendations	Suggested charge for initial cost sharing
Agyoli (semi-urban; gravity)	43	2835	4278	Users' WTP for sharing initial costs was found significantly and positively related to users' income	Only 7% have average WTP below Rs 2000, and majority have higher WTP	Users should be asked to pay some amount in cash; attempts to be made for extending facilities for private tap connections	Rs 2000/HH for public taps and equal to WTP for private tap connections
Wamgha (rural; gravity)	41	2508	3504	Users' WTP for sharing initial costs was found positively related to users' income	Except for 7% in the lower-income bracket, majority have WTP more than Rs 1900 WTP amount for private and public taps almost the same	Users should be asked to pay some amount in cash; attempts to be made for extending facilities to private tap connections	Rs 1200–1500 for public taps and equal to WTP for private tap connections
Sandi (rural; shallow tubewells)	12	1035	1790	Users' WTP for sharing initial costs was found positively related to users' income	Majority expressed WTP at between Rs 500 and 800 for private wells	Users should be asked to pay for full cost of the facilities; no efforts to be made for private tubewells	Rs 500/HH

218

Note
* This chapter is based partly on the author's work on the measurements of users' WTP in Rural Water Supply and Sanitation Project (RWSSP) areas jointly implemented by the RWSSP, Ministry of Local Development, Nepal, and the Finnish Development Agency. The study was carried out for the RWSSP during March–November 1997. The author would like to express his sincere thanks to the project officials and Plan Center Ltd. for providing financial support to carry out this study. However, the author alone is responsible for the views expressed in this chapter.

References
Bohm, R.A., Essenberg, T.J. and Fox, W.F. (1993), 'Sustainability of potable water supplies in the Philippines', *Water Resources Research*, **29**, 1955–63.
Briscoe, J., Castro, P.F., Griffin, C., North, J. and Olsen, O. (1990), 'Toward equitable and sustainable rural water supplies: a contingent valuation study', *World Bank Economic Review*, **4**, 115–34.
Commission on Sustainable Development (CSD) (1997), 'Freshwater resources', Ch. 18 in *Progress Review Report on Agenda 21*, New York: UNDPCSD.
Cropper, M.L. and Freeman III, A.M. (1991), 'Environmental health effects', in J.B. Braden and C.D. Kolstad (eds), *Measuring Demand for Environmental Quality*, North-Holland: Elsevier Science Publishers.
Cropper, M.L. and Oates, W.E. (1992), 'Environmental economics: a survey', *Journal of Economic Literature*, **30**, 675–740.
Davos, C.A. and Nienberg, M.W. (1980), 'A framework for integrating the health concerns into environmental decision-making', *Journal of Environmental Management*, **11**, 133–46.
Dinar, A., Balakrishnan, T.K. and Wambia, J. (1998), *Political Economy and Political Risks of Institutional Reforms in the Water Sector*, Policy Research Working Paper No. 1987, World Bank, Washington, DC.
Dorfman, R. (1977), 'Incidence of the benefits and costs of environmental programs', *Journal of American Economic Association*, **67**, 333–40.
Gianessi, L.P. and Peskin, H.M. (1980), 'The distribution of the costs of federal water pollution policy', *Land Economics*, **56**, 85–102.
Haneman, W.M. (1994), 'Valuing the environment through contingent valuation', *Journal of Economic Perspectives*, **8**, 19–43.
Harrington, W., Krupnick, A. and Spafford, O. (1987), 'The economic losses of a waterborne diseases outbreak', *Journal of Urban Economics*, **25**, 116–37.
Hershaft, A. et al. (1974), *Critical Review of Air Pollution Dose-response Functions*, Council on Environmental Quality, National Technical Services, USA.
Johansson, P. (1995), *Evaluating Health Risks: An Economic Approach*, Cambridge: Cambridge University Press.
Kask, S.B. and Shogren, J.F. (1994), 'Benefit transfer protocol for long-term health risk valuation', *Water Resources Research*, **10**, 2813–23.
Lindberg, K., Johnson, R.L. and Berrers, R.P. (1997), 'Contingent valuation of rural tourism development with tests of scope and mode stability', *Journal of Agriculture and Resource Economics*, **22**, 44–60.
Mitchell, R.C. and Carson, R.T. (1989), *Using Surveys to Value Public Goods: The Contingent Valuation Method*, Washington, DC: Resources for the Future.
New Era (1997), *Health Survey Report of Rural Water Supply and Sanitation Project*, Lumbini Zone, Nepal.
Organization for Economic Cooperation and Development (OECD) (1989), *Environmental Policy Benefits: Monetary Valuation*, OECD: Paris.
Tiwari, D.N. (1998), *Determining Economic Value of Irrigation Water: Comparison of Willingness to Pay and Other Indirect Valuation Approaches as a Measure of Sustainable Resource Use*, CSERGE Working Paper No. 98–05, CSERGE, University College London, UK.
USAID (1991), *Ranking Environmental Health Risks in Bangkok*, Washington, DC: Office of Housing and Urban Programs, USAID.

Vincent, J.R., Crawford, E.W. and Hoehn, J.P. (1991), *Valuing Environmental Benefits in Developing Countries*, Special Report, East Lansing, USA: Michigan State University.

Whitehead, J.C. and Houtven, G.V. (1997), *Methods of Valuing the Benefits of Safe Drinking Water Act: Review and Assessment*, Greenville, USA: East Carolina University.

Whittington, D., Briscoe, J., Mu, X. and Barron, W. (1990), 'Estimating the willingness to pay for water services in developing countries: a case study of the use of contingent valuation surveys in the Southern Haiti', *Economic Development and Cultural Change*, **38**, 293–311.

Whittington, D., Lauria, D.T., Wright, A.M., Choe, K. and Hughes, J.A. (1993), 'Household sanitation in Kumasi, Ghana: a description of current practices, attitudes and perceptions', *World Development*, **21**, 235–43.

World Bank (1993), *Water Resources Management: A Policy Paper*, Washington, DC: World Bank.

World Bank (1996), *Staff Appraisal Report, Rural Water Supply and Sanitation Project, Nepal, South Asia Regional Office*, Washington, DC: World Bank.

13 A holistic approach to the evaluation of socio-economic and environmental impacts of technological change in agriculture: an application in Bangladesh[1]

Sanzidur Rahman and Jayant Routray

13.1 Introduction

Technological change is an important factor in economic growth and development. The major technological breakthrough in agriculture in the twentieth century is the development of high-yielding modern grain varieties of wheat and rice which are highly responsive to inorganic fertilisers, insecticides, effective soil management and water control (Hayami and Ruttan 1985). The overwhelming belief in the pursuit of this 'high-input payoff' model of agricultural development, popularly coined as the 'green revolution', is due to its potential in increasing foodgrain productivity, employment as well as income (seen in many countries during the 1960s and 1970s), thereby alleviating poverty and hunger. Bangladesh, being a predominantly agricultural economy with an extremely unfavourable land–person ratio owing to high population density, also sought to pursue the policy of transforming agriculture through rapid technological progress to alleviate poverty and widespread hunger. Consequently, over the past four decades, the major thrust of national policies has been directed towards diffusing the green revolution technology (modern varieties of rice and wheat) with corresponding support in the provision of modern inputs, such as chemical fertilisers, pesticides, irrigation equipment, institutional credit, product procurement, storage and marketing facilities.

However, the impacts of this green revolution technology among the adopting nations have been mixed and are accompanied by controversies largely due to the approach utilized in the evaluation process and the extent of the issues covered in the analyses. Freebairn (1995), analysing the results of 307 studies undertaken during the period 1970–89, observed that about 80 per cent of these studies had conclusions that the new technology widened both inter-farm and inter-regional income inequality. The interesting point in this study is that the nature of the conclusions drawn from these evaluation studies was found to be influenced by the 'regional origin of the authors', 'location of the study area', 'methodology followed', and 'the geographic extension of the study area'.

Most of the early evaluations of modern technology and/or green revolution centred on the concerns of growth, productivity, efficiency and equity (Sidhu 1974; Parthasarathy 1974; Griffin 1974; Sen 1974; Harris 1977; Mellor 1978; Lal 1979; Bisaliah 1982; Prahladachar 1983; and Dantwala 1985). The anticipation that the modern technology can affect other spheres of life remained ignored. In particular, knowledge on the delayed consequences of this technological change on other spheres of the economy is nascent and has not been considered until more recently spurred by studies such as Shiva (1991), Redclift (1989), Brown (1988), Wolf (1986), Clapham (1980) and Bowonder (1979 and 1981). However, concern over sustainability in food production, owing to technological change, is gaining momentum (Alauddin and Tisdell 1991; Redclift 1989; Marten 1988; and Conway 1986). As a result there has been a growing interest in evaluating the merits of traditional agriculture as it was increasingly realized that modern technology, particularly the green revolution, although dramatically increasing food production in its initial years of inception, has been accompanied by a tapering off in production potential in later years.

Given this backdrop, the present study employed a holistic approach to evaluate the impacts of three decades of modern technology diffusion in Bangladesh agriculture, focusing on its economic, social/distributional and environmental impacts and the prospects for food production sustainability.

The chapter is organized into a number of sections. Section 13.2 presents the research design and evaluation methodology for the study. Sections 13.3–13.5 present the evaluations of the economic, social/distributional and environmental impacts of technological change in agriculture. Section 13.6 presents a synthesis of the empirical findings and the main policy implications to be drawn from the study.

13.2   Research design and evaluation methodology

The overall hypothesis of the study is that although the diffusion of modern agricultural technology has contributed to increased production, employment and income, its distributional consequences have been mixed. Also, this technological change in agriculture has exerted adverse impacts on the environment and its diffusion has not been uniform across regions. This has resulted in regional disparities. Moreover, long-run crop production levels are believed likely to reach a saturation level, thereby posing a threat to the sustainability of food production. Given this, the research is designed to provide a blend of economic (crop input–output), biophysical (soil fertility) and behavioural (farmers' perception) analyses to capture the diverse issues involved.

The study is based on time-series crop input–output data for 47 years (1948–94) and farm-level cross-section data for crop year 1996 collected from three agro-ecological regions. It also includes soil samples from representative locations and information on infrastructural facilities. The research is conducted at two levels: macro level and micro level, respectively. The macro-level analysis comprises all of the agricultural regions of the country. The following method was adopted for the selection of areas for in-depth micro-level analysis. First, relatively homogeneous agricultural regions with respect to a set of technological, demographic, infrastructure and crop production efficiency parameters were identified at the macro level, which were then classified into five levels of development.[2] Then, one region each from a 'high', 'medium', and 'low' level was selected.[3] The specific selected regions are those of Comilla, Jamalpur and Jessore. Once the regions had been selected, a multistage random sampling technique was employed to locate the districts, then the *thana* (subdistricts), then the villages in each of the three subdistricts and finally the sample households. A total of 406 households from 21 villages (175 households from eight villages of Jamalpur Sadar *thana*, 105 households from six villages of Manirampur *thana* and 126 households from seven villages of Matlab *thana*) forms the sample of the study. In terms of varieties of crops[4] produced, the total number of observations was 1448: 117 local rice, 829 modern rice, 103 modern wheat, 92 jute, 71 oilseeds, 59 potatoes, 70 pulses, 47 spices, 44 vegetables and 16 cotton.

A comprehensive assessment of the multifaceted impacts of technological change is a huge task. The present study attempts to provide an analysis of economic, social/distributional, and environmental impacts of technological change in Bangladesh agriculture using a holistic approach.

The term 'holistic' is used to signify the coverage of multiple issues (employment, income, poverty and environment) from multiple components (social, economic, biophysical and environmental) that are analysed at multi-levels (both macro and micro) by applying multi-techniques (spatial, quantitative and behavioural) using multi-period information (time-series and cross-section).

13.3   Economic impacts of technological change
One of the major arguments in favour of promoting the green revolution is its potential in increasing aggregate crop production by increasing crop productivity as well as cropping intensity. Also, as the green revolution technology is input intensive, its widespread adoption is expected to influence the demand for inputs as well as increase their prices. Finally, a positive influence on household income from increased agricultural production is expected.

Impact on aggregate crop production
The impact of technological change on production is analysed by estimating an aggregate crop production function with regionwise disaggregated data for

29 years (1960/61–1991/92). Data are taken from the *Statistical Yearbook of Bangladesh* (BBS 1980, 1989, 1991 and 1995), *Yearbook of Agricultural Statistics* (BBS 1978, 1986, 1992 and 1994), Hamid (1991 and 1993) and Deb (1995).

The Cobb–Douglas aggregate production function model is used for the estimation:

$$CROP = f(LAND, LABORFORCE, LIVESTOCK,$$
$$FERTILISER, HCAP, ROAD, PMVAR, PIRRIG) \qquad (13.1)$$

Note The explanatory notes for these variables, and for the variables in subsequent equations, are presented in Appendix 13A.

Three alternative models were estimated using different variables to represent technology. Model 1 uses the irrigation index (*PIRRIG*) as the proxy for the technology variable. Model 2 uses the proportion of area under modern varieties of rice and wheat (*PMVAR*) as the technology variable. Since both the irrigation index and area under modern varieties are complements, the multiplication of irrigation index and area under modern varieties (*PIRRIG*PMVAR*) is used in Model 3 to remove any potential multicollinearity problems. The OLS (ordinary least squares) estimation procedure, corrected for first-degree autocorrelated disturbances using the Prais–Winsten method, is used. All three models provided similar results.

Impact on prices
As the increased diffusion of modern agricultural technology increases the supply of foodgrains, the price of foodgrain is likely to remain low relative to other crops. This will lead to a rise in real wages for agricultural labourers for both adopting as well as non-adopting regions. Apart from the indirect favourable impact of modern agricultural technology on the labour and output market, a similar adjustment of income transfer can occur through the operation of the land market, particularly through changes in tenurial arrangements and rental income from land. Fertiliser is an integral component of the modern agricultural technology. Hence, a positive association between fertiliser demand and area cultivated under modern varieties of rice and wheat is expected. The increased demand for fertiliser may put an upward pressure on fertiliser prices.

In order to identify factors affecting labour wages, fertiliser prices, land rent and output prices, the following equations are fitted separately to the plot level data:

$$WAGE = f(LABOR, OWNLND, MVAR, INFRA, SOIL) \qquad (13.2)$$

$$FP = f(FERT, OWNLND, MVAR, INFRA, SOIL) \qquad (13.3)$$

$$LANDRENT = f(LANDPC, MVAR, IRRIG, TNC, CAPL, \\ INFRA, SOIL) \qquad (13.4)$$

$$OUTP = f(QTY, OWNLND, PMVAR, INFRA, SOIL) \qquad (13.5)$$

OLS estimation procedures were applied to estimate these price functions.

Impact on input demand
Since modern varieties of rice and wheat production are highly input intensive, the following demand functions for modern inputs are postulated:

$$FERT = f(FP, AMLND, MVAR, CAPL, AGCR, INFRA, SOIL) \quad (13.6)$$

$$LABOR = f(WAGE, AMLND, MVAR, AGCR, INFRA, SOIL) \quad (13.7)$$

$$ANIMAL = f(ANIMP, AMLND, MVAR, AGCR, INFRA, SOIL) \quad (13.8)$$

Furthermore, the adoption of modern varieties is dependent on the availability of irrigation. Therefore, the following equations are presented to explain the variation in adoption of modern varieties:

$$MVAR = f(IRRIG, AMLND, CAPL, AGCR, INFRA, SOIL) \qquad (13.9)$$

$$IRRIG = f(AMLND, CAPL, AGCR, INFRA, SOIL) \qquad (13.10)$$

Given the demand structure of modern inputs, it is clear that *IRRIG* and *MVAR* are endogenous variables since *MVAR* appears on the right-hand side of equations (13.6), (13.7) and (13.8) and *IRRIG* appears on the right-hand side of equation (13.9). This is, therefore, a case of a simultaneous equation model with recursive structure, where irrigation determines modern technology adoption, and modern technology adoption determines the demand for fertiliser, labour and animal power services. Therefore, the simultaneous estimation of five equations, (13.6), (13.7), (13.8) and (13.9) or (13.10) is conducted using the three stage least squares (3SLS) technique that allows correlation among disturbances in individual equations.

Credit is an important factor in agricultural development as the majority of the farmers lack financial liquidity. Therefore, the identification of factors determining the availability of agricultural credit can serve as a vital instrument in solving the liquidity crisis of farmers. The following equation is fitted to the data at the crop level:

$$AGCR = f(OWNLND, MVAR, IRRIG, TNC, CAPL, WORK, \\ FAMILY, EXPCE, INFRA SOIL) \qquad (13.11)$$

OLS estimation procedures were applied to the data.

Although pesticides have not been considered as a complementary input to be used in conjunction with new seeds, fertilisers and irrigation while promoting modern technology diffusion, nevertheless they have become a major input in present-day agriculture (Pingali 1995). In order to test whether there is a significant association between modern variety cultivation and subsequent pesticide use, a multivariate analysis is performed at the crop level. The following equation is fitted to the data:

$$PEST = f(AMLND, PMVAR, PIRRIG, AGCR, INFRA, SOIL) \quad (13.12)$$

The Tobit estimation procedure was applied to the data as some farmers do not apply pesticides and, therefore, have zero values for pesticide use.

Impact on income
Income of a household depends on a host of factors, such as land ownership, choice of crops, working members in the family, level of education and so on, and whose effects cannot be predetermined. Therefore, in order to assess the impact of modern agricultural technology on annual household income, the following equation is fitted to the household-level data.

$$INCM = f(AMLND, WORK, CAPL, AGE, TNC, PMVAR, \\ PIRRIG, EDUCH, INFRA, SOIL) \qquad (13.13)$$

OLS estimation procedures were applied to the data. Separate regressions are undertaken for total family income as well as for major component income: crop income, agricultural (crop, livestock, fisheries and land leasing) income, and non-agricultural income, respectively.

13.4   Social and distributional impacts of technological change
Literature analysing the impacts of modern agricultural technology mostly emphasizes the direct effects on income distribution and geographical regions, using the basic argument that technology is not scale neutral and mostly benefits areas endowed with favourable agroecological conditions (Lipton and Longhurst 1989). However, Hossain et al. (1990) argued that modern agricultural technology might also have indirect effects that operate through factor markets and enable transfers of income across socio-economic groups as well as regions. This could occur from a change in the nature of the operation of land, labour and other input markets that would smooth income

disparities across socio-economic groups through an adjustment process. The present section analyses the direct effects of modern technology diffusion on regional equity, employment, gender equity in employment, income distribution and poverty. The database, specification of models and procedures employed for individual impact areas are discussed briefly below.

Impact on regional equity
The impact of technological change on regional variations in the level of agricultural development is analysed using cross-section regionwise data for three periods covering a span of 20 years (1972/73–1992/93). A linear regression model is specified including indicators representing technological, infrastructural, agroecological, crop production efficiency, demographic and human capital factors. The basic assumption of the model is that there exists a linear relationship between the explained indicator and the set of explanatory indicators (Pokhriyal and Naithani 1996). The specification is given by:

$$GVFOOD = f(MVYLD, LVYLD, WHTYLD, FERTRATE,$$
$$PESTRATE, PMVAR, PIRRIG, CI, SEED, RAIN, DENS,$$
$$HCAP, CREDIT, ROAD, RDQLTY) \qquad (13.14)$$

A stepwise forward regression estimation procedure is used to identify the significant indicators. Three separate regressions, using triennium averages centred at the middle year for three periods; Period 1 (1973–75), Period 2 (1981–83) and Period 3 (1991–1993), is estimated. Then weighted standard scores are constructed utilizing the regression results, which are then used to delineate the regions in descending orders of development levels to identify homogeneous agricultural regions. The result is also used to determine sampling locations for the micro-level component in this study.

Impact on employment
It is widely established that modern varieties of rice and wheat utilize more hired labour than local varieties (Hossain 1989; Ahmed and Hossain 1990; and Hossain et al. 1990). In order to test this hypothesis and identify factors affecting labour demand, a multivariate analysis is performed at the household level. The following equation is fitted to the data:

$$LABOR = f(AMLND, MVAR, TNC, WAGE, INFRA, SOIL,$$
$$SUBP, WORK, WORKW, EDUCH) \qquad (13.15)$$

Both OLS and Tobit (two limit probabilistic regression) estimation procedures were applied to data on hired labour demand as well as total labour demand functions as farmers may have zero values for hired labour use.

. *Impact on gender in employment*

Rural women in Asia play a major role in the agricultural sector, particularly in the post-harvest processing. However, a major shift in technology has occurred in the post-harvesting processing sector, through the introduction of rice mills, which dramatically displaced employment opportunities of rural women involved in the manual husking operation of rice grains. Ahmed (1982) estimated that rice mills displaced 29 per cent of the total husking labour and almost all hired labour displaced were women who have limited alternative employment opportunities. His crude nationwide estimate suggests that, if rice mills are made adequately available throughout the country, a total of 45 million person-days of hired labour would be displaced leading to a reduction in the income of the rural poor of about Tk 450 million at its 1982 level.

In the present study, the issue of gender equity in employment is analysed by comparing the proportion of male and female family labour as well as hired labour used in connection with local and modern varieties of rice and wheat, respectively. Also, the mean difference between the labour wages paid to men and women is analysed and statistically tested.

Impact on income distribution and poverty

Analysis of the distributional impacts of modern agricultural technology is conducted by categorizing the villages according to their level of modern technology adoption. Villages with more than 60 per cent of land area under modern varieties of rice and wheat are designated as the 'high adopter' villages, between 40 and 60 per cent of land area under modern varieties as 'medium adopter' villages, and less than 40 per cent land under modern varieties as 'low adopter' villages. For purposes of analysing the distributional impacts of technological change, the concentration of income held by the top 10 per cent households, income inequality (gini-coefficient) and gini-decomposition analysis are computed for the different adopter categories of villages. For analysing the impact of modern agricultural technology on poverty, a number of poverty measures and indices, such as Sen's poverty index (1976), Kakwani's poverty index (1980) and Foster et al.'s poverty measure (1984) are utilized.

13.5   Environmental impacts of technological change

The environmental dimension of technological change in agriculture is a relatively neglected area of statistical analysis, despite the fact that the ecological integrity of the agricultural production system is a prerequisite for sustainability. The present study undertakes some initial analyses, which begin to fill this gap. First, it analyses the environmental impacts of modern agricultural technology as perceived by farmers in the sample of households and villages covered in the survey. This is supplemented by evidence derived from bio-physico-chemical tests of soil fertility and water quality, and from time-series data relating to fertiliser and pesticide use and the sustainability of rice and wheat yields. These are used as longer-term indicators believed to be impacted due to these technological changes. These are used to support (or refute) the conclusions drawn from farmers' perceptions.

Farmers' perceptions on environmental impacts were elicited in two steps. First, a list of 12 specific environmental impacts[5] that may be associated with technological change was read out to the respondents, who were asked to reveal their opinions on these impacts. Next, they were asked to provide scores, on a five-point scale, on the extent to which they considered that technological changes had resulted in the individually specified impacts. If a respondent considered that the specified environmental impact had not occurred, then it was scored zero. The methods used in the evaluation of environmental impacts are elaborated below and a summary of the principal findings is incorporated into the final section.

Impact on soil fertility

Concerns have been raised in recent years over declining soil fertility as reflected in the falling productivity of crops in Bangladesh (BASR 1989 and Yano 1986). Physical and chemical analyses of soil were conducted to evaluate the general fertility of the soil and inter-regional differences (if any) between the study areas. Fifteen composite soil samples (five from each region) of rice fields were randomly selected from within the total sample of households. The soil samples were taken from recently transplanted Boro rice fields.

Ten soil-fertility parameters were tested. These are: (i) soil pH, (ii) available nitrogen, (iii) available potassium, (iv) available phosphorus, (v) available sulfur, (vi) available zinc, (vii) soil texture, (viii) cation exchange capacity (CEC) of soil, (ix) soil organic matter content, and (x) electrical conductivity of soil. A composite weighted soil fertility index, based on the test results for the study area, was constructed and incorporated as an independent variable in all the models mentioned above. High index value refers to better soil fertility.

In addition, farmers' perceptions of 'soil fertility decline' were checked against their fertiliser application rates with an a priori expectation that a negative association exists between soil nutrient availability and fertiliser application rate. Also the relationship between fertiliser use and organic manure application was analysed. Additionally, a time-trend analysis of fertiliser use per hectare of gross cropped area and fertiliser productivity (aggregate output per kilogram of fertiliser application) at the regional level for 29 years (1961–92) was carried out.

Impact on other selected components of the environment
An analysis of the effect of technological change in agriculture on human health is beyond the scope of the study. However, an inference of one aspect of the relationship may be attempted by analysing the use of pesticides by farmers, and their perception of the use of this input. The pesticides used by the farmers were assessed with reference to the World Health Organization (WHO) prescribed chemical hazard categories.

Analysis of the effect of technological change on fish catch was attempted using time-trend analyses of fish catch in open water bodies (rivers, estuaries and perennial depressions) at the regional level for a period of 10 years (1983–94). Also, a review of the literature on the impacts of flood control drainage and irrigation (FCD/I) projects was undertaken to support the argument.

Insect/pest and disease infestation was examined by time-trend analysis of pesticide use rates at the regional level for 17 years (1976–93), in addition to the analysis of categories of pesticides used by the farmers mentioned above.

Although, in the case of Bangladesh, arsenic contamination is not due to the increased use of toxic chemicals as may be observed elsewhere, it is the drive for groundwater irrigation to support the diffusion of modern agricultural technology, which is primarily responsible for widespread and growing arsenic pollution in the country. This is supported by the findings from a recently conducted large-scale sample survey of arsenic pollution by BRAC (a national non-governmental organization: NGO) which also covered some of the study villages (BRAC 1997). Also, findings from the first international conference on arsenic pollution held in Bangladesh during March 1998 support this finding (Ullah 1998).

Impact on the sustainability of food production
In order to analyse the extent to which growth rates in food production are likely to be sustained in the future, a logistic function is applied to the data on foodgrain (rice and wheat) yield per net hectare for 47 years (1947/48–1993/94) and compared with the linear trend. Also, the long-term compound annual growth rates of food crops (rice, wheat and potato) were estimated for the entire period, distinguishing between the pre-technological change period (1947/48–1967/68) and the post-technological change period (1969/70–1993/94). The fitted equations are as follows:

$$Linear\ trend\ function \quad FOODYLD = \alpha + \beta T + \varepsilon \qquad (13.16)$$

$$Logistic\ trend\ function \quad FOODYLD = 1/(1 + e^{-(\alpha + \beta T)}) \qquad (13.17)$$

13.6   Synthesis of impacts and policy implications

The nature of the impacts of technological change in agriculture is complex and multidimensional (see Figure 13.1). Modern agricultural technology increases regional *crop production* but exacerbates regional disparities.[6] On one hand, an increase in aggregate crop production confirms the positive impact of technological change in raising productivity, implying that food production can be sustained in future.[7] On the other hand, the declining yield rate (−1.06 per cent per annum during 1968/69–1993/94) of modern rice varieties over time is raising doubt on sustaining food production through technological change alone. Again, the observed increase in modern wheat yield (3.63 per cent per annum during 1968/69–1993/94) over time will somewhat offset the effect of a depressing modern rice yield, thereby providing another source of hope for food production sustainability. Current increases in foodgrain production are largely due to switching from local to modern varieties of rice and wheat, which still provide higher yields than local varieties. Whether this can be sustained in the future remains to be determined.

Modern technology diffusion in the agricultural sector has exerted a distinct upward pressure on input and output prices as well as input demands.[8] The upward pressure on *output prices* raises the *income* of the farm producers while the upward pressure on *labour wages* may reduce income inequality through an indirect transfer of income from rich farmers to poor landless labourers, also supported by Hossain (1989). However, the increase in land rents raises equity concerns since landownership in rural Bangladesh is highly skewed, with more than 50 per cent of the farming population being landless and tenants. Higher land rents imply that the technological change opens up opportunities for the landed elites to raise their rental income through the tenancy market.

Although technological change raised *employment* significantly, it remained highly skewed in favour of men since only male labour are hired to meet the increased demand. Women, constituting half of the total population, have failed to get direct benefit from this technological progress as mostly men are hired to meet the increased demand. The few women (12 per cent of total households) who are hired are paid significantly lower wages than men (Rahman and Routray 1998). However, the failure to increase women's employment opportunities is not due solely to the nature of the technology. Rather it is social and cultural barriers that restrict their participation and their capacity to obtain benefits from this technological change. The simultaneous increase in wages and in the demand for hired labour due to technological progress may redistribute income, but the level of redistribution is unlikely to be sufficiently substantial to bridge the gap between the rich and the poor farmers.

Technological change has contributed significantly to increases in income but it has also contributed to worsening *income inequality*. The concentration

MULTIFACETED IMPACTS OF TECHNOLOGICAL CHANGE IN AGRICULTURE

Economic impacts	Social/distributional impacts	Environmental impacts	Impact on sustainability
Impact on crop production • Aggregate crop production: increase	**Impact on regional equity** • Regional foodgrain production: increase • Regional inequity: increase	**Impact on soil fertility** • Soil fertility: decline	**Trend in foodgrain yield** • Long-run modern rice yield: declining • Long-run modern wheat yield: increasing
Impact on prices • Labour wage: increase • Fertiliser price: increase • Land rent: increase • Output price: increase	**Impact on employment** • Hired labour demand: increase • Total labour demand:	**Impact on other selected components of environment** • Human health: increased hazards • Fish production: decline • Insect/pest attack: increase • Crop disease: increase • Water quality: deteriorate	**Prospects for sustainability** • Foodgrain production sustainability: undetermined

Economic impacts	Social/distributional impacts	Environmental impacts	Impact on sustainability
Impact on input demand	**Impact on gender equity**		
• Fertiliser demand: increase	• Employment: skewed in favour of male labour		
• Animal power demand: increase	• Family female labour supply: increase		
• Pesticide use demand: increase			
• Agricultural credit demand: increase			
Impact on income	**Impact on income distribution and poverty**		
• Crop income: increase	• Income distribution: higher inequality		
• Agricultural income: increase	• Poverty: higher poverty		
• Non-agricultural income: lower			

Note: Based on the analytical results obtained from utilizing equations (13.1)–(13.17) and other subsequent qualitative analyses mentioned in Sections 13.3–13.5.

Source: Rahman (1998).

Figure 13.1 Synthesis of socio-economic and environmental impacts of technological change in agriculture in Bangladesh, 1996

233

of income is estimated to be highest in the high adopter villages (the top 10 per cent households are estimated to control 30 per cent of per capita income while the bottom 50 per cent control only 19 per cent). Gini-decomposition analysis reveals that the cultivation of modern variety crops alone contributes 29 per cent to total income inequality.

The adoption of modern technology is also correlated with the incidence of village poverty. All the measures of poverty revealed that poverty is high in high adopter as well as in low adopter villages. It is in the medium adopter villages, characterized by a diversified cropping system, that the incidence of poverty and income inequality is estimated to be lowest.

The findings relating to the *environmental impacts* of modern agricultural technology are not encouraging. The detrimental effects of the modern technology on soil fertility are clear as evidenced from farmers' perception ranking (ranked one, index value 0.79), test results of soil nutrients, and negative growth rate of aggregate output per unit of fertiliser application at regional level for the period 1960/61–1991/92. Partially associated with this are the adverse effects on human health as well as decline in open water fisheries that served as a major source of animal protein for the rural poor in Bangladesh (Rahman 1998). The decline in fisheries resources may also be partly attributed to overfishing, increased population pressure and poor management. Increases in crop diseases, pests and insect attacks are also evident. In addition, the contamination of water bodies through chemical runoff and eutrophication associated with modern technology, although it cannot yet be conclusively proved, remains a major environmental concern for the future (ibid.). Arsenic pollution in groundwater, although it is caused by geogenic processes, is brought to the surface through anthropogenic processes stimulated by increased demand for irrigation for the modern variety cultivation in one hand and demand for safe drinking water on the other. Surface soils in intensively irrigated regions now contain high levels of arsenic (Ullah 1998). In summary, a complex intertwined mix of positive and negative consequences is associated with this highly proclaimed technological breakthrough in agriculture that needs to be carefully evaluated in order to pave the way for sounder-based, future agricultural development plans.

Characteristics of 'medium adopter' villages
Analyses of the distributive effects of modern technology diffusion clearly reveal that it is the medium adopter villages that experience least income inequality and the lowest incidence of poverty. In order to identify the conditions associated with the superiority of this category of village, a number of the socio-economic characteristics of the villages studied, classified by adopter category, have been examined. It was found that a number of features distinguish medium adopter villages from the other two categories. Striking

differences exist in the proportion of large farmers, farm size, level of irrigation development, level of modern variety adoption, cropping intensity, level of fertiliser use, and level of organic manure used in the medium adopter villages.[9]

Therefore, one possible strategy for sustainable agricultural development planning will be to internalize the salient features of the successful medium adopter villages and to replicate and/or create such conditions in high adopter as well as low adopter villages.

Strategies for agricultural development planning and policy options
In this subsection an integrated agricultural development plan is outlined which incorporates the following policies: (i) balanced modern technology diffusion, (ii) crop diversification, (iii) soil fertility management, (iv) strengthening bottom-up planning and agricultural extension services, (v) rural infrastructure development, (vi) price policy prescription and (vii) economic diversification. The first three components are interlinked with one other and need to be implemented simultaneously. The remaining four components will smooth the development process by: (a) enhancing effective input delivery and output marketing systems through developing appropriate infrastructure, (b) responding to price signals which reflect more appropriate pricing policies, and (c) engaging in non-agricultural income-generating activities through economic diversification.

The balanced adoption of modern agricultural technology along with crop diversification should be one of the major policies. This is based on the experience of medium adopter villages, which have achieved a balance between modern varieties of rice and wheat as well as with non-foodgrain crops. This suggestion contrasts with almost all earlier evaluations of the green revolution that suggested spreading modern technology to its fullest extent.

Additionally, the adoption of an effective pricing policy is pivotal to enhancing crop diversification by reducing the price risks associated with non-foodgrain production. On distributional grounds, subsidies are suggested on animal power services and output prices that can be implemented across the board. Also, the development of crop insurance policies, through public and private insurance agencies, and of marketing, transportation and infrastructural facilities, are proposed to reduce harvesting and marketing risks to encourage crop diversification.

Human resource development, to provide technical skills in growing non-foodgrain crops, to raise awareness of the adverse environmental impacts of technological change, and to improve enterprise development skills, are also proposed to encourage greater crop and other forms of economic diversification. Improving the technical know-how of farmers can be achieved by: (a) strengthening the existing agricultural extension network, utilizing a bottom-up planning approach, and (b) collaborating with national and regional level NGOs working at the grassroots level.

The key to success in realizing this planning strategy is coordination between the major facilitators: relevant government agencies, NGOs, financial institutions and the farming communities. The development programmes of individual agencies must be coordinated in order to enable the farming and rural communities to reap the full benefit from their interventions. This implies substantial changes in the attitudes of government agencies towards development programmes along with a major restructuring of individual programme scheduling, budgeting and implementation strategy.

In conclusion, Bangladesh needs agricultural technologies that are more labour intensive, which provide more equal opportunities for men and women, reduce income inequalities and poverty and impose fewer negative impacts on the environment. A properly designed crop diversification policy and its effective implementation would be an important first step towards the goal of achieving sustainable development. The implementation of an economic diversification policy and the improvement of rural infrastructure would enhance this process.

Notes

1. The present study is extracted from the first author's PhD dissertation completed at the Asian Institute of Technology (AIT), Bangkok, Thailand. The focus of this chapter is on elaborating the approach utilized for analysing the multifaceted impacts of technological change in agriculture. As such, details of the analytical results are avoided while a synthesis of the results is provided in these Notes (for details, see Rahman 1998).
2. Essentially, this is an outcome of the exercise conducted at national level to examine regional equity. The five levels are: 'very high', 'high', 'medium', 'low' and 'very low', respectively.
3. Regions from the two extremes, 'very high' and 'very low' levels are avoided. The justification is that the Chittagong region, falling under the 'very high' level, is already transforming into an urban–industrial region and the regions under 'very low' level, namely Khulna and Faridpur regions, suffer from agroecological and other biophysical constraints.
4. The crop groups are: local Aus rice, modern Aus rice, local Aman rice, modern Aman rice, local Boro rice, modern Boro rice, local wheat, modern wheat, jute, potatoes, pulses, spices, oilseeds, vegetables and cotton. Pulses in turn include lentils, gram, chola and khesari. Spices include onions, garlic, chilly, dhania, ginger and turmeric. Oilseeds include sesame, mustard and groundnut. Vegetables include brinjal, cauliflowers, cabbages, arum, beans, gourds, radishes and leafy vegetables.
5. The 12 specific environmental impacts of technological change are: (i) reduces soil fertility, (ii) affects human health, (iii) reduces fish catch, (iv) increases disease in crops, (v) compacts/hardens soil, (vi) increases insect/pest attack, (vii) increases soil erosion, (viii) increases soil salinity, (ix) contaminates water source, (x) increases toxicity in soil, (xi) creates water logging, and (xii) increases toxicity in water.
6. In identifying the significant variables explaining regional variation using equation (13.14), the technology indicators (*PMVAR* and *PIRRIG*) were found to significantly ($p < 0.01$) positively influence foodgrain output (*GVFOOD*) emphasizing their crucial role in regional crop production. BASR (1989) and Alauddin and Tisdell (1991) also attributed differential

access to irrigation as the major reason for regional variation in crop production growth (for details, see Rahman 1998).

7. In the estimation of aggregate crop production function utilizing equation (13.1), the technology variable (*PMVAR* as well as *PIRRIG*) was found to be significantly ($p < 0.01$) positively associated with crop production over time. The estimate of 'returns to scale' using conventional inputs reveals 'constant returns to scale ($1.08 \approx 1.00$)' prevails in crop sector in Bangladesh. When non-conventional factors, such as technology, infrastructure and education variable are incorporated, an 'increasing returns to scale ($1.17 > 1.00$)' to crop sector is observed. The output elasticity of this technology variable is estimated at about 0.09 (for details, see Rahman 1998).

8. The technology variable (*PMVAR*) is estimated to be significantly ($p < 0.01$) positively related to labour wage, fertiliser price (positive but not significant), animal power price, land rent, and output prices (equations (13.2–4)). The joint estimation input demand equation (equations (13.6–10)) revealed that *PMVAR* is significantly ($p < 0.01$ and $p < 0.05$) related to fertiliser, labour and animal power demand, respectively. Also, *PMVAR* is significantly ($p < 0.10$) related to agricultural credit demand (equation (13.11)) and *PIRRIG* is significantly ($p < 0.01$) related to pesticide use (equation (13.12)), respectively (for details, see Rahman 1998).

9. The proportion of large farmers (owning land > 2.00 ha) in medium adopter villages (MAV) are 16 per cent as compared to 6–7 per cent in high adopter villages (HAV) and low adopter villages (LAV). Average farm size in MAV is 0.96 ha as compared to 0.68 and 0.62 ha in HAV and LAV, respectively. The irrigation level is strikingly similar between HAV (62 per cent) and LAV (60 per cent) of total land area. Area under modern varieties is 75 per cent, 47 per cent and 32 per cent in HAV, MAV and LAV, respectively. The cropping intensity is highest in MAV (190 per cent) followed by HAV (177 per cent) and LAV (160 per cent). Fertiliser use is highest in HAV (224 kg/ha) followed by MAV (206 kg/ha) and LAV (164 kg/ha). Organic manure use rate is highest in MAV (1.5 ton/ha) as compared to 1.1 ton/ha in HAV and only 0.2 ton/ha in LAV, respectively (for details, see Rahman 1998).

References

Ahmed, J.U. (1982), 'The impact of new paddy post-harvest technology on the rural poor in Bangladesh', in M. Greely and M. Howes (eds), *Rural Technology, Rural Institutions and the Rural Poorest*, Comilla: Bangladesh Academy for Rural Development, pp. 15–25.

Ahmed, R. and Hossain, M. (1990), *Development Impact of Rural Infrastructure in Bangladesh*, Research Report No. 83, Washington, DC: International Food Policy Research Institute.

Alauddin, M. and Tisdell, C. (1991), *The Green Revolution and Economic Development: The Process and its Impact in Bangladesh*, London: Macmillan.

Bangladesh Agricultural Sector Review (BASR) (1989), 'Growth performance of cereal production since the middle 1970s and regional variations', *Bangladesh Agricultural Sector Review*, Dhaka: UNDP/BARC.

Bangladesh Bureau of Statistics (BBS) (1978), *Yearbook of Agricultural Statistics of Bangladesh, 1978*, Dhaka: BBS.

Bangladesh Bureau of Statistics (BBS) (1980), *Statistical Yearbook of Bangladesh, 1980*, Dhaka: BBS.

Bangladesh Bureau of Statistics (BBS) (1986), *Yearbook of Agricultural Statistics of Bangladesh, 1986*, Dhaka: BBS.

Bangladesh Bureau of Statistics (BBS) (1989), *Statistical Yearbook of Bangladesh, 1989*, Dhaka: BBS.

Bangladesh Bureau of Statistics (BBS) (1991), *Statistical Yearbook of Bangladesh, 1991*, Dhaka: BBS.

Bangladesh Bureau of Statistics (BBS) (1992), *Yearbook of Agricultural Statistics of Bangladesh, 1992*, Dhaka: BBS.

Bangladesh Bureau of Statistics (BBS) (1994), *Yearbook of Agricultural Statistics of Bangladesh, 1994*, Dhaka: BBS.

238   *Case studies*

Bangladesh Bureau of Statistics (BBS) (1995), *Statistical Yearbook of Bangladesh, 1995*, Dhaka: BBS.
Bisaliah, S. (1982), 'Technological change and functional income distribution effects in Indian agriculture: an econometric analysis', *Artha Vijnana*, **24** (1), 1–14.
Bowonder, B. (1979), 'Impact analysis of the green revolution in India', *Technological Forecasting and Social Change*, **15** (3), 297–313.
Bowonder, B. (1981), 'The myth and reality of HYVs in Indian agriculture', *Development and Change*, **12** (2), 293–313.
BRAC (Bangladesh Rural Advancement Committee) (1997), BRAC-RED/HPP/RDP Joint Study Project, Unpublished data, Dhaka: Research and Evaluation Division, BRAC.
Brown, L.R. (1988), *The Changing World Food Prospect: The Nineties and Beyond*, Worldwatch Paper No. 85, Washington, DC: Worldwatch Institute.
Clapham, W.B. (1980), 'Environmental problems, development, and agricultural production systems', *Environmental Conservation*, **7** (2), 145–53.
Conway, G. (1986), *Agroecosystem Analysis for Research and Development*, Bangkok: Winrock International.
Dantwala, M.L. (1985), 'Technology, growth and equity in agriculture', in J.W. Mellor and G. Desai (eds), *Agricultural Change and Rural Poverty*, Baltimore: Johns Hopkins University Press, pp. 110–23.
Deb, U.K. (1995), 'Human capital and agricultural growth in Bangladesh', unpublished PhD Dissertation, Los Banos: University of the Philippines Los Banos.
Foster, J., Greer, J. and Thorbecke, E. (1984), 'A class of decomposable poverty measures', *Econometrica*, **52** (3), 761–66.
Freebairn, D.K. (1995), 'Did the green revolution concentrate incomes? A quantitative study of research reports', *World Development*, **23** (2), 265–79.
Griffin, K. (1974), *The Political Economy of Agrarian Change: An Essay on the Green Revolution*, Cambridge, MA: Harvard University Press.
Hamid, M.A. (1991), *A Database on Agriculture and Foodgrains in Bangladesh (1947/48–1989/90)*, Dhaka: Bangladesh Agricultural Research Council/Winrock International.
Hamid, M.A. (1993), *A Database on Minor Crops, Cash Crops, Livestock and Fisheries in Bangladesh (1947/48–1991/92)*, Dhaka: Bangladesh Agricultural Research Council/Winrock International.
Harris, J (1977), 'Bias in perception of agrarian change in India', in B.H. Farmer (ed.), *Green Revolution: Technology and Change in Rice Growing Areas of Tamil Nadu and Sri Lanka*, London: Macmillan, pp. 30–36.
Hayami, Y. and Ruttan, V.W. (1985), *Agricultural Development: An International Perspective*, Baltimore: Johns Hopkins University Press.
Hossain, M. (1989), *Green Revolution in Bangladesh: Impact on Growth and Distribution of Income*, Dhaka: University Press Ltd.
Hossain, M., Quasem, M.A., Akash, M.M. and Jabber, M.A. (1990), *Differential Impact of Modern Rice Technology: The Bangladesh Case*, Dhaka: Bangladesh Institute of Development Studies.
Kakwani, N.C. (1980), *Income Inequality and Poverty: Methods of Estimation and Policy Implications*, New York: Oxford University Press.
Lal, D. (1979), 'Agricultural growth, real wages, and the rural poor in India', *Economic and Political Weekly*, **11** (28 June), A47–A61.
Lipton, M. and Longhurst, R. (1989), *New Seeds and Poor People*, London: Unwin Hyman.
Marten, G.G. (1988), 'Productivity, stability, sustainability, equitability and autonomy as properties for agroecosystem assessment', *Agricultural Systems*, **26** (4), 291–316.
Mellor, J.W. (1978), 'Food price policy and income distribution in low-income countries', *Economic Development and Cultural Change*, **27** (1), 1–26.
Parthasarathy, G. (1974), 'Wages and income of the weaker sectors in rural India', *Indian Journal of Agricultural Economics*, **29** (3), 78–91.
Pingali, P.L. (1995), 'Impact of pesticides on farmer health and the rice environment: an overview of results from a multidisciplinary study in the Philippines', in P.L. Pingali and P.

Roger (eds), *Impact of Pesticides on Farmer Health and the Rice Environment*, Boston: Kluwer Academic Publishers, pp. 3–21.

Pokhriyal, H.C. and Naithani, P. (1996), 'Identification of levels of agricultural development: a methodical inter-district analysis', *Journal of Rural Development*, **15** (1), 13–30.

Prahladachar, M. (1983), 'Income distribution effects of green revolution in India: a review of empirical evidence', *World Development*, **11** (11), 927–44.

Rahman, S. (1998), 'Socio-economic and environmental impacts of technological change in Bangladesh agriculture', Unpublished PhD dissertation, Bangkok: Asian Institute of Technology (AIT).

Rahman, S. and Routray, J.K. (1998), 'Technological change and women's participation in crop production in Bangladesh', *Gender, Technology and Development*, **2** (2), 243–67.

Redclift, M. (1989), 'The environmental consequences of Latin America's agricultural development: some thoughts on the Brundtland Commission Report', *World Development*, **17** (3), 365–77.

Sen, A. (1976), 'Poverty: an ordinal approach to measurement', *Econometrica*, **44** (2), 219–31.

Sen, B. (1974), *The Green Revolution in India: A Perspective*, New Delhi: Wiley Eastern.

Shiva, V. (1991), *The Violence of the Green Revolution: Third World Agriculture, Ecology and Politics*, London: Zed Books.

Sidhu, S.S. (1974), 'Economics of technical change in wheat production in the Indian Punjab', *American Journal of Agricultural Economics*, **56** (3), 2–21.

Ullah, S.M. (1998), 'Arsenic contamination of ground water and irrigated soils of Bangladesh', in *Proceedings of the International Conference on Arsenic Pollution of Ground Water in Bangladesh: Causes, Effects and Remedies*, held on 8–12 February, Dhaka: Dhaka Community Hospital Trust, Bangladesh and School of Environmental Studies, Jadavpur University, Calcutta, India.

Wolf, E.C. (1986), 'Beyond the Green Revolution: New Approaches for Third World Agriculture', Worldwatch Paper No. 73, Washington, DC: Worldwatch Institute.

Yano, T. (1986), *Identification of Problem Areas Based on Yield Trend Analysis: Investigation of Lands with Declining and Stagnating Productivity Project: Bangladesh, Burma, Laos, Thailand and Vietnam*, FAO Working Paper 2 (AG: GCP/RAS/107/JPN), Bangkok: RAPA/FAO, Thailand.

Appendix 13A   Definition of the variables used in the models

AGCR	amount of agricultural credit borrowed by the household ('000 taka)
AGE	age of the farmer (years)
AMLND	amount of land cultivated by the household (ha)
ANIMAL	amount animal power service used by the household (bullock pair day)
ANIMP	animal power price at the farm level (taka/bullock pair day)
CAPL	value of farm capital excluding land asset ('000 taka)
CI	cropping intensity (%)
CREDIT	agricultural credit disbursed per ha of gross cropped area ('000 Tk/ha)
CROP	value of rice (all varieties), wheat, jute, sugarcane, potatoes, pulses, oilseeds at 1984/85 prices of all region ('000 taka)
DENS	population density per ha of gross cropped area (persons/ha), a proxy measure for population pressure
EDUCH	completed years of formal schooling of the head of household (years)
EXPCE	years of experience of farmer in crop production (years)
FAMILY	number of family members in the household (persons)
FERT	amount of fertiliser used by the household (kg)
FERTILISER	total fertiliser (urea, phosphate, potash and gypsum) use in the region weighted at 1984/85 prices (taka)
FERTRATE	fertiliser used per ha of gross cropped area (kg/ha)
FOODYLD	weighted average yield per ha of all varieties of rice and wheat (ton/ha)
FP	fertiliser price at the farm level (taka/kg)
GVFOOD	gross value of all varieties of rice and wheat per ha of gross cropped area ('000 Tk/ha)
HCAP	percent of literate population (%), a proxy measure for human capital
INCM	total family income of the household ('000 taka)
INFRA	index of underdevelopment of infrastructure (the higher the index the more underdeveloped is the infrastructure)
IRRIG	amount of cultivated land under irrigation (ha)
LABOR	number of days of total labour used in crop production (days)
LABORFORCE	agricultural labour force of the region constructed from census data with trend extrapolation model (persons)

LAND	area under all crops included in output (*CROP*) is considered as the land area under cultivation (ha)
LANDPC	amount of land owned per capita (ha)
LANDRENT	amount of land rent per ha of cultivated land ('000 taka)
LIVESTOCK	total draft animals of the region estimated using linear trend extrapolation from livestock census data (number)
LVYLD	weighted average yield per ha of all local varieties of rice (ton/ha)
MVAR	amount of cultivated land under modern varieties of rice and wheat (ha)
MVYLD	weighted average yield per ha of all modern varieties of rice (ton/ha)
OUTP	price of crop output at the farm level (taka/kg)
OWNLND	amount of land owned by the household (ha)
PEST	amount of pesticide used by the household (taka)
PESTRATE	pesticide used per ha of gross cropped area (Tk/ha)
PIRRIG	proportion of cultivated land under irrigation (%)
PMVAR	proportion of cultivated land under modern varieties of rice and wheat (%)
QTY	amount of crop produced by the household (kg)
RAIN	actual total annual rainfall (mm)
RDQLTY	ratio of unpaved road to paved road (unit less), a proxy measure of the quality of road indicating accessibility
ROAD	road density per sq km of land area (km/km^2), a proxy measure of infrastructure at the macro or regional level
SEED	improved seed of rice and wheat distributed per ha of gross cropped area (kg/ha)
SOIL	index of soil fertility (the higher the index the better is the soil fertility)
SUBP	subsistence pressure measured as number of family members in the household (persons)
TNC	the amount of cultivated land rented-in (ha)
WAGE	labour wage at the farm level (taka/day)
WHTYLD	weighted average yield per ha of all varieties of wheat (ton/ha)
WORK	number of working members in the household (persons)
WORKW	number of female working members in the household (persons)

Index